The Genesis of the Modern Art Market in London, 1700–1900

Thomas M. Bayer

The Genesis of the Modern Art Market in London, 1700–1900

Rebels, Geniuses and Entrepreneurs

palgrave
macmillan

Thomas M. Bayer
Tulane University
New Orleans, LA, USA

ISBN 978-3-032-00593-9 ISBN 978-3-032-00594-6 (eBook)
https://doi.org/10.1007/978-3-032-00594-6

This Palgrave Macmillan imprint is published by the registered company Springer Nature Switzerland AG.
The registered company address is: Gewerbestrasse 11, 6330 Cham, Switzerland

This book is dedicated to The Fabulous Four:
Reily, Avery, Carys and Emerson.

Preface

Readers, understandably, might wonder why a book about the origin of the modern art market several hundred years ago in London has an image of Damien Hirst's much newer 2007 sculpture, *For the Love of God*, on the cover. What connects the two?

While this book is, indeed, about the genesis of the modern art market, it covers a lot more ground. It ties events and individuals in the distant past to events and individuals of our time. One owes its existence to the other. *For the Love of God* epitomizes this book's main point: artists and others in London's eighteenth- and nineteenth-century art milieu deliberately built a modern art market for recently re-branded art products to compete in an emerging consumer society. The art we see today is the result of their rebelliousness, their entrepreneurial ingenuity, and their business savvy. There is nothing new about the way Damien Hirst's diamond-encrusted skull was conceived, created, promoted and then 'sold' to a group of investors that included himself and other stakeholders. This modus had been conceived, tested and refined a long time ago. Viewed from this perspective, cutting-edge contemporary art is still rather Victorian.

For the book's cover, I wanted an image of an object that, juxtaposed with the title, illustrates this indebtedness to the past. *For the Love of God* meets this objective. It is the visual representation of the modern art market's entire history.

New Orleans, LA　　　　Thomas M. Bayer

Acknowledgements

After close to 40 years of investigating the art market and over 50 years of being active in it, I cannot acknowledge all those individuals and events that contributed to this book. The rebellious artist Whistler would have used the term 'the experience of a lifetime' rather than risk being guilty of omission. Barely 21 years old, I was welcomed with open arms into the international community of art dealers. I was introduced around, met other dealers, restorers, shippers, auctioneers, experts, and countless personalities whose roles in the market did not fit any of these traditional categories. I visited famous artists in their studios, and I gained access to individuals and families of great wealth who owned equally great art works and preferred to do business away from the public eye.

Art dealing cannot be learned at university. Knowledge is acquired through informal apprenticeships and mentor-mentee relationships. Fortunately, the art business attracts gregarious personalities who enjoy sharing their passion for art and, much to my benefit, also their knowledge. Life-long friendships resulted from these encounters. This book would not have been written without their contribution.

My experience in academia followed similar lines. I also received a warm welcome. My professors were intrigued with my art market experience and encouraged me, from the onset, to focus my graduate research on issues that related to art marketing. I have followed their recommendations to this day. Without their guidance and support, I would not have realized that my familiarity with the commercial world of art dealing offered the opportunity to examine art history from a largely uncharted perspective.

They too must be acknowledged. At the risk of being biased, Marylin Brown, the chair of my dissertation committee, and John Page, who showed me how numbers tell stories, deserve a special shout out.

I also owe thanks to Emily Russell, the history editor for Palgrave Macmillan. I had never pitched a manuscript before and dreaded the prospect. In the past, someone usually asked me to write something for their publication or series. Now, the shoe was on the other foot. I had to do the asking. Contrary to the horror stories I had heard about the submission process, I received Emily's positive response the next day. And here we are—one year later. I can categorically state that without her, you would not be reading these lines. I want to thank Emily for her professionalism, her patience and her positive spirit as she helped me maneuver through the process of publication. Any mistakes in the text are mine. More than 15 eye surgeries have left my vision impaired, and, likely, one or two typos may have escaped my notice.

My most profound gratitude, however, is reserved for Laura D. Kelley, fellow historian and my long-time sweetheart. As they say, 'it takes one to know one.' We support each other in our obsession with the past.

Contents

About the Author

Thomas M. Bayer was born in Germany in 1953. In 1974, he moved to New Orleans to start a career as an art dealer. He worked for 4 years as an assistant for Kurt Schon, the owner of one of the largest galleries in the South. In 1978, with three partners, he founded the International Fine Arts Association, Inc. (IFAA, Inc.), a fee-based consultancy, to advise private and institutional buyers and sellers of art. In 1979, the consultancy received a Private Letter Ruling from the Department of Labor which established fine art as a qualified investment under the ERISA code, and allowed, IFAA, Inc. to acquire art works for certain types of pension plans.

In 1983, Thomas started The Fine Arts Gallery of New Orleans which sold mainly European art from the nineteenth and early twentieth centuries. He curated different theme exhibitions to show in different US cities. After the gallery closed in 2005, Thomas continued operating the International Fine Arts Association with Robert McHarg until the latter's death in 2015.

In 1989, Thomas decided to pursue graduate degrees in Art History and Economics. He received his Ph.D. with distinction from Tulane University in 2001 and began teaching Art History. During his studies, he published multiple papers, two of which won awards. After completing his degree, he continued to publish numerous scholarly articles and presented papers on art market topics. He also wrote the authoritative book on the economics of the English art market, the subject of his dissertation.

List of Figures

CHAPTER 1

Introduction

Art follows wealth for its rich rewards.
—Karel van Mander (1548–1606), Schilderboek

[Karel van Mander (1548–1606), Flemish painter and art historian. Little is known about his early years and his training, but in 1568, on a trip to Italy, he encountered the works of Michelangelo, Raphael, and Titian. He settled in the Netherlands, in Haarlem, after his return from Italy and became a well-regarded member of the local artists' community and a founding member of the Haarlem Guild of St. Luke. Van Mander is perhaps best known for his book 'Schilder-boeck', an early art history text that, in addition to the above quote, contains biographies of Netherlandish and Flemish artists, as well as treatises on art theory and practice.][1]

In 2005, a few months before hurricane Katrina nearly destroyed the city of New Orleans, a small, badly overpainted painting on a damaged oak panel sold for $ 1175 at a local auction house. I usually go to presale viewings and may have seen it. But frankly, I don't remember. If I did notice it, it left no lasting impression. It should have. Because a few years later, in 2013, the same painted oak panel was sold privately, this time as a Leonardo da Vinci, for $ 127.5 million. Then, in 2017, the same painting was sold

T. M. Bayer, *The Genesis of the Modern Art Market in London, 1700–1900*, https://doi.org/10.1007/978-3-032-00594-6_1

at an auction at Christie's in New York. The new owner paid 450,000,000, the highest price paid for any painting—ever. An increase in value from $ 1175 to $ 450,000,000 in twelve years (Figs. 1.1 and 1.2).

The painting may have been commissioned by King Louis XII of France around 1500. In 1638, a work with that title was recorded in the collection of James Hamilton, 1st Duke of Hamilton, at Chelsea Manor in London. However, there is no provable link between the painting in the collection of the French king and the one in the Duke's possession. After the Duke's execution in 1649, his painting was sold to a creditor in 1651 and subsequently returned to the British royal family in 1660. It was then inherited by James II and may have been part of his bequest to his mistress, Catherine Sedley. A painting assumed to be the one in question was sold at auction and eventually ended up in the collection of Francis Cook of Doughty House in Richmond, London. It was then sold at auction in 1958 for £45 as an attribution to Giovanni Antonio Boltraffio, who was among Leonardo's studio apprentices. The painting reappeared at auction in New Orleans in 2005 as part of the estate of a roofing contractor from the nearby Louisiana state capitol, Baton Rouge. In 2017, that painting was sold at Christie's auction house in New York for a record-breaking $450.3 million to Prince Badr bin Abdullah Al Saud, who ostensibly made the purchase on behalf of Abu Dhabi's Department of Culture and Tourism]

This amount translates into $ 1.1 million per square inch—probably the most valuable assembly of square inches in the world.

But this is not all. At a size of only 25.8 × 19.2 inches, the sturdy oak panel is also a remarkably compact form of discreetly transportable wealth. One would have to lug around some six thousand kilograms of gold—depending on current price—to match the pound or dollar value of the small picture. This painted piece of wood, however, wrapped in bubble-plastic, would inconspicuously fit into a Delta Airline Business Class overhead luggage compartment on any international flight. Or if you have a high-risk tolerance, you could just stick it in your hardcover suitcase and check it.

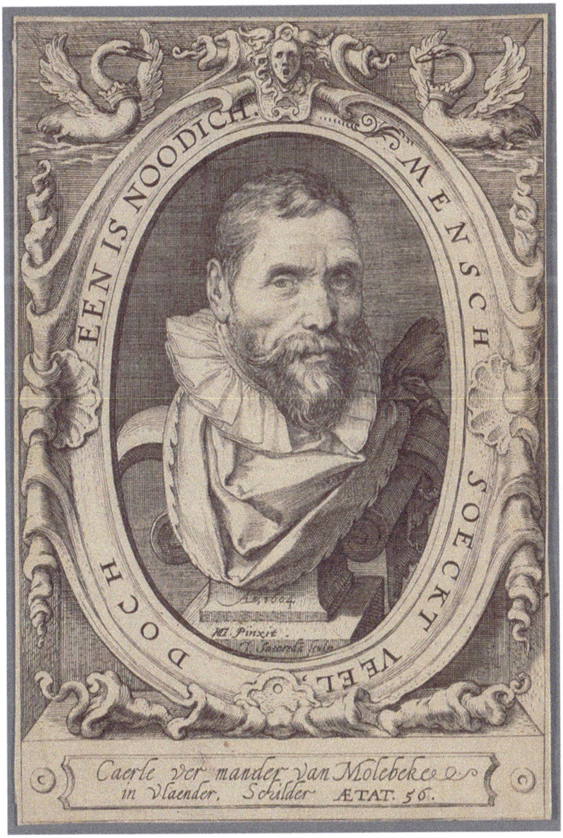

Fig. 1.1 Portrait of Karel van Mander (1548–1606), after Hendrik Goltzius

But artists don't even have to be dead for hundreds of years or universally famous to have their work command stratospheric prices. David Hockney, a Yorkshire painter from Bradford, born in1937 and very much alive at this writing, can attest to that fact. One of his paintings sold at Christie's in 2018 for $ 90.3 million.

What is going on?

Why are artworks of such high value secretly locked away in special warehouses in tax free zones instead of gracing the walls of their owners' mansions?

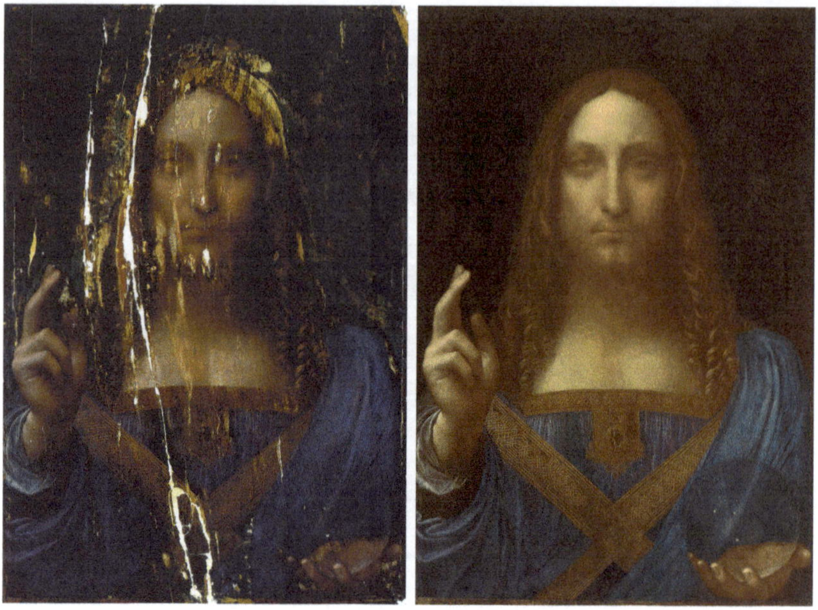

Fig. 1.2 Leonardo: Salvator Mundi, unrestored – restored

What kind of a market makes this possible? And why? Have we all gone mad?

We visit galleries and wander through magnificent museums, our temples of art, mesmerized by the display of the opus of divine genius. We read reviews composed by learned art critics using words that leave us bewildered. We attend art auctions, intrigued by the glitter, the competition, and the staggering sums of money. We might successfully bid on something. Some of us have studied art history in college, confused by the countless 'isms' that describe the multitude of styles of contemporary art. Among us are artists, curators, collectors, students, teachers, auctioneers, art dealers, art critics, art historians, or just lovers of art. Art is inextricably woven into the fabric of our society. We take it for granted. Yet if someone were to ask how this art market became what it is today, how it functions and for what purpose, how would we answer? Despite art's ubiquity, the operations of the art market and how it was created—its genesis—remain a mystery.

This fact came to full display when the news of the Leonardo sale made international headlines. Friends and acquaintances inundated me with questions about how this could happen. How can one work of art, in fact, a quite modest example of a great master's work, command a price of $ 450,000,000. That is a lot of money for a smallish and over-restored oak panel that still has experts disagreeing on who worked on which section of it and when. The painting's disappearance right before it was to be unveiled in the fall of 2018 at its new home in Abu Dhabi had tongues wagging and fueled the mystique surrounding the work's astonishing history. Media coverage was phenomenal; several books about it have been published;[2] a documentary has been produced, and surely a screenplay must be in the works. Latest news has it that it will soon be unveiled. Finally, in Al-Úla, it has been rumored.

Besides the Leonardo price, I was also questioned about other art works that had sold for similar exorbitant sums: the Hockney I mentioned earlier, a Cezanne for $250 million in 2011; a Willem de Kooning for $ 300 million in 2015; a Gauguin for $ 229 million in 2016. The list goes on. Every time the media reported such sensational sums I was bombarded with questions.

The reason was that my old friend and research colleague, John Page, and I had been investigating economic issues related to the art market since the mid-1990s, when I began writing my doctoral dissertation on this topic. John, an accounting professor at Tulane University in New Orleans, has a background in Economics, information systems, and Mathematics as well as the high level of expertise in data mining that I, an academic art and economic historian and professional art dealer, do not have. Our combined experience, we felt, would be useful for taking deep dives into the genesis of the modern art market. We wanted to know how it started, and how it became what it is today. By teaming up to scrutinize the social history of art through the lens of economic data, we hoped to learn something new about the art and the art markets of the past and their impact on the art and the market of the present. What we had in mind was a series of econometric and statistical analyses of art sales extending over a long period of time. We wanted numbers to tell us stories about the past. To do this, we needed data, lots and lots of data, the kind that accountants and economists customarily use to examine businesses and markets. Unearthing such records from days gone by is challenging, tedious, and time-consuming. And fun.

As it turned out, the solution was on one of the shelves of my gallery's library. It was a set of books, called *Art Sales*, that I had often used to research provenances of different paintings that passed through my hands. A wealthy Londoner, Algernon Graves (1845–1922), a nineteenth-century publisher of popular engravings, had taken on the admirable task of compiling these records. I owned a 3-volume reprint of the original books published between 1918–1921. They list in miniscule detail the individual auction sales of over forty-three thousand paintings done by 1837 different artists, celebrated and unknown, spanning across two centuries, from around 1700 to 1900. These sales had predominantly taken place in London, the center of the European art trade during these two hundred years. Thanks to those records, we were able to create an extraordinary database, unprecedented in scope and detail, and optimally suited for our enterprise.[3]

To augment our data further, I went to London to mine the extensive archives kept in the basement of Christie's, the world-famous British auction house on King Street in London. It was originally founded by James Christie in 1766 and is currently owned by François Pinault, a prominent French mega-collector and very high-net-worth individual. The archive's extensive collection of annotated auction catalogues, going back to December 6, 1766, Christie's very first sale, yielded another extensive amount of additional data, and, in many instances, it allowed me to verify the data in Graves' records. The keepers of this vast treasure of catalogues, the archivists, Lynda McLeod and Jeremy Rex Parkes, turned a normally monotonous task into a daily pleasure with their helpfulness, their enthusiasm, humor, and their general good cheers two levels below the streets of London. Unfortunately, since 2021, the archives are accessible by appointment only.

Later, a friend who had recently started working at the Getty Research Center in Los Angeles and knew of my interests called to let me know that she had found something that should spark my curiosity. While familiarizing herself with the archival holdings, she had discovered among the Getty's document collection the original day books—the handwritten records of the daily business activities—of one of the leading London art dealers of the second half of the nineteenth century, Arthur Tooth. So off I went to Los Angeles to spend a week at the Center. During my stay, I was able to transcribe by hand the original entries line by line. Back in New Orleans, I itemized the data into categories, and John digitized them.

All these data—Graves' auction sales, the information I had extracted from Christie's auction catalogues, and the entries from Arthur Tooth's day-to-day business records—were then merged into one massive data set. It contains well over 1.5 million individual pieces of information spanning the art market of the eighteenth and nineteenth centuries including many hitherto unfamiliar names of individuals who were active in it. Besides their names, the data also provided a window into their activities. We stored these records in a way that allowed us to run different analyses using programs John Page wrote—I wouldn't know a regression from a recliner—to get specific answers to an extensive list of questions we had. Compiling, entering, and sorting these data took us over five years and seriously tested our eyes as well as the patience of our lovely spouses.

We made fascinating discoveries, encountered intriguing and colorful characters, ingenuity, brilliance, and remarkable entrepreneurial skill. And we gained unprecedented insight into the economics of the art market, and who the 'makers and shakers' were. I presented papers at academic conferences, and we published numerous articles. I was also invited to write the first comprehensive scholarly book on the economic history of the English art market, which had also been the topic of my dissertation many years earlier. John took care of the analyses and graphs, and I wrote the text. It was well worth the effort. To this day, we get inquiries related to this data from graduate students and the scholarly community.[4]

And then the headline-making sale of Leonardo's panel happened. The bafflement this event caused and the animated and sometimes intense discussions that ensued among my friends and colleagues suggested that there was a story that should be told that goes beyond a historical account of events and individuals from a few hundred years ago. Instead, the story should connect this past to the present and, perhaps, even to the future. How did specific events and actions that occurred during the past three hundred years set a dynamic into motion that has brought us to this point?

The answer to this question is within these pages.

I focus on specific milestones in the past that formed the foundation for the genesis of a modern consumer market for one of mankind's most extraordinary products—art. In London, between 1700 and 1900 certain events occurred which fundamentally transformed the traditional market for art and laid the tracks for the modern art market of the present. I revisit game-changing occurrences and key individuals that were crucial to this monumental undertaking and highlight their impact on the arts environment of today. These pages also tell a story about enterprise, about genius and about rebellion against the doctrines of the past; it is about the liberation of artistic creativity, and the forging of economic emancipation. We can witness cultural legacy in the making. Heroes and rebels come in many guises. Some, instead of donning shining suits of armor or waving pitchforks, wear a painter's humble smock, their armor a brush and paint.

But this book is not just about artists. It is also about what opportunities this new consumer market offered then and what it offers now. What information does this market provide? How does it change? Why does it change? How does it initiate changes, and how does it react to changes? How does this never-ending dynamic shape our culture?

I describe this interaction of interests, personalities, and their decisions that helped make creating, buying, owning, and selling art as accessible, desirable, and as profitable as possible. Personal choices shaped the modern art market and, inadvertently, the products in which the market trades.

The art market is an exciting place, enriching, amusing, spectacular, provocative, mysterious, and perpetually surprising, like a whirlwind, unregulated and chaotic. It is full of colorful, adventurous, and entrepreneurial characters, famous and infamous, involved in a complex mixture of activities to advance their interests. By connecting the past to the present—even to the future—this book illuminates the modern art market's genesis. It highlights the historical, social, and economic circumstances that led in London between 1700 to 1900 to the creation of a complex modern consumer market which, in the twenty-first century, makes it possible to sell a decorated piece of wood done by a dead celebrity artist for 450 million dollars, and where other works of art routinely command prices in the tens and hundreds of millions. How was this modern, tailor-made market for art objects constructed and how does it operate? This book tracks this phenomenon from its modest beginnings in London in the early eighteenth century to the start of the art market's globalization at the end of the Victorian age. Along the way, I discuss specific instances that illustrate how the innovations and operations introduced to the art market in London during these 200 years continue to define its modus operandi to the present day and, most likely, in the future. It is because of these events and the individuals involved that we now witness a few hundred dollars worth of canvas and paint, or wood, change hands for hundreds of millions of dollars.

This story is full of astonishing tales and enlightening insights, extraordinary talent, sharp wit, keen humor, rebelliousness, astonishing ingenuity, remarkable entrepreneurial drive, and outright gall. It is an encounter with imagination beyond the artistic kind, with a creativity rooted in rational economics, working parallel and in synergy with the elusive muses of artistic inspiration—a creativity that ultimately broke all constraints imposed on artistic expression. It is also an insight into the transformation of a traditional market for wall decoration into a sophisticated exchange mechanism for an internationally traded asset involving financial speculators, investors, and shrewd operators in a world awash with cash with nowhere safe to go. Globally, trillions of dollars of assets are producing more and more trillions of booked values, all chasing the same thing—a secure home. Over the past 300 years, art has become such a place.

This book provides an account of the circumstances and the individuals who fundamentally changed the definition of art and how they accomplished this astonishing feat: the brilliant minds that apotheosized art, the entrepreneurial painters who first conceived of art exhibitions; the clever auctioneers and the art auction system that became the nexus of today's market; the art press and the art critics with the power to make and break careers, even shape our cultural legacy; the scholars and experts who influence the market, as well as the curators and museums that apotheosize the product of artistic labor. All worked, and continue to work, in tandem to shape our cultural legacy and reap their share of the enormously rising global wealth. Along the way, this collaboration initiated an unprecedented liberation and explosive growth of creativity in the market for cultural commodities and proactively established the modus operandi of the modern market for art. What they constructed brought about fundamental and far-reaching changes in our definition of art, so radical that they blew apart centuries-old dictates of tradition, conventional propriety, and taste.

Nowadays, we take all this for granted: world-famous museums; blockbuster exhibitions; ubiquitous art galleries; verbose art critics; glitzy auctions; artistic superstars; experts and learned scholars with PhDs; and art collectors spending hundreds of millions. How did it all get started?

It was the unstoppable desire of artists 300 years ago to rebel against dictates and traditions, their determination to create a market for their products, and their drive to earn an independent livelihood. These were the midwives to the birth of the great diversity that characterizes modern art.

Art and Value

Before we proceed, I want to cover certain background information and context as well as make some observations about art as an asset category. A useful way to make sense of the history of the art market and the personalities who helped create it is to think of it as a man-made evolution—a commoditization process, if you like—towards a progressively dynamic, flexible, and versatile structure that serves the explicit purposes of increasing liquidity and establishing prices. This interaction between supply and demand, i.e., the market's velocity (sales), is particularly important for art. Art lacks intrinsic utility. Only when we sell art do we know its actual value. The market is the determinant of value and, by implication, decides what is and is not art.

[The concept of commoditization as a process was first discussed by Igor Kopytoff in a seminal essay published in 1986. He viewed commoditization as a market-inherent force that drives a market towards greater efficiency. Participants in a market, any market, are motivated to seek changes that improve the market's purpose: transferring ownership and establishing prices. Viewed in the context of commoditization, the different actions undertaken over these 200 years by the art market's various participants reveal themselves to have been rational decisions aimed to improve—subjectively or objectively—the market's function.][5]

To no one's surprise, the employment of art in the service of wealth is as old as recorded history. Armies plundered art because it was easy to transport and easily traded. The small stuff went into the bags of the ordinary soldiers; the big stuff was handled by supply trains for the generals and leaders. Obelisks from Egypt and entire tympanum sculpture groups from Greece safely made the journey across perilous sea lanes to their final destinations in Paris, London, or Berlin. I should note, however, that currently, the legitimacy of their present locations is being reconsidered in response to demands for their return by the countries of origin. The once proud symbols of imperial conquests have become embarrassments. 'O tempora, o mores'.

These days, in most circles it is no longer chic to plunder other nations' art. It is still done, of course, and fueling a thriving black market. But looted art is merely a byproduct of the market. More important is a somewhat more civilized role that art plays in today's world.

There are people with enormous personal fortunes who made their money in countries and political systems which, unlike the US and most European nations, offer no real protection for the legal ownership of wealth. As a result, these high-net-worth individuals continuously look for safe ways and secure places to store portions of their vast riches. They like art as an asset because it possesses certain uniquely convenient qualities.

Even in countries where personal property enjoys robust legal protection, high-net worth types find it useful to warehouse money in art works. For one, it's nice to look at. Yet, often, these valuable art assets are not actually hanging on the walls of the folks who own them. But even if masterpieces do indeed grace one's mansion(s), they are easily whisked away before the Feds, or the sheriff knock on the door. Bank accounts can be frozen, but art has legs.

These days, works of art can safely change hands without ever having to switch physical location. Access to special storage facilities in officially designated freeports around the globe will do the trick. An electronic code and encrypted authorization are all anyone needs. What is the benefit? Well, if you want to sell a company and reduce the official selling price, partial payment in art can make it happen. Do you want to leave a few hundred million to your offspring without going through all that irritating estate tax nonsense? Art can do it for you. Do you like that sprawling penthouse in Miami, New York, Paris, or London? It can be yours if the art is right. Even if you need some quick cash, your friendly art lender is ready to collateralize your conveniently and safely stored collection.[6]

The leitmotif that presently drives the art market's top end is an aspect of art's commodity character. Specifically, it is artwork's capacity to store and move discreetly and efficiently great amounts of exchangeable wealth and store them safely, out of others' reach, to do with as one wishes. Remember how many kilos of gold it takes to make up the price of the Leonardo panel?

Works of art are portable and unregulated international assets.

Art was deliberately turned into a storage for abundant wealth. It is the result of methodical actions that reshaped art's commodity character from pretty wall décor 300 years ago to high-value financial asset in the twenty-first century. It is the outcome of a process involving numerous participants—players—all working together, deliberately, and sometimes also inadvertently, towards maximizing the economic potential of the product we call 'art'.

What is 'value' in the context of art? Successful storage of value requires a consensus among at least two individuals that whatever asset is selected for the job—art, for example—can be exchanged for another asset with the understanding that the value stored in one type of asset can be transferred to the other. A 'thing', even fiat money, only has exchangeable value if someone other than the original owner agrees that it holds value in the first place. What that value turns out to be is up to the two parties to negotiate who engage in the exchange—one representing the supply side and the other the demand side.

Paper money, for example, has no intrinsic worth beyond its utility as a financial asset. If you hand someone a perfectly good $100 bill for food you want to buy, and that person is unwilling to take the bill in exchange for the food, you are stuck with a piece of paper and a growling stomach. The bill has become worthless because the other person does not accept it as a storage of exchangeable value for the purpose of this transaction. Similarly, if you have the equivalent of $100 million deposited in Botswana in local currency, the Pula, in a bank vault in the capital, Gaborone, the buying power—the exchangeable value—of this money is geographically restricted to Botswana, unless you can find someone somewhere else in the world who is willing to accept the Pula's exchange value. If you were to try exchanging Pulas for Euros at a bank in, say, Dingle, Ireland, you would fail. And, as my personal research showed, no local pub would accept them as payment for a pint of Guinness, either.

In a global context involving much higher values than $100 million, the dilemma becomes obvious. Our wealth depends on the agreement that whatever assets we own—cash, gold, real estate, loans, stocks, bonds, derivatives, Crypto, NFTs, etc., or art—possess transferable value.

Constructing an asset with exchangeable value, introducing it successfully to the market, and then protecting our faith in it require skillful and constant management. The Tulip Mania in Holland in the seventeenth century or, more recently, crypto currencies and NFTs are instructive examples. For conventional assets, we have central banks, various versions of a Security and Exchange Commission, official records of mortgages, hosts of rules and regulations, and, of course, the interplay of supply and demand in the market.[7]

Art is no different. Like any other asset's market, the market for art, the place where art's exchangeable value is established and transferred, also requires skillful and constant management.

Art's pedigree and its qualifications as a safe storage for tradeable value are impressive, well-established, and well-known. In Antiquity, owning a bronze sculpture by, for example, Lysippus (395–305 BCE), one of the celebrated sculptors of the Hellenistic Age, was just as good as, in fact, even better than, officially issued coinage the value of which was manipulated and subject to frequent debasement. Wealthy Romans, over 2000 years ago—like the great statesman and orator, Marcus Tullius Cicero (106–43 BCE) —collected, bought, and sold art.[8] Quickly and easily hidden from the occasional marauding barbarians or overzealous tax or debt collectors, art could potentially be sold at auction or privately, to other wealthy individuals anywhere in the Roman world, even borrowed against. Art was also a protection against the frequent debasement of the Roman currency (inflation) just like it is today. Throughout history, as we will see, in times of war and peace or economic ups and downs, art has demonstrated its reliability as an asset.

Owning art is also fun and exciting. Art is beautiful to look at, cool to own, stimulating to contemplate, heady to discuss, inspiring to learn from, erudite to know about, intellectually provocative, and culturally enriching. It is impossible to get the same level of enjoyment from the ownership of a bond or a stock certificate.

And it is rare, too. Everyone rich these days has a yacht or two, a few jets, homes everywhere. These things are a dime-a-dozen. But who has an introspective Rembrandt portrait, a sensuously reclining Modigliani nude, a contemplative Acrobat by Picasso, or a lyrical Rothko? Very, very few. Supply is severely constrained. Only a select group of the mega-rich role models of global Capitalism can vie for their possession.

Art represents wealth, be it personal or sovereign. And it has a long and impeccable provenance as a storage of exchangeable value. There isn't a single civilization in history that has not assigned value to art. Indeed, isn't this one of the qualifying conditions for the term 'civilization'?

Art always enjoyed good liquidity—at the right price, of course. Throughout history, many transfers of wealth were orchestrated by employing art as a storage of value. Whether statesmen's collections, imperial collections, papal collections, or bankers' collections, all of them represent wealth transferred and stored in art. Depending on how one defines art, it could be said that art is the oldest currency. Art preceded coins and paper money by thousands of years. Unlike a sword, a tool or real estate, art has no practical use, no intrinsic value, except the aesthetic enjoyment it stimulates and the storage and convenient transport for wealth/value it offers. Oscar Wilde's comment that 'all art is quite useless' was off the mark—an exception for the Irish wit.[9]

What is less well-known, however, is how this market for art objects developed to become what it is today, and what is involved in maintaining collective faith in it. This is one of the central topics I explore in this book.

The apotheosis of art that our western cultures constructed implies that these 'consecrated' objects must be removed from vulgar associations with mammon. Is not the most flattering compliment we can give to an artwork to describe it as 'priceless'? Yet, as many gallery aficionados and art collectors can confirm, such 'priceless' objects usually do have a price, albeit a high one. The savvy Uber-art dealer Lord Duveen (1869–1939) once countered with great wit to Paul Mellon's complaint about the steep price of Thomas Lawrence's (1769–1830) *Pinkie* (1794) by explaining that 'when you are paying high for the priceless, you are still getting it cheap' (Fig 1.3).

[Joseph Duveen was one of the leading art dealers in Europe in the early decades of the twentieth century. A superb salesman, he cultivated relationship with wealthy Americans, such as Mellon, Rockefeller, Morgan, Kress, and others and sold them European Old Master for extraordinary prices. Many of the great works in US museums have passed through Duveen's hands. There is even a wing named after him in the National Gallery in London.][10]

We can discuss a building in an aesthetic context as a piece of architecture or as a construction project in engineering terms, but also as a commodity traded in the real estate market. Art, similarly, can also be examined in different ways. This book considers art as a unique product category that was created specifically for a market that was ingeniously constructed by stakeholders to liberate artistic creativity and maximize the economic and financial potential of the resulting art products.

It may be true that these commodity-centered ruminations demythologize the apotheosis of art. But the apotheosis of art is man-made

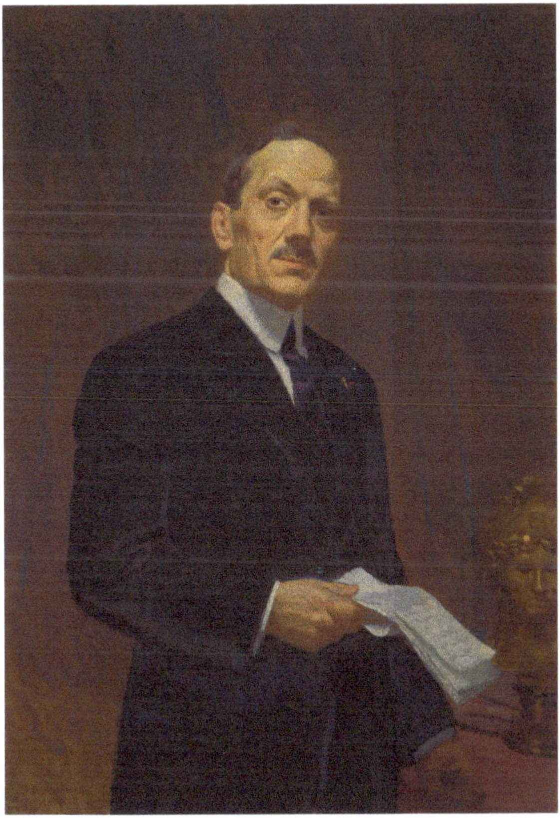

Fig. 1.3 Augusto Bastianini (1876–1940); portrait of Joseph Duveen, 1st Baron Duveen

and intentional. It is, to use a modern vernacular, simply part of the commodity character of art, its ‘brand’. We should be able to appreciate art in whatever physical and intellectual contexts we encounter it, even as a commodity for a modern consumer society.

Notes

1. Dictionary of Art Historians. https://arthistorians.info/manderk/ (last accessed March 2025).
2. For example, Ben Lewis, The Last Leonardo (N.Y.: Ballantine Books, 2019).

3. Algernon Graves, Art Sales, 3 vols. (N.Y.: Burt Franklin, 1970).
4. Thomas Bayer and John Page, “Arthur Tooth: A London Art Dealer in the Spotlight, 1870–71”, Nineteenth-Century Art Worldwide (Spring, 2010), Bayer and Page, The Development of the Art Market in England: Money As Muse, 1730–1900, (London: Pickering and Chatto, 2011); Bayer, Page, Yaron Raviv, Joshua. Rosett, “Age, Human Capital and the Quality of Work: New Evidence from Old Masters,” The Berkeley Electronic Journal of Economic Analysis and Policy, Vol. 13, No. 2 (July 2013): 687–708; Bayer, Page, “The ingenious marketing of modern paintings,” Journal of Historical Research in Marketing, vol. 6, no 2 (2014): 211–233; Bayer, Page, Raviv, Rosett, “Seasonal Affective Disorder and Seasoned Art Auction Prices: New Evidence from Old Masters,” Journal of Behavioral and Experimental Economics, vol. 59 (December 2015): 74–84; Bayer, “Arthur Tooth”, Bloomsbury Art Markets (formerly Art Market Dictionary), Johannes Nathan, Inge Reist, Thomas Gaehtgens, eds. (online, 2022). Readers of our earlier book of the British art market, my dissertation, M.A. thesis, and other published writing will encounter familiar events and individuals in this book. My research relies to varying extents on the primary and secondary data I have described above, but the purposes vary. In my years of investigating and writing about the British art market, I have regularly revisited specific occurrences and data to examine them in different contexts and to differing degrees of detail. Rather than copiously citing myself, I provide my original sources. Whenever observations throughout the book are based on analyses of the Bayer/Page data, I cite accordingly.
5. Igor Kopytoff, ¨The Cultural Biography of Things: Commoditization as Process,¨ The Social Life of Things: Commodities in Cultural Perspectives, ed., A. Appadurai (Cambridge, MA: Yale University Press, 1986): 64–91.
6. Once a guarded insider secret, Freeports have recently received more attention, likely not welcome by all their stakeholders. For more information on these Freeports see, Talia Berniker, “Behind Closed Doors: A Look At Freeports”; https://itsartlaw.org/2020/11/03/behind-closed-doors-a-look-at-freeports/ (last accesses March 2025); Leena Kim, ¨Where the Superrich store their Art to avoid Taxes,¨ Town and Country, (April 2023) https://www.townandcountrymag.com/leisure/arts-and-culture/a35032655/what-is-a-freeport-art-collections/ (Last accessed March 2025)Famke A. Loos, ¨Freeports as ecosystems for the preservation of fine art value and the acceleration of related businesses,¨ (Rotterdam: Erasmus University Rotterdam (2017) MA thesis, supervisor: F. VermeylenJohn Zarobell, “Freeports and the Hidden Value of Art”, International Studies Faculty Publications. (2020): 27, https://repository.usfca.edu/international_fac/27 (last accessed March 2025).

7. For more information about the Tulip Mania see Anne Goldgar, Tulipmania: Money, Honor and Knowledge in the Dutch Golden Age (Chicago: University of Chicago Press 2007); Charles River, Tulip Mania: The History and Legacy of the World's First Speculative Bubble during the Dutch Golden Age (Charles River Editors, 2018).
8. https://www.academia.edu/43570364/Did_Cicero_Care_About_Art_An_Apology (last accessed March 2025); Anne Leen, "Cicero and the Rhetoric of Art," The American Journal of Philology, vol, 112, No. 2 (Summer 1991): 229–245.
9. Oscar Wilde, The Picture of Dorian Gray (N.Y.: Random House (1909): viii.
10. Samuel N. Behrman, Duveen (N.Y.: Random House, 1951): 30–31.

CHAPTER 2

For Art's Sake: A (Very) Brief History of the Modern Art Market

If we were to think of the history of the modern art market as a stage play, the first act would be set in the Netherlands sometime in the sixteenth century. It would focus on the fundamental change in the way artists, specifically painters and sculptors, made their living. For the arts, this was an existential and defining event. The old patronage system was waning. Commissions from wealthy individuals—aristocrats, church leaders, rich merchants, and bankers—to do specific works were declining. To make up for this loss of income, artists began to produce artworks with the hope of selling them to someone yet to be identified—an anonymous consumer. This shift from the old system to a market-based economy demanded that artists, for better or worse, start thinking like businessmen. Cost-and-benefit considerations, consumer-orientation, entrepreneurial knack, and marketing savvy became as important to success as artistic skill.

Without doubt, a vibrant trade in art existed already in antiquity. There were celebrated artistic superstars, their works highly prized and much sought after. Names like Apelles, Aristides, Zeuxis, Praxiteles, or Lysippus are enshrined in the pantheon of artists, much like Rubens, Rodin, Picasso, or Pollock. Unfortunately, we do not have such comprehensive primary data for the ancient times as we have for the period that frames this book. However, scholars focusing on the art market of the ancient Mediterranean world have found evidence that allows certain conclusions about the dynamics of the art market in ancient times.[1]

T. M. Bayer, *The Genesis of the Modern Art Market in London, 1700–1900*, https://doi.org/10.1007/978-3-032-00594-6_2

There is also ample evidence that artists created works for an anonymous market during the period of the Renaissance and the Baroque in the art centers of Europe. It makes business sense to display a few smaller works and sketches around the workshop that could be bought on the spot. Prints, also, were being produced for mass-distribution. The German artist Albrecht Dürer (1471–1522) was particularly successful in this regard.[2] Our art and archeology museums are filled with prints, sketches, reduced versions of famous statues, and small statuary groups often depicting ancient mythological subjects. Many of these themes have served as inspiration for artists long before the Renaissance and continue to do so today. We usually take such objects as an indication that artists, besides working on commission, also produced for a market of consumers personally unknown to them.[3]

However, the type of data-driven market analyses underlying this book, requires a vast amount of very detailed information directly related to the sale of identifiable works of art. In fact, each individual transaction included in the data I use here comprises twelve different variables. Such granular records like dealers' daily business ledgers; detailed auction sales records spanning centuries; sellers' and buyers' names and social status; how much they paid; dimensions, title, and medium of each work; exhibition catalogues, etc., are not available to us for these earlier periods. Far better data for economic investigations of the art market can be found among the archival records and contemporary anecdotal accounts from the trading cities of the sixteenth and seventeenth centuries in the region of today's Netherlands.

The Art Market in the Netherlands

For well over a century, art historians and economists have mined the copious surviving records relating to the production and marketing of art in the Dutch Republics during this era.[4] The period is particularly significant, because it marks the time when we can first detect the influence of business-oriented thinking, i.e., economic considerations characteristic of a modern consumer society, on many of the works of art created.

In the Netherlands, the decline in patronage of church leaders and members of the social and monied elite had made way for its replacement by an increasingly affluent middle class. There were import/export traders, commercial money lenders, shipping agents, wholesalers; retailers; tavern owners and countless others who fancied an attractive artwork to decorate their homes. Keeping up with one's neighbors was a significant market driver.

Without the traditional patrons, artists lost the relatively low-risk position that comes with working on commission. Instead, they had to start producing works on speculation and find ways to sell their products to a largely unknown and heterogeneous consumer group. It was made up of individuals of different degrees of wealth, different tastes, types and levels of education, professions, and social backgrounds. Like all other producers who sold their products on the open market, they adapted to meet the demands of the developing competitive environment. Artists became independent entrepreneurs. They tested new ways to make and market their products, in other words, they engaged in process innovation. Furthermore, in response to the growing, competitive, and increasingly diverse market, they also began exploring new subject matters and styles, i.e., they employed product differentiation. Both, process innovation and product differentiation, are competitive practices characteristic of a modern consumer economy.

For example, artists switched from painting on wooden panels to using canvas.[5] Canvas was easier to prepare, lighter to transport, less vulnerable to weather, and cheaper than aged oak panels. The average size of paintings became smaller to fit the spatial limitations of the urban residences of the new buyers. Furthermore, smaller sizes made it possible to offer a larger selection of less labor-intensive pictures for sale. In addition, there was a noticeable tendency towards specialization in subjects as painters sought to carve out their niche—their brand, as it were. The same trends would show up later in England.

Paulus Potter /1625–1654), for instance, had a thing for animals, especially cows, whereas Jan Steen's (1626–1679) brand were bawdy tavern interiors and brawling peasants; Jan de Heem (1606–1684) specialized in luxurious still life while Pieter Saenredam (1597–1665) produced church interiors. In fact, a casual look through any dictionary of Dutch painters of the 'Golden Age of Dutch Painting' confirms that this specialization was such an effective differentiation for art producers that it became one of the defining aspects of the art of this period. Further evidence of the influence of business-oriented thinking was the popularity of formula painting, as well as the practice of copying and mechanical repetition of designs for workshop production.[6] Thousands of nearly identical *Landscape with Windmill* pictures or *Vanitas* still life images were mass-produced for the market. A painter's tool kit of this period typically included specially designed brushes used exclusively for creating certain visual effects, such as wind-swept trees and clouds.

This market orientation even led to stylistic changes. One group of painters, for example, called the 'tonalist', became known for their near monochromatic landscapes. With only a bare minimum of colors, these works could be finished quickly and cheaply. Others only painted in shades of gray to produce cheap 'grisailles', as these pictures were called.

To market their art, some painters set up stalls in commercials fairs and markets. Even taverns and inns occasionally doubled as proto galleries. In fact, the painter Jan Steen owned a brew pub in Delft for a few years and supposedly used his walls to display his own pictures and possibly those of other artists. Paintings were also offered for sale on the 2nd floor of the Amsterdam stock exchange, marking a portentous early juxtaposition of these two speculative assets.

The fortunes of painters during the Dutch Golden Age experienced a steady decline towards the end of the first half of the seventeenth century.[7] There were several causes. The sluggish economy around mid-century; the costly conflict with France that started in 1672; and an increasing tendency of collectors to buy paintings by old masters rather than contemporary works, all contributed to the market's contraction. Demand dropped, as did the number of specialist artists. Johann van Gool (1685–1763), a painter and artists' biographer, wrote in 1750 that this decline had intensified due to speculation and corrupt activities of dealers.[8] Unfortunately, the author did not elaborate on the nature of these shady practices. However, the trend of acquiring Old Master paintings in favor of contemporary works suggests that Van Gool's comment was on point.

Unfortunately, for an in-depth quantitative study of the construction of a modern art market, the Dutch Golden Age was too short-lived. The region was also exposed to frequent wars which interfered with the secular development of a market infrastructure. It also does not offer the detailed records of art sales needed for such a time-spanning investigation. But it alerts us to what indicators we need to look for in an environment in which market dynamics can play themselves out fully, without interruption and impediments.

The Art Market in England

The chance to study the development of an art market under more favorable historical conditions is in England, specifically in London. There, between 1700 and 1900, an art market of increasing complexity and sophistication developed unhindered. With a population of over 500,000 people, London, by 1700, was Europe's richest and largest city with a lively, consumer-oriented economy that was creating vast new wealth. The high density of consumption in that bustling city, its size, wealth, and social diversity were perfect conditions for developing new commercial techniques to encourage consumption and direct demand into specific areas of the economy. This was the revolutionary stage in the development of the modern consumer society familiar to us today.[9] Importantly, the island was never affected directly by the widespread destruction resulting from the wars fought on the Continent. Its economy progressed unencumbered and, therefore, presents ideal conditions for systematic study.

For all these factors, London presented an excellent opportunity to construct the foundation of a consumer-oriented, competitive modern art market and, over the next two centuries, nurse it to full maturity. The English art market was centralized in London, and it was less developed or regulated than the different regional markets on the Continent, like the Dutch Republic's or France's. The London market could grow unconstrained by any of the institutional nuisances that still retarded business on the Continent, like guilds or different restrictions on sales. In fact, some of the best artists from the Netherland sought their fortune across the Channel.[10]

Moreover, art collecting was no novelty in England. The 'grand tour' to the Continent was coming into fashion during the seventeenth century, and young upper-class Englishmen saw, for the first time, the luxurious lifestyles of their peers in different European countries. On these grand tours, British aristocrats and members of wealthy families would traverse the Continent to see personally the great architectural, artistic, and cultural treasures of Europe. France, Germany, Italy, the Netherlands, Portugal, Spain, and Switzerland were typical destinations. The impact of such conspicuous display of wealth and artistic patronage on impressionable young men from an island with little native tradition of painting must have been extraordinary.[11] Think of Americans traveling to Europe in the late nineteenth or early twentieth century—or even today—and seeing, for the first time, the incredible diversity of art and architecture and its ubiquitous presence. Germany still has more castles than the US has McDonalds outlets.

Of course, this 'grand tour' had to show some tangible evidence, a souvenir, that would testify to the journey's success. Or, perhaps, if it was not possible to make the journey personally, or if it was deemed too risky to lug an expensive art piece across bandit-riddled Europe, then, maybe, a picture or two bought from one of the Dutch dealers, who had recently begun to arrive in London, would do just fine.[12]

According to contemporary sources, dealers and private owners of art on the Continent knew very well that the English were prepared to pay high prices.[13] It was also widely known that these visitors' knowledge of art was often in reverse proportion to their enthusiasm and the sizes of their purses. Not surprisingly, as a result, many of the imported canvases were of dubious authenticity.

[This same opinion among sellers of art prevails to this day with similar consequences. But the label of ignorance shifts over time to different nationalities. In the late nineteenth and early twentieth century, it was the Americans who wore it—and, to some extent, they still do. In the 1970s, the label was used to describe the newly arriving Arab art consumers; ten years later, it was attached to the Japanese; more recently to Russians and Chinese art buyers. Wherever vast wealth is abundantly created, there are usually solicitous art dealers ready to provide prestige and status—at a cost, of course. Conspicuous consumption is essential to signaling wealth.]

The sleazy reputation resulting from unscrupulous business practices would have far-reaching consequences. It was also a source of negative publicity and lack of trust that fed a gossip-hungry audience. The same holds true today. When there is that kind of money floating around, even if—or because—it involves consecrated objects of our culture, there is great temptation and opportunity for questionable practices.[14]

Yet despite the reputational problems of the trade, imports of art thrived in England at the dawning of the eighteenth century—unfortunately at the expense of native English artists. This situation was further exacerbated by the fact that Dutch artists had increasingly migrated to

England. Better trained and more popular, these Continental competitors worsened the already tenuous situation of native English painters.[15] Ironically, at the same time, collecting in general was growing, and the period saw the beginning of a regular trade in works of art. However, instead of benefitted local artists, these buoyant conditions attracted enterprising dealers who put their marketing talents to work, selling old works of art at auctions, lotteries, and even raffles.[16]

The art market in England at the beginning of the eighteenth century can best be described as a market in a state of tension. Wealth's 'rich rewards', to use van Mander's earlier observation, were unevenly spread among painters. As a result, the arts environment in England during this century can be characterized as a competition involving competitively disadvantaged native artists for a share in an expanding market for art products. To thrive, painters had to explore and exploit new opportunities like other independent producers of luxury goods. They also had to compete with an established trade in older pictures and cheap locally produced or imported copies.

The ingenious ways in which these challenges were met are responsible for the development of the infrastructure that makes up the modern art market—not just in Great Britain. The modus operandi spread to neighboring Europe and beyond and defines how the international art market works to this day.[17]

Notes

1. Sarah E. Bond, Trade and Taboo: Disreputable Professions in the Roman Mediterranean, (Ann Harbor: University of Michigan Press, 2016); for an excellent overview of Greek art, including its production and trade see John Pedley, Greek Art and Archeology, (N.Y.: Pearson, 2020), 5th ed.
2. Eva Cobb, "Renaissance Printmaking: How Albrecht Durer Changed the Game", The Collector (Nov 2, 2024), https://www.thecollector.com/how-albrecht-durer-changed-printmaking-renaissance/ (last accessed March 2025); also, David Landau and Peter Parshall, The Renaissance Print: 1470–1550 (New Haven & London: Yale University Press, 1994).
3. Marcello Fantoni, Louise C. Matthew and Sara F. Matthew-Grieco, The Art Market in Italy, 15th–17th Centuries, (Modena: F.C. Panini, 2003); Francis Haskell, Patrons and Painters (New Haven and London: Yale University Press, 1980), offers the first example of systematically relating the art of a particular period—the Baroque—to the patronal environment in which it was produced.

4. The study of the art market in sixteenth and seventeenth century Netherlands is benefitting from increasing scholarly attention. The first modern systematic study of the period's art market was undertaken by Abraham Bredius, "De kunsthandel te Amsterdam in de XVIIe eeuw,"Amsterdam Jaarboekje (1891): 54–57. This publication was followed by Hans Floerke, Die Formen des Kunsthandels, das Atelier und die Sammler in den Niederlanden vom 15.–18. Jahrhundert (Munich and Leipzig: Georg Muller 1905); here are some examples of more recent contributions to the subject: John Michael Montias, Artists and Artisans in Delft: A Socio-Economic Study of the Seventeenth Century (Princeton: Princeton University Press,1982); Montias, "Cost and Value in Seventeenth-Century Dutch Art", Art History, 10, no. 4 (December 1987): 455–466 for an examination of this period's paintings under a supply and demand model. Montias argues that certain stylistic changes are, indeed, attributable to market forces; Montias "Socio-economic Aspects of Netherlandish Art from the Fifteenth to the Seventeenth Century: A Survey", The Art Bulletin, LXXII, 3 (September 1990): 358–373; the increasing presence of dealers is addressed in Montias, "Art dealers in the seventeenth-century Netherlands", Simiolus, 18, 4 (1990): 244–256; Montias, Vermeer and His Milieu: A Web of Social History (Princeton: Princeton University Press 1991); Thomas Bayer, "The Seventeenth Century Dutch Art Market: The Influence of Economics on Artistic Production.", Athanor, X (Tallahassee: Florida State University, 1991): 21–28 and Bayer, "Socio-economic Aspects of Netherlandish Painting during the Sixteenth Century, Athanor, XII (Tallahassee: Florida State University, 1994): 55–59 also take a market oriented approach and list additional sources; Niederlandische Jahrbuch, "Painting for the Market," (1999); De Marchi and Van Miegroet, ¨Rules Versus Play in Early Modern Art Markets,¨ Louvain Economic Review, 66 (2000): 146–148; also their essay ¨The History of Art Markets,¨ Handbook of the Economics of Art and Culture, (Amsterdam: Elsevier, 2006)), V. Ginsburgh, ed., are also important contributions to the topic. This list is a small sample.
5. Dianne Wolfthal, The Beginning of Netherlandish Canvas Painting 1400–1530 (Cambridge: Cambridge University Press, 1989): 12–14.
6. Floerke: 129–134, 154–155, 158; Karel van Mander, Dutch and Flemish Painting (New York: MacFarlane, 1938): 158–160.
7. David Ormrod, ¨The Art Trade and Its Urban Context, England and the Netherlands compared, 1570–1770¨, Auctions, Agents and Dealers, J. Warren and A. Turpin, eds. (Oxford: The Beazley Archives and Archeopress, 2008): 11–12, and n. 9.

8. Jan van Gool, De Nieuwe Schouburg der Nederlandische Kunstschilders en Schilderessen, 2 vols. (The Hague: 1750), vol. 1:105, 360–361, vol. 2: 112–113.
9. Neil McKendrick, John Brewer and J. H. Plumb (eds.), The Birth of a Consumer Society (Bloomington: Indiana University Press, 1982).
10. Horace Walpole, Anecdotes of Painting in England (London: Henry G. Bohn, 1849): vol. 1, ix.
11. John Evelyn, Diary & Correspondence of John Evelyn, Frs., W. Bray, ed (London: G. Bell and Sons, 1883–1887); 15; Walpole, vol. 2: 9, 'While many works of art in England have suffered so greatly from neglect, ignorance, and fanaticism, added to accidental damage and natural decay, the names of our countrymen, to whom many of these works must be assigned, perished with them'. Walpole, vol. 1: ix, further observes that 'this country, which does not always err in vaunting its own production, has not a single volume to show on the works of its painters. In truth, it had rarely given birth to a genius in that profession'.
12. Frank Hermann, The English as Collectors (New York: W. W. Norton & Co., 1972): 9, and n. 1; Richard Redgrave, A Century of Painters of the English School (London: Sampson Low, Marston & Co. Ltd, 1890): 11; Michael Foss, The Age of Patronage (Ithaca: Cornell University Press, 1971), p. 74.
13. Foss: 74.
14. Sidney Hutchison, The History of the Royal Academy 1768–1968 (London: Robert Royce, Ltd., 1968):13/14; Louise Lippincott, Selling Art in Georgian London (New Haven & London: Yale University Press, 1988): 108, mentions the practice of Arthur Pond, painter, dealer, and publisher, to provide a written guarantee of authenticity; Ronald Paulson, Hogarth: His Life, Art, and Times (New Haven & London: Yale University Press, 1971): vol. 1: 372, vol. 2: 330; John Pye, Patronage of British Art, A Historical Sketch (London: Longman, Brown, Green and Longmans, 1845): 43, and n. 43, 242; David Solkin, Painting for Money (New Haven & London: Yale University Press, 1993): 251, 254, 5; John Steegmann, The Role of Taste from George I to George IV (London: Macmillan and Co. Ltd., 1936): 27; Walpole, vol 3: 730; William Whitley, Art in England, 2 vols. (N.Y.: Hacker Art Books, 1973): vol. 1: 110, 156, 210.
15. Walpole, vol. 1: ix; Pye: 44, note 46.
16. Bernard Denvir, The Eighteenth Century (London &N.Y.: Longman, 1983): 167–169 mentions Rouquet's emphasis of the spectacular growth of the art trade in London; also, Pye: 28. The painter Hogarth claimed that the British, as a commercial people, were more interested in the trade in art than painting itself. See John Ireland and John Nichols, Hogarth's Work, 3 vols. (Edinburgh & London: Oliphant, Anderson & Ferrier, 1874), vol

3: 64 ff. On lotteries involving art see Sven H.A. Bruntjen, John Boydell (1719–1804) A Study of Art Patronage and Publishing in Georgian London (N.Y., Garland Publishing, Inc., 1985): 148, and n. 98; Whitley, vol 2: 241, mentions that the first raffle of art in England was organized by members of the 'St. Luke's Club', sometimes also called 'Society of Virtuosi' in 1689.

17. For additional information affecting the London-based art market during its early stage, see Bayer and Page, The Development of the Art Market in England: 16–23.

CHAPTER 3

Ingenious Marketing

The ingenious and novel methods the London artist community devised under unfavorable conditions are textbook examples of entrepreneurial thinking. The common thread is the artists' collective focus on maximizing their potential as producers of luxury goods in a highly competitive, buoyant, and consumer-oriented environment. These were the first steps on the long path of the market's increasing efficiency in trading works of art—its commodification.

The depiction of artists as tormented geniuses in numerous "biopics" has resulted in the often-misleading impression that business savvy and artistic talent are incompatible. However, the history of the art market proves this assumption to be erroneous. Artists throughout the ages have been extraordinarily inventive and successful in selling their products. Apparently, the Muses who inspire artists appear to have a knack for branding and marketing as well. Perhaps, money, 'pecunia' in Latin, should be crowned the tenth muse? There is little doubt that the desire and need to sell their works have driven artists to ever more resourceful means to innovate and differentiate, to be original and distinct—in other words, to increase their competitiveness.

As their brethren had done on the Continent, the artists in London also catered to the wealthy. However, by the time the eighteenth century came around, these painters began to use several new strategies that would be decisive not just for their individual future, but to the future of the entire

T. M. Bayer, *The Genesis of the Modern Art Market in London, 1700–1900*, https://doi.org/10.1007/978-3-032-00594-6_3

art market. The focus of the market started to shift away from the social elite and move in the direction of the ordinary Englishman and woman. From that point forward, the business of art was increasingly defined by the dynamics of the relationship between art and a new audience—the public at large. This dialectic set a development—a commoditization—into motion that has shaped the production of art ever since.[1] On one side was a heterogeneous group of consumers from different social backgrounds, with different levels of education, wealth, different political views, different tastes, and different types of dwellings and, on the other side, were the artists who wanted to sell their works to them.

For the first time, painters staged public exhibitions and, also for the first time, they took full advantage of the media. The success of this combination—public exhibition and popular media—ultimately leads to the birth of the all-important middleman, the professional, profit-seeking art dealer whose presence would fundamentally alter the trajectory of not just the market, but, as I argue, inevitably the arts as well.

These artists' deliberate shift of focus to the anonymous mass of consumers, similar to their Netherlandish colleagues, occurred among other occupations too. Different makers of luxury goods, Wedgewood, Chippendale, Hester Bateman or the silver smith, Paul de Lamerie, for example, were pursuing similar paths.[2] Paintings as wall décor for a numerically larger and demographically more diverse group of potential buyers were in competition with these products. The 'Consumer Revolution' had created opportunities for many luxury goods producers, not just painters. Besides porcelain and sterling silver there were fancy mirrors, pricey clocks, hand-painted silk wallpapers, expensive cabinetwork, etc., that were aggressively and imaginatively marketed to the same clientele.

Painters were aware of this competition. To stand out they had to act. Something was needed, something special and unique, something that would set their product noticeably apart from all the other luxury goods on the market. Consumers had to perceive paintings as much more than just another luxury product, but as something different, much better than a common Chippendale desk or a set of silver candelabras. To achieve this, painters set out on a deliberate and brilliant path to create for art a new image, one that consisted of a distinctive, intangible dimension—an aura.

[The concept of 'aura' as an aspect of a work of art was first introduced by the German philosopher, Walter Benjamin (1892–1940), in his 1936 essay 'Das Kunstwerk im Alter seiner technischen Reproduzierbarkeit'.[3] *Benjamin used the term aura to describe an intangible, unique, even apotheotic aspect of original art works. He argued that this aura is the result of an artwork's historical and cultural context combined with its physical presence. In non-scientific terms, it is whatever gives us goosebumps when we are in the presence of a great work of art. Mark Rothko's (1903–1970) fourteen paintings in the Rothko Chapel in Houston, TX, for example, or Vermeer's (1632–1675) Girl with a Pearl Earring (c. 1665) are among my personal favorites. In Benjamin's opinion, reproducing an original artwork can weaken, or even outright destroy, this aura. Benjamin published his essay during the rise of Nazism when the dissemination of reproductions of original works often explicitly served propagandistic purposes. However, the mass-produced reproductive engravings that fueled the Mid-Victorian art economy had the opposite effect: original works achieved celebrity status precisely because they were familiar to millions of people from their reproductions. A Madison Avenue-style campaign made sure that the aura of the original work was continually reinforced. Lady Elizabeth Butler's (1846–1933) Scotland Forever (1881, Leeds Art Gallery), one of the most reproduced paintings of its era and a masterfully painted glorification of battle and patriotism, also served similar ends, yet without discernable loss of its aura.]*

Along with this redefinition of their art, English artists also managed to reinvent themselves professionally. Rather than endure the life of humble practitioners of a manual trade, like furniture makers or silversmiths, they succeeded in becoming respectable professional men of ideas and members of polite society.

These artist-entrepreneurs were well-aware of the magnitude of their undertaking and tackled it with passion as well as pragmatic business sense. Their new idea about the character of art—its aura—needed to be nurtured, disseminated, and promoted to have any lasting impact. To that end, painters formed specific organizations for the explicit purpose of bankrolling and staging art exhibitions to which anyone was admitted—as long as you could afford the entrance fee which usually included a nice exhibition catalogue.[4] During the next century, this competition for attention in a public arena would give birth to modern art dealing and radically new types of art products. The modern history of art developed within the context of producers competing for consumers' attention. This same direct engagement of art with the public also gave rise to the academic discipline of art history as well as professional art writing and art criticism. And it factored into the later use of contemporary art as a form of investment.

Over the period of a century, British painters, individually and collectively, removed crucial social and economic obstacles that obstructed their progress. They erected in their place a whole new market mechanism without which the current art market would have developed differently. A remarkable feat, indeed, and a testimony to their entrepreneurial ingenuity.

Creating a Brand

The value of artistic labor today is not measured by input of hours and material costs. But that is a recent achievement. The radical change in the definition of art and the related valuation of artworks were gradually constructed only recently, starting in the 1700s and concluded at the end of the nineteenth century. And it took an impressively skillful, strategic, and multi-faceted public relations campaign to accomplish it. Without this redefinition, the modern art market could not function the way it does today. Impressionism, Post-Impressionism, Surrealism with its own Manifesto, Expressionism, Cubism, Abstract Art, Non-Objective Art, and the many other 'isms' that define the landscape of twentieth and twenty-first century art, would not exist; and neither would the extraordinary prices that modern works of art command today.

This deliberate construction of a new brand identity for 'art'—a unique 'aura'—had two purposes. One was to create for art a competitive edge over other luxury goods and, as a result, enlarge its market share. As merely attractive wall décor for a larger and socially more diverse number of potential buyers, paintings were in direct competition with a host of other luxury goods.

The other objective was to remove the earning constraints imposed by the traditional custom of enumerating artists based on time and material. The goal was to replace it with an ambiguously calculated method, one that priced the product of divine genius gloriously inspired by the Muses of Artistic Creativity. This far more elastic system would be quite handy in negotiations. The mega-dealer Duveen's quip to Mellon about the high price of the priceless is a telling example. By that notion, even Leonardo's *Salvator Mundi* was cheap.

This was a quest for economic liberation and professional self-determination. Artists wanted to be in charge of the definition of their brand and in control of negotiating their own compensation, independent of quantifiable variables, such as time and material costs.

For these very reasons, their discussion centered around the intangible aspects, the 'aura' of paintings. It is no coincidence that during the eighteenth century, the Age of Enlightenment, the meaning of the term 'genius' changed from 'characteristic disposition' to 'exalted special ability'.[5] The times were right. Interestingly, the average age of geniuses among artists has declined over the years, to the point where the term has now been applied to children to promote their art.

The exorbitant value society is prepared to assign nowadays to artistic labor is predicated on a societal consensus to accept, promote, and sustain works of art as objects with a worth that lies in the intangible realm. Art has no inherent price limit. It underwent an economic apotheosis. As with any faith, its canon is whatever its apostles and followers choose to make it. Without such a consensus, payments of tens and hundreds of millions of dollars for the labor of certain artists would not exist.

It was in London, during the eighteenth century, where this consensus matured unencumbered, grew beyond society's elite, democratized gradually and, over the next 200 years, globalized. It is no coincidence that this public relation and branding campaign also included shrewd ways to turn this intangible quality into tangible cash. After all, Adam Smith, one of the great moralists of the time and father of classical Economics, wrote in 1776, that we are creatures with a 'preponderance to truck, barter and exchange'.[6] There was no reason to limit this urge to tangible objects and services.

The late seventeenth and eighteenth centuries were a time when philosophical discussions were frequently concerned with the moral dimension of 'work' and of buying things. Economists explored, among other topics, the moral aspects of consumption. And one of the popular themes happen to be the moral pros and cons of paintings as a consumer good.

For us, living in a time when consumption is glorified beyond moral or ethical bounds, the eighteenth-century preoccupation with these issues seems odd. But it was a vastly different time. Europe was in the midst of the Enlightenment, when our views of society were fundamentally redirected and, for the first time, gave importance to the individual. A framework for the actions of these newly valued individuals had to be established, one that provided moral direction and guidance for the freshly emancipated multitudes. This was the time of the writing of the US Constitution.

While not quite as contentious as the opinions concerning the creation of a new nation, the views among the learned men of the age on the topic of consumption were by no means in agreement. What is remarkable in this drawn-out discourse is the active role taken by painters in directing the discussion step by step to the conclusion they desired. They wanted to be able to take charge of defining the merit of their individual contribution to society as artists and to take control over their own economic fate.

The eminent Anthony Ashley Cooper, the 3rd Earl of Shaftesbury (1671–1713), led the conservative camp.[7] A prominent art theorist during the early part of the century, he took the position that the purpose of paintings was to display themes of moral significance. He insisted that such themes be chosen by members of the aristocracy. Furthermore, they had to flatter the patrons' civic virtues as stewards of the nation for the professed benefit of all citizens—undisguised political propaganda, in other words. The role of painters was simply to paint these themes. The Earl proposed that the standards by which paintings would be judged should be how successfully they complied with these requirements. By implication, the value of the individual artist to society was similarly determined. Sir Anthony Ashley Cooper was of the opinion that ordinary portrait painting required no 'liberal knowledge, genius, education, converse, manners, moral-science, mathematics, optics, [but was] merely practical and vulgar'.[8]

Understandably, painters were not thrilled with being delegated the role of glorifying the fortunate folks who, by luck of parentage, ran the country. It was hardly exciting to paint yet another rich and vain person placed in an allegory based on some ancient story of Roman Republican virtues. Maybe one could take some liberties with the symbols, perhaps give them a little personal interpretation. But overall, painting portraits of the nation's elite clad in togas standing next to a Corinthian column beholding a marble bust of Cato were rather boring. And, quite frankly, the Earl's unkind comments about portrait painting—describing it 'merely practical and vulgar'—were bad for business.

Painting portraits, at that time—the first half of the eighteenth century—was one of the most lucrative activities for painters.[9] Everyone who thought they were somebody—and that covered a vast multitude—and could pay for one—a considerably smaller number—had to have one. Portraiture was too important of an income source for artists to allow it to be excluded from the trappings that project civic virtue. But how could a portrait of an ordinary person, whose only qualification was their ability to pay, promote civic virtue?

Jonathan Richardson (1667–1745), one of the popular portraitists of the period and, apparently, a rather practical man, came up with a solution. He posed a simple question: since civic virtue was the issue, shouldn't portraits of aristocratic men or women of high moral standing who by virtue of their elevated social standing alone were deemed significant to the well-being of the nation meet the Earl's standards? His clever reasoning worked. The proposal had two benefits. It conveniently flattered the sitter by giving her or him high moral standing simply by being portrayed and, at the same time, put money in the artist's pocket. The sophisticated theoretical discourse turned out to be quite receptive to the idea and readily included portraiture and their makers among ranks of the civically virtuous.

[As most of his fellow artists at the time, Richardson was predominantly a portrait painter. He was also a well-known collector of Old Master drawings. Richardson wrote extensively on a variety of art-related topics and published several influential works, for example, 'An Essay on the Theory of Painting' (1715); 'An Essay of the Whole of Art Criticism as it Relates to Painting' (1719); and 'An Account of Some of the Statues, Bas-Reliefs, Drawings, and Pictures in Italy' (1722).]

While Richardson's astute reasoning aided portrait painting specifically, it unfortunately did nothing for landscapes, seascapes, animal, or narrative paintings. These categories were all still excluded from being considered noble promoters of moral righteousness. But they would get their opportunity in due time.

Capitalizing on his win, Richardson pressed further. What about portraits of wealthy merchants and entrepreneurs? Were they not promoting civic virtues? Were they not stewards of the nation's wealth? Shouldn't their portraits, therefore, also be of public benefit? Yes! Of course! Who would disagree with such an astute observation? Theory accommodated once again. It was good business.

Recognizing his chance, Richardson then took the argument to its next logical step. Since portraits of such men advocated civic virtues, then, logically, those responsible for painting them also promoted civic virtues by their very labor. Therefore, Richardson argued, painters should be included among the ranks of this civically minded social elite. The great minds of art theory yielded to his brilliant reasoning and obliged once again.[10]

William Hogarth (1697–1764), arguably the greatest of the early artist/entrepreneurs, took a different route to liberate his work from the dictates of the aristocratic elite. Together with colleagues from his club, the St. Martin's Lane Academy, he launched several undertakings that promoted their work to a larger and heterogeneous audience in new contexts.[11] Let the public at large decide what kind of art they like, rather than be subject to the whims of a small group made up of the governing class. Hogarth presented portraiture that showed the sitters engaged in ordinary activities surrounded by the accouterments of their status rather than moralizing references to their civic virtues.[12] His well-known 1730 group portrait of the Wollaston Family is a typical example: it depicts members of an obviously affluent family in luxurious surroundings engaged in conversation.

The enterprising Hogarth also began to get involved in the lucrative publication of engraving of original works specifically designed to appeal to the public. Popular subjects, in-house printing and creative marketing, made the artists a household name. His immensely popular 'modern moral' series, while still implicitly didactic, were also humorous and satirical commentaries on life in early eighteenth-century England.[13] However, Hogarth also groomed his intellectual bona fides, a prerequisite to being accepted among the ranks of professional men of ideas. His publication of *The Analysis of Beauty* in 1753 is a sophisticated discourse on such esoteric aesthetic issues as the six Principles of Beauty and the varying qualities of the different curvatures of lines. He referred to this book as his 'War with the Connoisseurs'.[14]

Hogarth's conspicuous demonstration of superior sensibilities and intellect capable of sophisticated contemplation of complex aesthetics coupled with promotional exhibitions was original and persuasive. Individuals' worth to society was being redefined during this Age of Enlightenment. William Hogarth succeeded in showing that painters could contribute positively to the moral makeup of his country through their works and, thus, possessed the qualification to join the ranks of his nation's polite society.

The importance of this accomplishment to the development of the art market cannot be overstated. Starting out as no more than flattering illustrators of some social superior's thoughts to promote their class status, painters had now attained full recognition as professional men of ideas—moral ideas—which, once made visible by their own superior skill and intellect AND exhibited publicly, would be a benefit to all who beheld them. Hogarth, thus, expanded the product character—the brand—of art to include hitherto unacceptable qualities, such as satire, caricature, and telling stories about regular folks for them to enjoy. By doing so, Hogarth vastly expanded the economic potential of his occupation.

This brilliant eighteenth-century public relation campaign achieved two defining victories: it succeeded in ennobling artists and, by establishing art as a public benefit, it morally consecrated it. Artists and art had officially become good for society. Private vices—such as conspicuously flaunting wealth through the art on your walls—turned into public benefits, simply because of the chance that looking at art would make someone a morally better person.[15] William Congreve's (1670–1720) words 'Music calms the savage beast' from his 1697 play, *The Mourning Bride*, could henceforth be applied to painting as well.

[The topic of private vices versus public benefits was a popular subject in eighteenth-century philosophical discourse. An economy increasingly focused on producing goods for private consumption by a growing middle class had to reconcile a moral paradox: protestant ethics and conspicuous consumption of luxuries. An enjoyable read in that regard is Bernard Mandeville's work published in 1714, The Fable of the Bees or Private Vices and Public Benefits (F. D. Kaye, ed., 2 vols. (Oxford: Clarendon Press, 1924). Mandeville argues that selfishness and certain vices can, indeed, contribute to public benefit.]

For works of art to be sold for prices in the hundreds of millions, they must possess something that lies beyond their decorative utility, outside the quantifiable reality of labor and material. They must be universally recognized as having the additional quality of storing value that can be exchanged for other assets of similar character. Being a product that is beneficial to society and created by learned men of superior intellect and skill is an excellent start for a purely decorative object intent on climbing up the ladder to becoming a blue-chip asset. But, as we will discover, it would require several more steps.

In a global financial environment that constantly creates new values, there exists a corresponding need to establish ways of storing these values. This is part of the market-inherent commoditization, described earlier. Among the newest stores are cryptocurrencies and NFTs. Among the oldest are works of art. As long as a critically necessary number of individuals accept them as tradable assets, everyone is happy. But as the Tulip Mania in the Netherlands, the South Sea Bubble in Great Britain, the French Companie d'Occidente, the US stock market crash of 1929, or the global financial crisis have shown, assets are only as good as our faith in them. Art's impressive pedigree across millennia competes with the seductiveness of novelty.

A remarkable development in this context is the recent acceptance of specific crypto currencies as payment for specified works of art sold through the leading international auction houses. The 'new kid on the block'—crypto—is establishing its bona fides as a qualified store of exchangeable value in relation to art, one of the oldest. It is equally noteworthy, that among the works of art that have sold for crypto currency so far, is one composed of a real banana that was prominently displayed at Art Basel in 2019, taped to wall. Recognizing the evanescent nature of his work, the artist, Maurizio Cattelan (b. 1960), known for his humor, issued a certificate that stated that the legal owner of said certificate is the legal owner of the property rights of Maurizio Cattelan's work of art and can personally tape a real banana to a real wall—both of their choice—and, voila, here is art work. In 2024, at an auction at Sotheby's, it was sold for $6.2 million to crypto entrepreneur, Justin Sun, and paid for in crypto currency. An astute art market observer might consider this sale a possibly choreographed event to send certain signals to the public. Indeed, the occasion yielded worldwide publicity. Justin Sun's purported comment that he will 'eat the banana' when asked what he intended to do with it rings of a studied response created by a PR team. But just like the slicing of Banksy's *Girl With a Baloon*, during its auction sale at Sotheby's in 2018, the banana event, too, marks a historic step. I should point out that the *Girl With a Balloon* was purchased for 1,042,000 pounds by an anonymous collector, rumored to be a German lady, as it was being shredded. It was sold again, also at Sotheby's, in 2021, still shredded, but retitled, *Love is in the Bin*, for 21 million pounds. It had become history. The coup had been successful.

The art market relies on innovation and publicity. The manifestations of innovation extend, by definition, beyond the familiar ones and seek uncharted ground. Where we go in this journey into unknown territory defines us, and art is one of our mirrors.

For the fact that we pay such vast sums of money for art, both contemporary and old, we must give due credit (or blame) to this group of determined English artists who recognized the changing times, organized themselves and took their cause all the way to the finish line. Hogarth, a great satirist if there ever was one, must have patted his own back on the day, some 200 years later, when a fellow Englishman, a painter from Yorkshire by the name of David Hockney, saw one of his own paintings sell for $90 million.

Sir Joshua Reynolds, the first president of the Royal Academy, presided over the official conclusion of this nearly century-long campaign. In his typical florid wordiness, the reigning king among British painters presented in 1780 his famous Discourse IX to the esteemed members of the recently established institution.[16] In one impressively long sentence, he summarized the results of the campaign and their implications.

Painters, he posits, are professional *men of ideas*, not manual laborers hired to illustrate the thoughts of their social superiors. Moreover, as *intellectuals*, these men use their skill to search for an *abstract, even mysterious, concept of beauty*, an *idea* that *resides deeply within* each artist and *defines the very core of his being*. Yet *perfect expression* will always *elude* the artist. He is a *hero* in a life-long, all consuming, yet *futile, quest*. The only reward for his noble struggle is the chance that beholding his paintings—the physical evidence of his quest—may *elevate the minds* of *enlightened* spectators. The effects of this encounter can, in the great master's own words, 'extend themselves into *publick benefits*, and be among the means of bestowing on whole nations *refinements of taste*'.

Certain phrases in the preceding paragraph are italicized to draw attention to Reynold's word choices. He employs a type of language that is still used in descriptive and critical art writing today. Reynolds uses specific terms to reinforce the heroic and missionary character of artists, which to this day forms part of their collective identity, their aura.

In his Discourse IX, the founding president of this royally sanctioned body of artists publicly pronounced the end to the aristocratic hegemony over the judgment of the quality of painting and placed it squarely into the hands of his profession. Artists assumed control over the design of their paintings and the appraisal of their public benefit—the agreed-upon valuation standard. It was left up to each spectator's level of 'refinement of taste' to recognize and comprehend the public benefit inherent in each individual painting's intrinsic search for beauty. Naturally, only the enlightened would qualify for citizenship in this 'republic of taste'.

There are several intriguing tangents to Reynolds' Discourse IX. For example, the notion of public benefit of art is echoed in the US tax code. Making art assets accessible to the public earns significant tax benefits. One way is to give them to an existing museum; another is to start your own. The latter is all the rage these days for reasons that I will discuss later.

This public benefit of art is also reinforced by our museums. It is, in fact, their *raison d'etre*. The museum industry has extended the benefit of art from the public, the heterogeneous mass of people living in a country, to the sovereign, homogeneous nation as a separate entity. Art provides such extraordinary public benefits that a nation's image is, in part, defined by the art its museums own. The $ 450,000,000 price tag of the old oak panel painted, in parts, by the great Leonardo, included a premium for precisely that reason. It is destined to be introduced to the world with great pomp and fanfare, the rays of its fame to illuminate the greatness of the Saudi nation—a remarkable testimony to the global value of art. An iconic depiction of Jesus becomes a focal point and visual testimony of the sovereign wealth of a nation that strictly follows the teachings of Mohammed.

A further example of our society's acceptance of art's public benefit are the financial incentives offered to real estate developers to include art works in the public spaces of their projects. Moreover, municipalities create art districts as an urban renewal strategy and offer monetary incentives to artists and galleries to move there.

The roots for all this reach back to the days of Hogarth, Richardson, Reynolds and the determination of their community of artist to take full advantage of new opportunities that came along with the thriving consumer economy of their day.[17]

I mentioned earlier that the story of this campaign at the time was mirrored in similar phenomena in other sections of society. For example, it was also reflected, in theoretical terms, in the nascent field of political economy, Adam Smith's playground. The old social hierarchy had to accommodate the economy of a new commercial age. Production, marketing, and selling evolved to take maximum advantage of the many new opportunities offered. The path of painters is only one example, but a particularly creative and instructive one.

Notes

1. The eighteenth-century arts environment in Britain has been the topic of numerous publications. Of specific interest to this topic are John Barrell, The Political Theory of Painting from Reynolds to Hazlitt (New Haven and London: Yale University Press 1986); Lawrence Lipkin, The Ordering of Arts in Eighteenth-century England (Princeton: Princeton University Press, 1970); David Solkin, Painting for Money (New Haven and London: Yale University Press1993); Iain Pears, The Discovery of Painting: Yale University Press 1988).
2. On similar structural innovations within the pottery industry, specifically in the enterprises of Wedgewood and his competitor, Bentley, see Neil McKendrick, John Brewer and John Plumb, The Birth of a Consumer Society (London: Europa Publication, Ltd., 1982): 100–145.
3. Walter Benjamin, Das Kunstwerk im Alter seiner technischen Reproduzierbarkeit (Frankfurt: Surkamp Verlag, 1977), English title: The Work of Art in the Age of Mechanical Reproduction.
4. John Brewer "Commercialization and Politics", Neil McKendrick, et al.: 197–262, points out that these organizations aimed to advance their members' economic interests.
5. Raymond William, Culture and Society, 1780–1950 (N.Y.: Columbia University Press1983): 30–48.
6. Adam Smith, The Wealth of Nations, R. H. Campbell and A. S. Skinner, eds. (Oxford: Oxford University Press 1976): 26–27.
7. Anthony Ashley Cooper, 3rd Earl of Shaftesbury, Characteristics of Men, Manners, Opinions, Times, 1711, John M. Richardson, ed., 2 vols. (Indianapolis and New York: University of Indiana Press, 1964).
8. Cooper, Second Characters, or the Language of Forms, B. Rand, ed. (Cambridge: Harvard University Press, 1914): 135.
9. For Hogarth's comment to that effect see, John Pye, Patronage of British Art, A Historical Sketch (London: Longman, Brown, Green and Longman, 1845): 34, n. 24, referring to Jill Ireland, Hogarth (London: J. & J. Boydell, 1794–1798), supplement, without providing a page number.
10. Johnathan Richardson, Essay on the Whole Art of Criticism as it relates to Painting (London: 1719): 15–16, 26–28.

11. Ronald Paulson, Hogarth: His Life, Art, and Times, 2 vol. (New Haven & London: Yale University Press, 1971), vol. 1: 369–375 quote (347) is attributed to Vertue without providing a source. Additional information on Hogarth's St. Martin's Lane Academy can be found in Sydney Hutchison, The History of the Royal Academy 1768–1968 (London: Robert Royce, Ltd., 1968): 10–13; Pears: 124; Nicolas Pevsner, Academies of Art, Past and Present(Cambridge: Cambridge University Press, 1940): 125–126; Pye: 22/3; Whitley, vol. 1: 27. For a chronological overview of these early organizations, see Bayer, Page, The Development of the Art Market in England: 45–55.
12. Solkin,: 78.
13. Walpole, vol. 3: 721, also Paulson: 192–220.
14. Johnathan Conlin, ¨At the Expense of the Public': The Sign Painters' Exhibition of 1762 and the Public Sphere". American Society for Eighteenth-Century Studies, vol. 36 (Fall 2002): 6.
15. J. John Sekora, Luxury: The Concept of Western Thought, Eden to Smollett (Baltimore: John's Hopkins University Press, 1977).
16. Sir Joshua Reynolds, Discourses on Art, R. R. Wark, ed. (New Haven & London: Yale University Press, 1959): 171.
17. Beyond the individuals discussed here, there were many others who actively contributed to this debate in different ways. Richardson, Hogarth, and Reynolds represent milestones on a path, but they were part of a community. For a more extensive discussion of the 'branding' of art during the eighteenth century, see Bayer and Page, The Development of the Art Market in England, ch. 2: 29–40. A comprehensive survey of the art-related literature (Kunstliteratur) of this period can be found in Johannes Dobai, Kunstliteratur des Klassizismus und der Romantik in England, 3 vols. (Bern: Bentelli Verlag, 1974).

CHAPTER 4

Selling to the Public

As I describe in the previous chapter, at the onset of the eighteenth century, the accustomed way for English artists to drum up business was by vying for the attention of wealthy aristocratic or middle-class patrons to seek commissions. Judging from contemporary auction records, these commissions appear to have been mainly portraits. There were also a few painters who specialized in other subjects, the sea painter Peter Monamy (1681–1749) or the horse portraitist and sporting artist John Wotton (c.1682–1764), for example.[1] There was money to be made with paintings of sailing ships in stormy seas for wealthy shipowners, or portraits of horses for the horse-obsessed landed aristocracy. Typically, commissions were obtained by word-of-mouth networking, personal introductions, and/or advertisements in newspapers. The better-known artists, like Godfrey Kneller (1646–1723) or the already introduced Jonathan Richardson, moved among the higher levels of society and acquired status, fame, and wealth. Kneller was made a 'Sir' and even received a baronet.[2]

Selling paintings to an anonymous public was just beginning. Yet already certain artists explored different avenues that bucked tradition. In the absence of art galleries, as we know them today, painters displayed their works in popular coffee houses and pubs, much like their colleagues in the Netherlands had done earlier. These locales, while not ideal, offered exposure, and, in exchange, their walls were nicely decorated with paintings for free. Even today, such spaces still offer their walls for the display

T. M. Bayer, *The Genesis of the Modern Art Market in London, 1700–1900*, https://doi.org/10.1007/978-3-032-00594-6_4

of art to young and beginning artists whose careers have not reached the level where they are represented by a commercial gallery. These facilities offer an important low barrier opportunity to enter the market (Figs. 4.1, 4.2, and 4.3).

There is evidence of consumer orientation early on. Certain locations were frequented by people with specific political persuasions. Much of the contemporary theoretical discourse on art at the time had political aspects. Therefore, painters chose to reflect different partisan views and philosophical alliances in their works and display them in locations popular with sympathetic patrons. Issues dealing with economics, morality, luxury, consumption, and class resonated in their works.[3]

Artists' deliberate focus on their audience became a major influence on the physical appearance of art works from this point forward, and it has remained a dominating impact on the arts to this day. Many of the famous

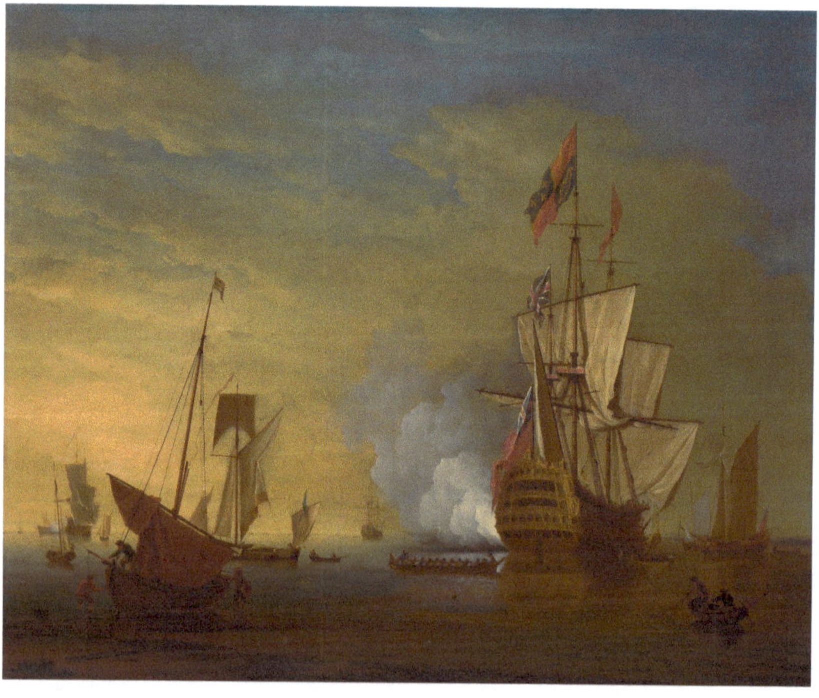

Fig. 4.1 Peter Monamy (1681–1749)

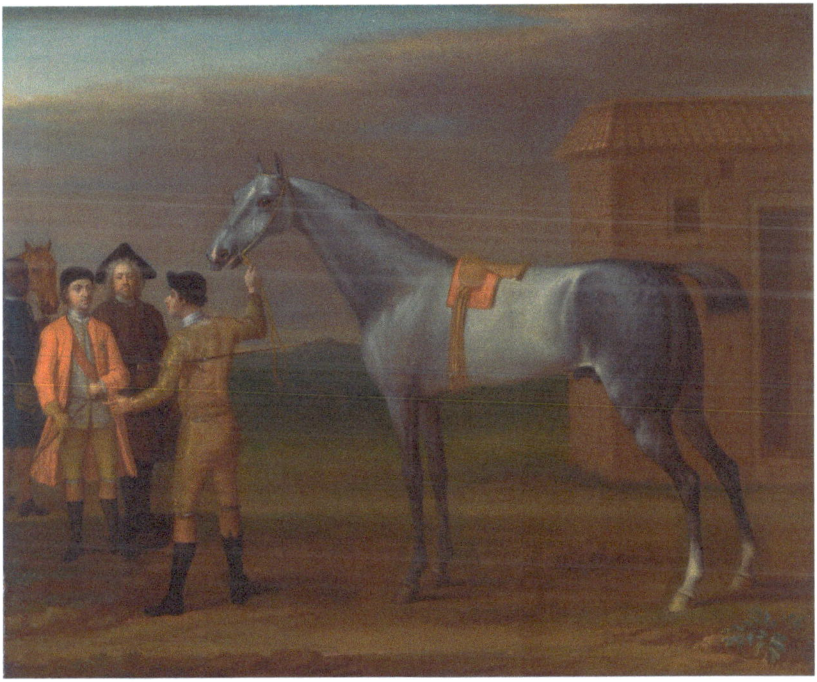

Fig. 4.2 John Wootton (1682–1764), Lamprey with his owner Sir William Morgan, at Newmarket

paintings from the late eighteenth century onward, throughout the nineteenth century and up until the present day, were, and still are, painted with undisguised attention to publicity potential and audience appeal. Among the many examples are such famous paintings as Benjamin West's (1738–1820) *Death of General Wolf* (1770) or in the next century, Rosa Bonheur's (1822–1899) *Horsefair* (1853), Daniel Maclise's (1806–1870) *Marriage of the Strongbow* (1854) or William Powell Frith (1819–1909) *A Railroad Station* (1861). Not coincidentally, these are often the same paintings that are illustrated in standard art history texts and displayed prominently in our museums. Many of these works once stood out on the walls of the Royal Academy in London, the Salon in Paris, or other public exhibition venues. They all have in common a distinct orientation towards audience appeal (Fig. 4.4).

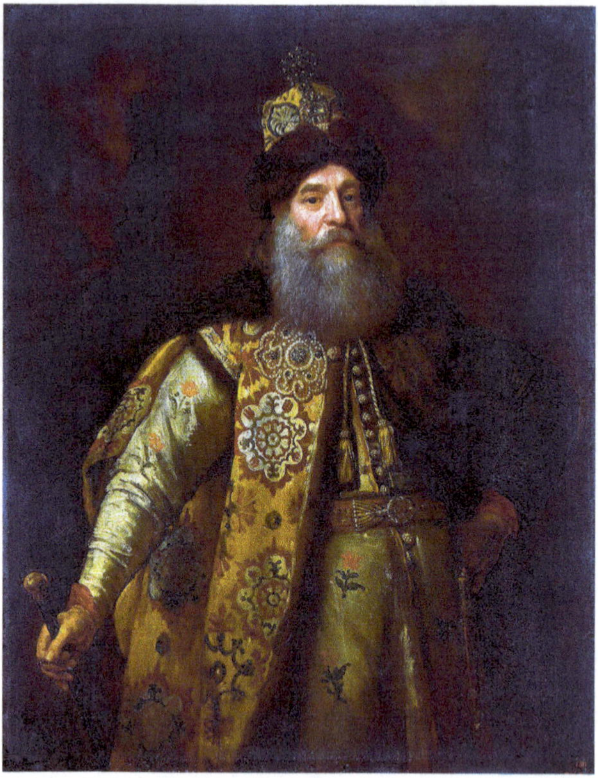

Fig. 4.3 Godrey Kneller (1646–1723); portrait of Piotr Potyomkin (1617–1700)

This conspicuous focus on popularity did not make everyone happy. Reflecting on this audience orientation, the writer and satirist Anthony Pasquin (1761–1818) complained:

> The mightiest evil to be regretted is that the vulgar, who have no knowledge of propriety, should, from their numbers, their riches, and consequently their power, have the national patronage of their dominion; and yet these bipedal reptiles must be uniformly soothed and solicited, under such forcible designations as THE PUBLIC.[4]

Undoubtedly, these harsh words must have hurt certain people's feelings. (Perhaps, this was the reason why the writer had traded his original

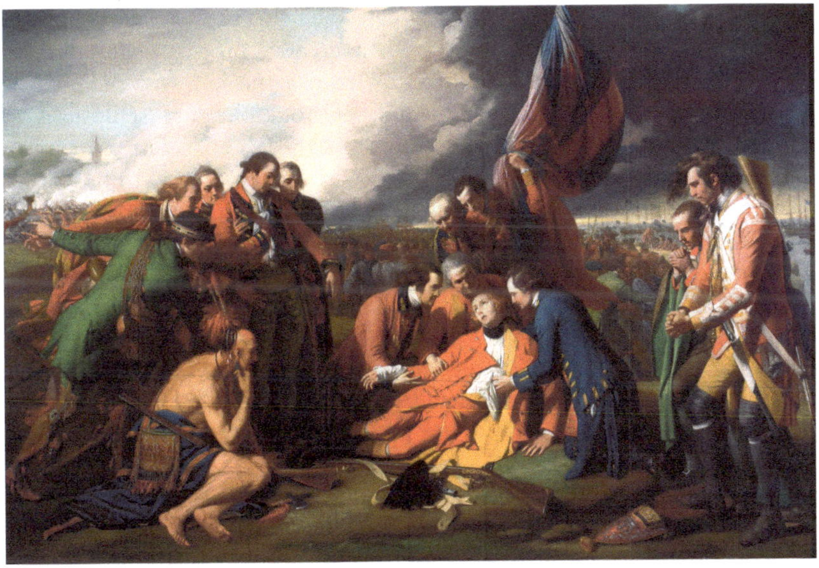

Fig. 4.4 Benjamin West (1738–1820), death of General Wolfe

and rather ordinary-sounding name, John Williams, for a more exotic French-sounding one.) Pasquin's contempt for the vulgar rich and powerful echoes loudly in the current criticisms targeting the twenty-first-century art environment.

The heavily promoted annual or biannual art exhibitions of the twentieth and twenty-first centuries that have sprung up around the world are potentially career-launching events, much like the Royal Academy was in earlier days. At these hyper-glitzy occasions, there are works on display that were deliberately produced to generate the utmost monetizable attention. Jeff Koons' (b.1955) display of his *Made in Heaven* series at the 1990 Venice Biennale is an excellent example of an art product intentionally designed to maximize publicity and turn the resulting notoriety into hard cash. It took Porn Hub only nineteen days to capture over 100 million users. While this internet site did not exist in 1990, the commercial value of attention through graphic sexual imagery certainly did, as persuasively demonstrated by Jeff Koons.

Is this art? Well, the market ultimately determines if an object is a work of art. In 1957, at a lecture at the Houston Museum of Fine Arts, the great French artist/provocateur Marcel Duchamp (1887–1968) opined: 'The artist performs only one part of the creative process. The onlooker completes it, and it is the onlooker who has the last word'. And the onlookers accepted Mr. Koons' huge photographs and sculptures of explicit sex acts with his then wife, Ilona, as art. After all, isn't this biannual event one of the greatest exhibitions of art? How can anything shown there not be art? Context matters. Duchamp had allegedly also claimed that 'Anything is Art if an artist says it is'. As we know, it was Joshua Reynolds, the eminently popular British painter, co-founder, and 1st president of London's Royal Academy, who laid the foundation for this assertion. Sir Reynolds would have agreed wholeheartedly with the French artist's claim. Whether or not he would have approved of Duchamp's art cannot be stated with similar certainty (Fig. 4.5).

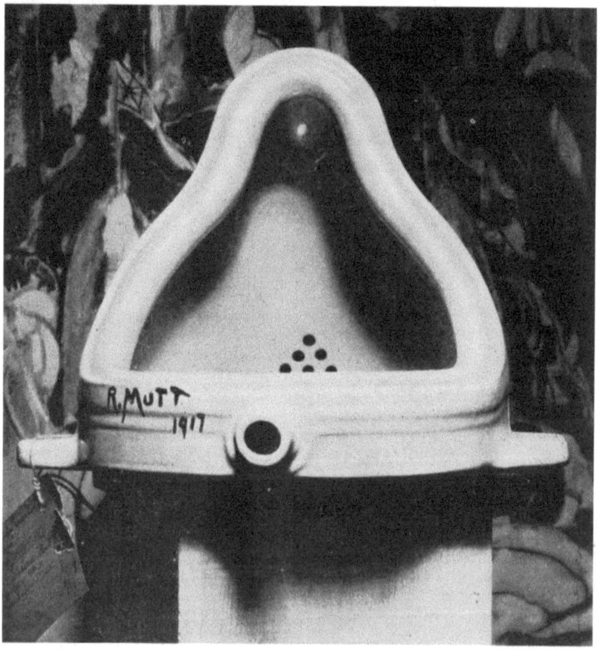

Fig. 4.5 Marcel Duchamp (1887–1968); fountain, photo by Alfred Stieglitz

To See and To Be Seen: Vauxhall Spring Gardens

Pubs and coffee shops did indeed provide wall space to display paintings, but they were not suitable as venues for artists to earn money. Hanging a work in any of these places was at best advertisement for the painter and may have resulted in an occasional commission or sale. But most likely, the paintings were just decorative backdrops. But without commercial art galleries, what could painters do to make money? It was logistically impossible to bring the paintings to all the homes of possible, but as yet unidentified, buyers. The only option was to entice potential customers to come to an accessible location where a variety of paintings could be seen—a proto-gallery. Ideally, such a locale should offer some type of entertainment or attraction so that a small entry fee could be charged. The task was to find the right location and display the right kind of pictures, ones that folks would enjoy and be willing to pay to see them.

Timing for such an experiment was excellent. One of the by-products of middle-class growth in the eighteenth century was the professionalization of a burgeoning leisure industry that served consumers who had uncommitted time on their hands and surplus means to enjoy it.

William Hogarth, not only an uncannily sharp social commentator, but ever the entrepreneur, took the first crucial step. In 1732, he negotiated an arrangement to display his works together with those of several of his fellow artists from his club in the elegant dining spaces—individual 'supper boxes'—of Spring Gardens at Vauxhall.

The Vauxhall Spring Gardens was a private entertainment business owned by Jonathan Tyer, an entrepreneur in the expanding leisure industry, who had remodeled an existing facility and turned it into *the* fashionable place in London. Instantly hugely popular, the Gardens became a melting pot of English society. Even the Prince of Wales was a regular; so were the working classes and all levels in between. The paintings displayed at the Gardens showed through their choice of subjects a distinct orientation towards appealing to middle class taste (Figs. 4.6, 4.7, and 4.8).[5]

For many of the Garden's visitors, it was the first time that they saw paintings like these in such elegant settings. The environment promoted familiarity with art, being surrounded by it, talking about it, and showed in what settings paintings could be displayed. The message to the visitors was simple: if you had the money, you were qualified to own art, no matter your family background. For the painters who exhibited there, Spring Gardens was the first significant and far-reaching step in their strategy to

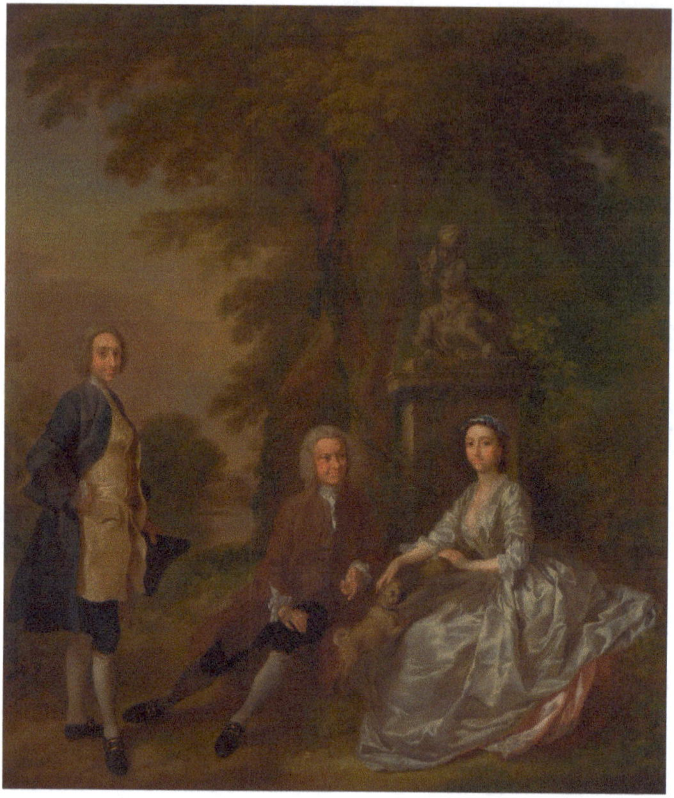

Fig. 4.6 Francis Hayman (1708–1776), Jonathan Tyers, with his daughter Elizabeth, and her husband John Wood

expand the market for their product. No records have come to light that indicate that the participating painters received any compensation from the garden's owner. Hogarth, supposedly, did get a lifetime entry ticket from Mr. Tyler. But the event served as excellent publicity and was a big step up from a smoky tavern's walls.

It warrants mentioning here that the ubiquitous flashy art exhibitions of today owe their existence to Hogarth's stroke of marketing genius. His ingenuity cannot be overemphasized. It set off a development that would lead directly to dealer-managed exhibitions in the nineteenth century and beyond, the establishment of contemporary art museums, and the 'block

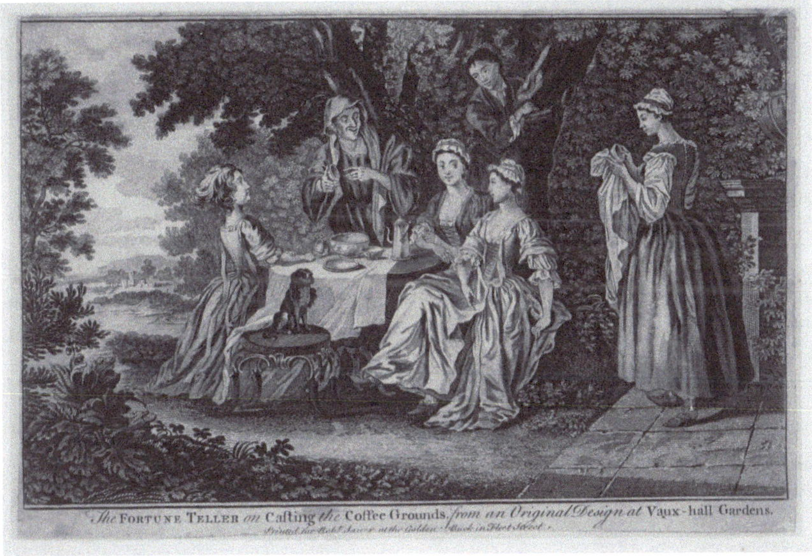

Fig. 4.7 Robert Sayer (1725–1794), after Francis Hayman; The Fortune Teller on Casting the Coffee Grounds

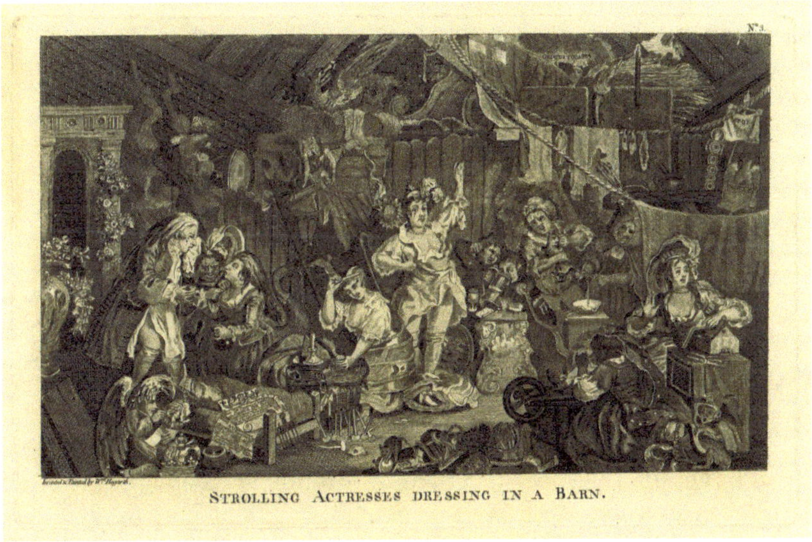

Fig. 4.8 William Hogarth (1697–1764); Strolling Actresses Dressing in a Barn

buster' shows and biennales of the late twentieth and early twenty-first centuries. These art market institutions perform vital functions in today's art market. Furthermore, Spring Gardens also initiated one of the most important characteristics of the modern art market: a demand for innovation. To entice the public to keep coming back, artists presented new themes; and to differentiate themselves from the other painters, they developed recognizably different personal styles. The public was not likely to be in interested in paintings that looked the same.

The Vauxhall Spring Gardens exhibition can be best described as the first major promotional event that introduced paintings as middle-class wall décor, effectively breaking down the social barriers that had stood in the way (Fig. 4.9).

But there was another project, also orchestrated by Hogarth, one that served specifically as a conspicuous demonstration of the all-important public benefit of paintings. By implication, it also placed painters explicitly among the respectable ranks of English society.

Philanthropy and Art Marketing: The Foundling Hospital

One of the offshoots of the Enlightenment was a growing participation in philanthropic endeavors by members of the middle-class as well as middle-class aspirants. Whether they were attracted by the prospect of emulating their social elite or motivated otherwise, the middle ranks of English society were enthusiastic about conspicuous philanthropic enterprises. For that reason, the eighteenth century is sometimes called the 'Age of Philanthropy'. It bore witness to a construction boom of charity schools, hospitals, and orphanages, all financed by private individual donations. The contributors were not just middle-class professionals. Members of the aristocracy—even the royal family—were also among them.[6] Publicly recognized contributions to these projects became a measure of social respectability and class distinction. Moreover, the proximity to their social superiors at charitable events further elevated the reputation of middle-class subscribers.

Again, it was Hogarth, ever keen on public relation opportunities, who recognized the potential benefits of an involvement of painters in charitable projects. In 1744, he succeeded in securing an appointment to the Board of Governors of the recently established Foundling Hospital. Five

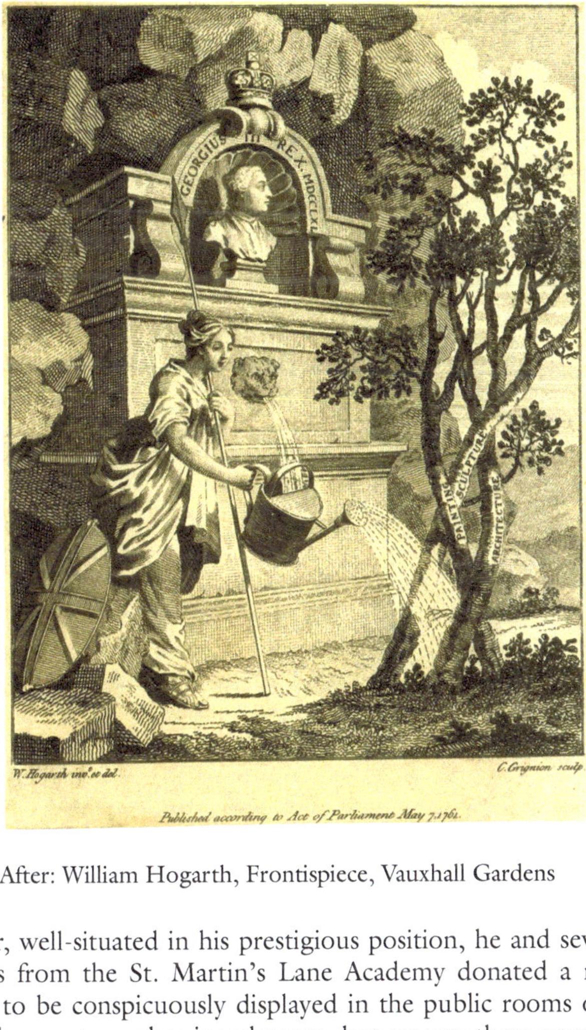

Fig. 4.9 After: William Hogarth, Frontispiece, Vauxhall Gardens

years later, well-situated in his prestigious position, he and several of his colleagues from the St. Martin's Lane Academy donated a number of paintings to be conspicuously displayed in the public rooms of the new facility. The exact number is unknown, but among them were works by Frances Hayman, and Joseph Highmore, as well as the famous portrait bust of Georg Friedrich Handel sculpted by Louis-Francois Roubilliac (1695–1762).[7] Prominent inscriptions on the frames listed each artist/donor by name and identified the depicted biblical acts of charity. These public gestures of philanthropy resulted in several paybacks for the artists.

For one, the hospital was open to the public and, thus, was a kind of proto public museum. There was no other place where the public could go for free to see works of art. Then, the biblical themes would, hopefully, stimulate emulation and, thereby, reinforce Richardson's argument that art, and those who make art, yield benefit to society.[8] But the Foundling Hospital was also a significant milestone in the artists' campaign for full acceptance among fashionable society as a professional community of painters. It was the first conspicuous demonstration of their acceptance of the responsibility—charity—that came with this status. Even George II was among their fellow donors.

Since then, Hogarth's idea has been imitated countless times and is fully commercialized by now. Art and charitable events have merged into single occasions. Today's society agrees that art is such an important contribution to the public wellbeing that our philanthropic support must also extend to the institutions and individuals who patronize art. Richardson would have argued that since art yields public benefits, and those who make art do so as well, then buying art must also be a virtuous deed. After all, it facilitates the existence of both artists and more art.

Philanthropy thrives on an old Latin proverb, 'pecunia non olet'—money does not smell. The act of giving removes all noxious odors. On top of that, philanthropy offers a protective cloak, one that can shield the charitable individual from the overly inquisitive masses. Our society is quite forgiving and forgetful in exchange for overt acts of philanthropy. However, some cracks are beginning to show in this shield. Increasingly, the morals, character, and conduct of the individuals behind charitable acts are being examined. Rooms, even entire wings, of different museums named after mega-donors, are affected by the fallout of this scrutiny. The Sackler family's involvement with Purdue Pharma, the maker of OxyContin, and the removal of their name from the walls of the Guggenheim, the Metropolitan Museum, and the National Gallery in London, despite the family's generous donations, are but one example. Different artists, too, have been reevaluated because of actions considered morally unacceptable.

Where this will lead is difficult to say. Will we denounce the serenely beautiful faces of Friar Filippo Lippi's (1406–1469) numerous *Young Mary* portraits, because he had an affair with one of the models, a nun? Will it soon be problematic to visit Caravaggio's (1571–1610) *Calling of St. Matthew* (1599–1600) in its original setting in the church of San Luigi dei Francesi in Rome because the artist had a price on his head for murder?

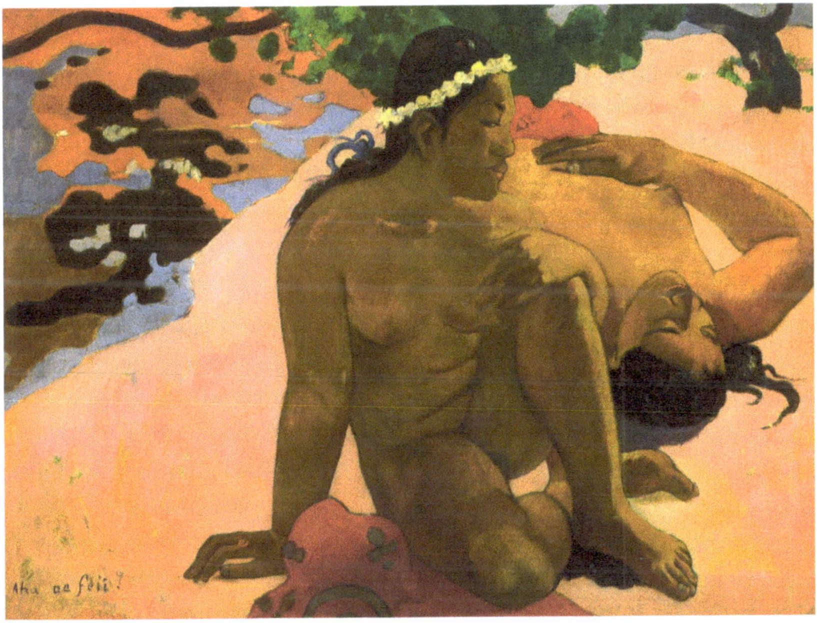

Fig. 4.10 Paul Gauguin (1848–1903). Aha Oe Feii?

Will Gauguin's famous painting, Aha Oe Feil (1892), be removed from public view because of the artist's relationship with Teha'amana, a young woman alleged to have been thirteen years old at the time? How will we deal with Egon Schiele's (1890–1918) arrest for seducing a minor? (Fig. 4.10)

Notes

1. Bayer/Page data sorted by artist name and sales date.
2. For more information on the arts environment in England during this time see James Barry, Inquiry into the real and imaginary Obstructions to the Acquisition of the Arts (London: T. Becket 1775); William Buchanan, Memoirs of Painting, J. Greig, ed, (London: Ackermann, 1824); Cynthia Gibson-Wood, 'Picture Consumption in London at the end of the Seventeenth Century', The Art Bulletin, vol. 84, no. 3 (Sep. 2002); Frank Hermann, The English as Collectors (N. Y.: W. W. Norton and Co., 1972); Louis Lippincott, Selling Art in Georgian London (New Haven & London:

Yale University Press, 1983); David Ormrod, "The Origin of The London Art Market, 1650–1730", Michael North and David Ormrod, eds., Art Markets in Europe, 1400–1800 (Aldershot: Ashgate Publishing 1998); Ormrod, "The Rise of the London Art Market, 1660–1769", Economica e Arte, secc. XIII-XVIII (March 2000): 305–321; Jonathan Pye, Patronage of British Art – A Historical Sketch (Longman, Brown, Green and Longman, 1845; Jean-Andre Rouquet, The State of the Arts in England (London: Jay Nourse, 1755): 22–24; David Solkin, Painting for Money: The Visual Arts and the Public in Eighteenth-century England (New Haven & London: Yale University Press, 1993); Horace Walpole, Anecdotes of Painting in England, 3 vols. (London: Henry G. Bohn, 1849).

3. An excellent cross-section of paintings from this period can be found in Ellis Waterhouse, *British Painting in the Eithteenth* Century, Tate (1957), Phadon (1957) https://www.google.com/search?sca_esv=053903a76464d342&rlz=1C5CHFA_enUS1083US1083&q=catalogue+of+British+Painting+in+the+eighteenth+century+Tate+1957&udm=2&fbs=ABzOT_AqAj1UoYQh8kglFXNyluWOqa5Byjz8gYDQhQlAIuFG_RXyZCeU2CGLlRRY-8c8ThOompI0geecy3YALCAf5ZhHV6qua5jl204OPWnAiPvz95Fx2-2qJF0BBDrGOOjf29oW6eNxGKOOUmmzaFMS9dY8yb0k0qWUVGZLH33m-uyWcefmxNWn8u78Rmhi2OHdbtqy51wKAV_fhhvSu2P-lVzH3Xqt4g&sa=X&ved=2ahUKEwi775-GrqWLAxWvmIQIHQYmAnUQtKgLegQIExAB&biw=1351&bih=673&dpr=2.(Last accessed March 2025.); Additional information on artists' organizations can be found in Nicholas Pevsner, Academies of Art, Past and Present (Cambridge: Cambridge University Press, 1940): 15, 124; Sidney Hutchison, The History of the Royal Academy 1768–1968 (London: Robert Royce, Ltd., 1968): 5; William Whitley, Artists and their Friends in England, 1700–1790, 2 vols. (London and Boston: The Medici Society, 1938), vol. 1: 7, 74; Ronald Paulson, Hogarth: His Life, Art, and Times, 2 vols. (New Haven & London: Yale University Press, 1971), vol. 1: 347, vol. 2: 43.
4. Anthony Pasquin, Memory of the Royal Academicians; being an attempt to improve the national taste (London: 1796).
5. A Brief Historical and Descriptive account of the Royal Gardens, Vauxhall (London, 1822): p. 7. A detailed history of the Gardens can be found in Warwick Wroth, F.S.A., The London Pleasure Gardens of the Eighteenth Century (London: Macmillan and Co., Ltd., 1896): 287–326; see also Solkin, Painting for Money (London & New Haven: Yale University Press, 2001): 137–156; on the art displayed, see David Coke and Alan Borg, Vauxhall Gardens: A History (New Haven & London: Yale University Press, 2011).

6. Pye: 25; for a detailed history of the Foundling Hospital see Robert Nichols and Francis Wray, The History of the Foundling Hospital (London: Oxford University Press, 1935).
7. Paulson, vol. 2: 35–37, 49; Pye: 87–90; Rouquet, The State of the Arts in England (London: J. Nourse, 1755): 25–27; Solkin: 165; Whitley, vol. 1: 163. The exact date is difficult to establish. Whitley mentions a remark made by Vertue in 1745, concerning the painter Hardin who 'has lately painted some pieces of landscape in rounds, which he has presented to the Foundling Hospital to adorn their room'. Paulson, vol. 2: 49 describes a dinner held on 1 April 1747 at the Foundling Hospital where four paintings by, respectively, Hayman, Hogarth, Highmore, and Wills could be seen.
8. Rouquet: 27.

CHAPTER 5

Artist Organizations and Commercial Art Exhibitions

Despite the many upsides, there was a problem with decorating elegant places, like Vauxhall Gardens, where fancy folks mingled, or the walls of a charity hospital as an eye-catching demonstration of self-interested philanthropy. These projects did not put any money into the participating painters' pockets. To deal with this serious shortcoming, London's artists transformed old-fashioned artists' clubs that had been around for many years into quasi-corporate enterprises.

Here is an example. In 1759, one of Hogarth's friends, the painter Francis Hayman (1708–1776), contacted William Shipley (1715–1803), a gentleman and drawing teacher who headed an organization with the cumbersome name, 'Society for the Encouragement of the Arts, Manufacture and Commerce'. It was commonly known as the 'Society of Arts'. Shipley's organization received its money from several rich art aficionados for the purpose of organizing a variety of annual competitions—including one for drawing—and award prizes to the winners of the different categories. For the display of the different winning entries, Shipley had recently acquired rooms on the Strand.[1] That exhibition space was the reason for Hayman approaching Shipley. The artist wanted to discuss renting the facility for a group exhibition tentatively planned for the following year.

T. M. Bayer, *The Genesis of the Modern Art Market in London, 1700–1900*, https://doi.org/10.1007/978-3-032-00594-6_5

[Francis Hayman was a theatrical, decorative, and portrait painter as well as a founding member of the Royal Academy. Hayman created stage designs and costumes for the theatre on Drury Lane, and he also introduced a Boucher-influenced French Rococo style to England.]

Francis Hayman was part of a group of artists that regularly met at the Turk's Head Tavern. Contemporary accounts indicate that beyond a general improvement of the individual members' capacity for drinking and smoking, not much else had been accomplished during these regular get-togethers (Fig. 5.1).

But things were about to change. Earlier that year, the members had gathered for an important meeting at the Foundling Hospital during which they had agreed to organize a big public exhibition of the club members' paintings—an independent group exhibition, as it were. The publicity generated by the Vauxhall Gardens exhibition and the philanthropic PR campaign at the Foundling Hospital was among the reasons for launching the project. It was time to capitalize on these events.[2]

['Foundling Hospital, Nov. 5, 1759. At a meeting of the Artists, resolved: That a general meeting of all Artists in the several branches of Painting, Sculpture, Architecture, Engraving, Chasing, Seal-Cutting, and medalling, be held at Turk's Head Tavern, in Gerrard Street, Soho, on Monday the 12th inst., at Six in the evening to consider a proposal for the honor and advancement of the Arts, and that it be advertised in the Public and Daily Advertiser. John Wilkes, President. Fra. Milner Newton, Secretary'.[3]

If the president's name rings familiar, it is because it belongs to none other than the John Wilkes who became famous for his acrimonious relationship with King George III and the Massacre in St. George's Field in 1768. It fits his rebellious personality to serve as the president of a progressive artist's organization. He had been elected to Parliament just two years earlier in 1757 and was known for his radical views.]

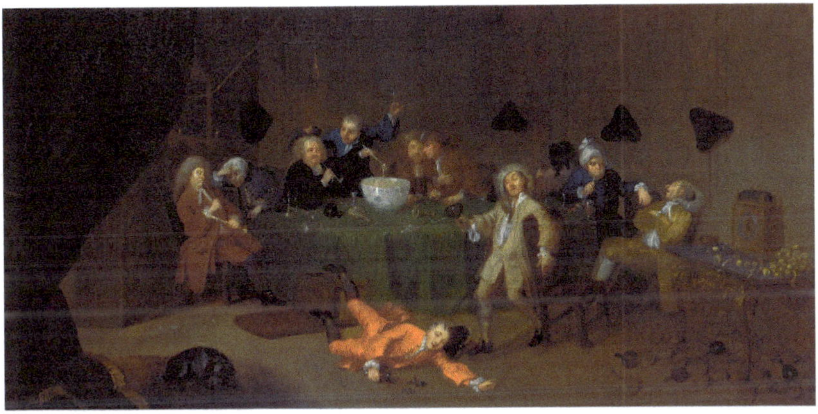

Fig. 5.1 William Hogarth (1697–1764), A Midnight Conversation

Since there still existed no commercial art galleries in London, Shipley's room on the Strand could provide wall space for Hayman's project in a good location with an already established reputation for popular and interesting exhibitions.[4]

All was agreed, and with a nod to the success of the Foundling Hospital project, Hayman promoted this new event also as a philanthropic affair to get additional P.R. mileage. The catalogue proclaimed that the exhibitors' noble intention was to 'raise a sum of money for the purpose of charity, by the annual exhibition of their works…'.[5]

The impact of this enterprise on the history of the art market was defining and far-reaching. The public's response was phenomenal. The level of excitement among the visitors must have been enormous. Most of them had likely never seen that quality level of art; many may have had no previous exposure to paintings at all. Now they could look at 130 different paintings done by 69 professional painters including such well-known artists as Francis Hayman and the famous William Hogarth. According to the local press, spectators 'continuously overcrowded' the room 'to inconvenience'.[6] This 'inconvenience' was very much appreciated. Catalogues, rather than sales of the exhibited paintings, was the income source. There was even something slightly scandalous about the physical closeness of so many people of different social backgrounds and sex. An impressive total of 6582 catalogues was sold generating a revenue of 164 pounds 11 shillings, around 30 times the annual income of a schoolteacher. Hayman and company were clearly onto something. There was money to be made.

This seemingly ordinary event was ground-breaking. It demonstrated irrefutably that there was additional earning potential for artists and other owners of paintings that did not require selling them: exhibiting them. The income from catalogue sales, while it was in small increments, came from a vastly larger demographic group than a few rich and finnicky art buyers. The key to success was getting the crowds in.

Not surprisingly, painters began to consider mass appeal and entertainment value when choosing subjects, composition, colors, and style of their works. Furthermore, there was the added benefit of demonstrating their capability to generate an income of their own, just like other businessmen, that was independent of the generosity of wealthy patrons. This economic freedom was a cornerstone among the qualification of an Englishman's respectability.[7] As long as they could make money with their art, their social standing was secure.

Not surprisingly, within a few months after the first exhibition by the Turk's Head 'Society of Artists of Great Britain' (as it came to be known), plans for a second exhibition were in the making.[8] However, disagreement over money triggered dissension among the group's members. The cause of the dispute was largely the phenomenal success of the first undertaking. Apparently, the rooms had been crowded and incommoded by the intrusion of great numbers whose stations and educations made them no proper judges of statuary or painting. They were made idle and tumultuous by the opportunity of a show and consequently '[g]reat inconvenience [had] resulted from inferior people crowding the exhibition room last year'.[9] To avoid such congestion by 'inferior' people, someone suggested that admission to the planned event would be granted only to those individuals who purchased a catalogue. There would be no more free entry. Philanthropy had to go. Whatever money would be made would go straight into the pockets of the artists. This was problematic for certain individuals, and they decided to form their own group and organize a separate exhibition, again with Shipley at his facility on the Strand. The other group, the one set on making money for themselves, found space at Christopher Cock's, one of the early fixed location art auction businesses in London. Then, in the spring of 1761, London art lovers were able to enjoy two competing events in London. And many more were soon to follow.

It was these second events that caught the attention of the press. From this point forward, journalists were hooked. Coverage was extensive and diversified. Some writers just labored on and on comparing the two exhibits; others focused on individual works; still others took a more didactic approach and offered erudite commentary; some went off into the aloof realms of theory and aesthetics, whereas yet others engaged unapologetically in puffery of all sorts. This wide range and different types of press coverage, offering something for every reader, reveal a lot about the size and variety of the audience that existed for popular writing about art. It also corroborates the widespread success of this new type of cultural entertainment venue: commercial exhibitions of paintings.[10]

No records have come to light that indicate that these, and later similar events, served as direct sales platforms for the displayed works. These exhibitions were not well-suited for that. There was no established custom for selling art in this setting. It would have been unacceptable for painters themselves to mingle among the visiting masses with sharpened pencil and order pad ready in hand. Such brash commercialism would have undermined artists' social aspirations. Professional salesmen of modern art did not come into existence until later. Instead, money was made from catalogue sales and/or entrance fees. Of course, there must have been instances where immediate sales took place or subsequent business developed. But that was likely the exception. The business model of these exhibitions was not dependent on such transactions.

Between the Vauxhall exhibition in 1734 and the early 1760s, in less than three decades, paintings had evolved from decorative backdrop to star attraction, from wall décor to commercial enterprise. These artist-financed and managed events became the dominant modus operandi of the contemporary art world for the next 80 or so years until professional art dealers took over. In England, more artists groups got started during this time, and they all began competing for a share of the buoyant demand for this exciting and fashionable thing to do on one's leisure time: looking at art while socializing.[11] These types of artists-run exhibition societies have survived to this day.

Rivalry among the various exhibition groups was keen, and the individuals and issues involved were amusing fodder for journalists and art writers as well as their audience. The ultimate prize for the members of the winning group in this contest was a royal sanction and the all-important advantage of being able to call themselves 'Members of The Royal Academy'. Finally, English painters would no longer have to feel inferior to their colleagues in France, where a Royal Academy had been established over one hundred years ago, in 1648.

By late 1768, one group emerged as the victor. In April 1769, presided over by Joshua Reynolds—soon to be bestowed with the title of 'Sir of the British Empire'—the first exhibition of the newly minted Royal Academy took place, featuring the great works of the equally newly minted Royal Academicians. What a nice ring these two words had! No wonder someone would be willing to pay more for a nice painting by one of those ROYAL ACADEMICIANS, not just by some common dauber (Fig. 5.2).

At the Academy exhibition, one could behold such sophisticated works as *Diana Disarming Cupid*, a *Death of Adonis*, or a *Hector and Andromache* and similar depictions of erudite classical topics. By contrast, distinctly down-to-earth depictions of a *Horse and Mare*, a *Girl by Candlelight* or a *Ship on Fire* were displayed at the Society of Artists exhibition at Spring Gardens.[12] Each organization aimed at a different target audience. We are witnessing product differentiation in a growing market environment. Differentiation and novelty remain fundamental to the art market.

To no one's surprise, this Royal Academy scheme turned into a big hit. More and more painters vied for the opportunity to show their work in this celebrated and prestigious showcase. Competition was fierce.

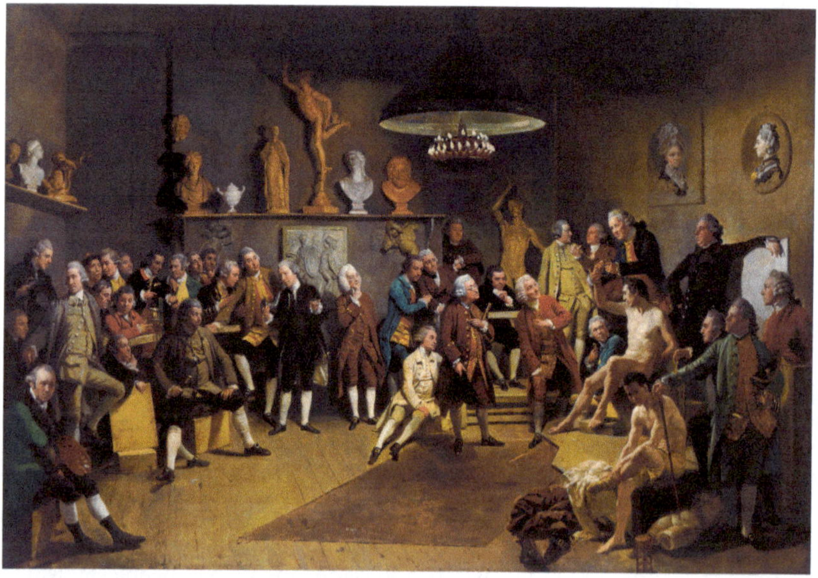

Fig. 5.2 Johann Zoffany (1733–1810), The Academicians of the Royal Academy

Unfortunately, it was also stacked in favor of those painters who followed the ever-so-conservative dictates of the Academy. The infamous 'Hanging Committee' tyrannically controlled the decisions over whose work would be hung on the walls and whose career on a nail.

For artists, exhibiting at the Academy was considered essential to maintaining their career. But there was a problem. The Academy, like the other exhibitions, was not really working well as a sales venue. According to contemporary sources, there were many years, when not a single work sold during the annual exhibition, the Academy's feature event.[13] This was not a matter of etiquette. The purpose of the occasion was to provide an exclusive opportunity for the social elite to mingle, view, and purchase, if they wish, what was considered that year's best production by England's most esteemed painters. But no one was in charge of sales.

Lack of sales was not the only shortcoming. There was also the discomforting fact that career-make-or-break decisions over whose work would be displayed at the grand annual event were in the hands of a dreaded and scorned group of old men, the feared Hanging Committee.

But by now, artists had plenty of experience in dealing with dictates, royal or otherwise. And there were many of them who wouldn't have any of it. After finally winning the status of independent professional men of ideas, they had no interest to have, yet again, someone else lord over them. Instead, they turned elsewhere for better sales outlets. They also started their own exhibition organizations, this time to rival the Royal Academy.

These competing groups were not just symptoms of a growing market. They were also engines of growth: they paved the way for a steadily rising number of artists to enter the market. And, as I have emphasized, to get noticed, painters increasingly specialized not just in terms of subjects, but, more importantly, also in stylistic aspects. All the old norms were coming under attack. Innovation became progressively important to become the market's fundamental driver.

[Over 11,000 artists are listed in Christopher Wood's dictionary. The reproduced works present a vast panorama of the great variety of stylistic and technical nuances as well as subject matter. The biographical entries underscore this variety. Most of the painters had in addition to their names also their specialization and unique characteristics listed.

Here is an incomplete account of some of the exhibition groups that were active in the nineteenth century: New Society of Artists; British Watercolor Society; New Watercolor Society: Old Watercolor Society; Pastel Society; Royal Society of British Artists; Royal British Colonia Society of Artists; The Royal Institute of Painters in Watercolor; Royal Spciety of Miniaturist Painters; Royal Institute of Painters in Oil Colors; Royal Society of Portrait Painters; Society of Women Artists. There were also smaller groups in the provincial centers of the country.]

The founding of The Royal Academy concluded the near century-long public relation campaign. With a royally endorsed profession, a royally sanctioned exhibition organization, a royal exhibition facility, and a royally hosted annual event that attracted Britain's social elite, painters had finally achieved full membership among the ranks of their nation's polite society. To accomplish this extraordinary feat, they had laid crucial foundations on which the subsequent development of the modern art market was built. The decision to seek their fortune among the public, rather than the elite—the many, not the few—started a dynamic—a commoditization process—that moved on a new track. All subsequent developments in art history can be traced to this decision.

Notes

1. For additional information on the 'Society of Arts' see Derek Hudson and Kenneth Luckhurst, The Royal Society of Arts, 1754–1954 (London: Murray, 1954); Robert Koch, Die Kunstaustellung (Berlin: Walter de Gruyter & Co., 1967): 201–202; Luckhurst, The Story of Exhibitions (London, New York: Studio Publications, 1951): 63 ff; John Pye, Patronage of British Art – A Historical Sketch (London: Longman, Brown, Green & Longman,1945): 60–61.
2. Anonymous, The Conduct of the Royal Academician with Members of the Incorporated Society of Artists of Great Britain (London, 1771): 8; also,

Sydney Hutchison, The History of the Royal Academy 1768–1968 (London: Robert Royce, Ltd., 1968): p. 16; Pye: 91–94 and n. 8 (Pye records the date as 12 November.); David Solkin, Painting for Money (New Haven & London: Yale University Press, 1993): 174.

3. William Whitley, Art in England (N.Y.: Hacker Art Books,1973), vol. 1:165.
4. Pye: 92, citing the original letter.
5. For this quote and data on the actual event see Pye: 91–95; Solkin, Painting for Money: 174–175; Whitley, vol. 1: 165–167; also, The London Chronicle (April 3–5, 1760): 1; The London Evening Post (April 3–5, 1760): 1; Whitehall Evening Post (April 5, 1760): 1; Public Advertiser (April 18, 1760): 2; The London Chronicle (April 12, 1760): 362, (April 17, 1769): 378.
6. Pye: 94, and n. 12, 91 and n. 8, referring to the Minutes of the meeting at Turk's Head, citing The Literary Panorama (1808), vol. 3: 1013–1014, 1226–1228, 1295 and n. 13 referring to the Literary Panorama (1808), vol. 3: 1226.
7. The St. James Chronicle (May 2, 1761): 4; Public Advertiser (May 6, 1761): 4.
8. Pye: 96–99.
9. Here is a chronological listing of publications that refer to the above-discussed events. London Chronicle (April 3–5, 1760): 1; London Evening Post (April 3–5, 1760): 1; Whitehall Evening Post (April 5, 1760): 1; London Chronicle (April 12, 1760): 362 and April 17, 1760, p. 378; Public Advertiser (April 18, 1760): 2; London Chronicle (April 16–18, 1761): 375; Whitehall Evening Post (April 16–18, 1761): 1; Public Advertiser (April 17, 1761): 1; London Chronicle (April 18, 1761): 400; London Chronicle (April 23–25, 1761): 394–395; London Chronicle (April 23–25, 1761): 393–394; London Evening Post (April 23–25, 1761): 1; St. James Chronicle (April 23–25, 1761): 3; St. James Chronicle (April 25–28, 1761): 3; Whitehall Evening Post (April 25–28, 1761): 2; Public Advertiser (April 27, 1761): 3; London Chronicle (April 28–30, 1761): 2; St. James Chronicle (April 30–May 2, 1761):2, (May 2–5, 1761) : 2, 4; Public Advertiser (May 5, 1761): 4, (May 6, 1761): 4; St. James Chronicle (May 5–7, 1761): 2, (May 7–9, 1761): 2–3, (May 9–12, 1761): 2; Public Advertiser (May 11, 1761): 4; Public Ledger (May 11, 1761): 1; London Chronicle (May 11, 1761): 460–461; St. James Chronicle (May 14–16, 1761): 2, 4; London Evening Post (May 14–16, 1761): 1; St. James Chronicle (May 23–26, 1761): 2; London Evening Post (May 27–29, 1761): 504–505; St. James Chronicle (May 28–30, 1761): 3,(June 2–4, 1761): 2; General Evening Post (June 4–6, 1761): 1.
10. Pye: 94–95.

11. Reviews of these exhibitions can be found in Lloyd's Evening Post and British Chronicle (May 1–3, 1769): 427, (May 3–5 1769): 4. For a detailed history of the early years of the Royal Academy, see Hutchison: 23–44. Other texts on this topic include Charles Holme, The Royal Academy from Reynolds to Millais (London, New York: The Studio, 1904); Walter R. Lamb, The Royal Academy (London: A. Maclehose & Co., 1935); William Sandby, The History of the Royal Academy of Arts from its Foundation in 1768 to the Present Time (London: Longman, Green, Longman, Roberts, & Green, 1862); David Solkin (ed.), Art on the Line (London and New Haven: Yale University Press, 2001).
12. Samuel Carter Hall, Retrospective of A Long Life from 1815–1883 (New York: D. Appleton and Company, 1883): 195, 199.
13. Ibid., 197.

CHAPTER 6

Books, Periodicals and Newspaper

Eighteenth-century writers were making a living by selling reading as entertainment and education to anyone who could afford the cost of a journal, a newspaper, or a book. Essays about paintings were popular content, and as exhibitions of art became more frequent, writers' role in the art market became increasingly important.

In addition to the writers on art, book sellers were also significant contributors to the popularization of art appreciation among the new audience. The retail book trade was one of the eighteenth century's growth industries, and bookstores were spreading across the island. Reading was a status-defining and trendy pastime among the expanding middle class. Painters were conscious of the link between bibliophiles and lovers of art. Several of the leading intellectuals of the age, the Earl of Shaftesbury and Bernard Mandeville, for example, wrote discourses on theoretical matters of art. William Hogarth, we may remember, also contributed to the debate with his *The Analysis of Beauty*.

Books were not cheap. Therefore, buyers of books—luxury goods, not unlike paintings—were a good market for painters to target. To tap into this lucrative market of bibliophiles, artists published prints of paintings they had done for prominent clients and offered these for sale in bookstores.[1] Their proprietors must have been pleased to have an additional thing to sell. For the artists, the prints were not only a source of revenue but also advertisements for their original works.

T. M. Bayer, *The Genesis of the Modern Art Market in London, 1700–1900*, https://doi.org/10.1007/978-3-032-00594-6_6

Newspapers, too, were growing in popularity. So were fashionable magazines, like the *Spectator* or the *Tattler*. London dailies alone had weekly sales of 100,000 copies which were regularly shared with as many as 20 different individuals.[2] The opportunity of reaching such a large and mixed audience cost-effectively via inexpensive classified ads appealed to painters, and they began advertising in newspapers and journals, much like other producers of luxury goods or tradesman. However, as artists, they designed these advertisements in a manner that made them stand out among the other published notices.

This differentiation was important. During the eighteenth century, painters were still involved in the professional image and branding campaign I discussed earlier. Due to the nature of this campaign, there were valid concerns that the special status to which painters aspired—and were on the way to acquiring—might be jeopardized if they advertised their wares like any common merchant. To counter that impression, they designed these advertisements as announcements in the news section that often elaborately described their works in the most flattering terms. Then and there was the birthplace of the often excessively wordy language typical of exhibition invitations sent out by commercial galleries or museums to their clients, patrons, and the media in our time.[3]

This new form of marketing appealed to writers who were also looking for an outlet for their skills.[4] The public relation campaign to change artists' professional image included a lot of discussion about the theoretical foundations of paintings. This was heady stuff. How does one convince an entire consumer class that the product of a painter's manual labor should not be valued by the amount of time and the cost of materials involved? If it is not something measurable, like time and materials, then obviously something intangible needed to take its place, something intellectual and theoretical, something for learned people to read, talk, and write about. This elusive, mysterious element, part of art's aura, whatever it may be, had to show convincingly that painters were different from any other makers of luxury goods. At the same time, this new realm of intangibles could also be useful among competing artists or artists' groups to differentiate themselves individually.

To be successful, this campaign and its delicate points on theory and aesthetics had to be shared with a wider public. After all, these conversations about aesthetics and exotic theories of art and related stylistic and technical aspects had a specific purpose: to sell art. To accomplish this goal, artists needed the help of professional men of letters. These writers were always looking for work, and they welcomed the new opportunity with great enthusiasm. This meeting of needs marks the beginning of a fruitful and lasting relationship between writers and professional artists that has lasted to this day. Modern art criticism and today's writings about the history of art can be traced back to this eighteenth-century alliance between these two professions. As a result, both, paintings and writing about paintings, adapted (commoditized) to improve this relationship with a common objective: expanding their respective markets.

An analysis of the subjects of paintings and their respective dates shows that from the mid-1750s onward, paintings' themes were noticeably more narrative or literary.[5] Why? It was much easier for writers to write about paintings based on books or well-known stories, and easier for their audience to appreciate these works. It would be another two centuries before art writers had to find a new vocabulary to write about art that was non-objective and told no discernible story.

Over time, writers became more conversant with art theories, iconography, and stylistic nuances, and they spread their knowledge to an appreciative and growing audience. They loved discussing contemporary painters within a sweeping historical context that extended from the legendary painters of antiquity to the Renaissance and the Baroque. This approach was not original. It intentionally imitated Georgio Vasari's (1511–1574) schematic way of thinking about art described in his famous book, *The Lives of the Most Eminent Paintings, Sculptures, and Architects* published in 1550.

Today's academic art historians and art critics, their counterparts in journalistic writing, are direct descendants of these early writers on art. Their specific function in the operations of the art market is addressed as a separate topic later.

Notes

1. Abraham Raimbach, *Memoirs and Recollections of Abraham Raimbach* (London, 1845): 22–23.
2. The Spectator, no. 10 (March 12, 1710–1711). Also Michael Harris, London Newspapers in the Age of Walpole (London: Associated University Presses, 1987): 190.
3. Louis Lippincott, Selling Art in Georgian London (New Haven & London: Yale University Press, 1983): 48/9; Paulson, Hogarth: His Life, Art, and Time (New Haven and London: Yale University Press, 1971), vol. 1:

213–214, 372, vol. 2: 344. On other artists advertising invitations to the public to come to their houses, see William Whitley, Artists and Their Friends in England 1700–1790, 2 vols. (London & Boston: The Medici Society, 1938), vol. 1: 115; Lippincott: 32 ff. Michael Foss, Man of Wit to Man of Business (Bristol: Bristol Classical Press, 1988): 177–178.

4. David Solkin, Painting for Money (New Haven & London: Yale University Press, 1993), ch. 7 and notes. Paulson, vol. 2: 307; Whitley, vol. 1: 167–168, vol. 2: 271 for names of several of the early art critics and the publications for which they wrote. See also the art-related materials from the London Press from the 1760s in the Paul Mellon Center for Studies in British Art, Yale University, assembled by Claire Lloyd-Jacob.
5. Bayer/Page data.

CHAPTER 7

Changing Economics: A Relentless Demand for Novelty

With the Royal Academy established, the focus of artists shifted from collective recognition to individual rivalry. This was no longer a quest for the opportunity to compete as a group. Instead, painters, both within and outside the ranks of the Academy, vied for the public's attention in an annual exhibition spectacle that catapulted artists to fame, fortune, and celebrity status.

Artists responded to this new challenge again with sound business sense, entrepreneurship, and creativity. They recognized the need for a new genre of painting, one that would truly captivate the audience: large-scale, visually stunning works that dazzled with their display of exceptional skill, erudition, drama, and bravura. Baroque-like visual sensations that would make the audience gasp and art writers use superlatives. The time was ripe for this new style, with a vast array of subjects—from literature and mythology to politics and eroticism—waiting to be interpreted.

Journalists covering the art scene found these subjects equally captivating, and competition among artists to create the most attention-grabbing visual sensations intensified. This competitive landscape would shape the art world for generations to come, influencing the trajectory of painting even beyond the emergence of modern art.

These new market conditions signify one of the crucial turning points of art. Many of the paintings we consider among the greatest contributions to our cultural history are works specifically created for a market that

T. M. Bayer, *The Genesis of the Modern Art Market in London, 1700–1900*, https://doi.org/10.1007/978-3-032-00594-6_7

demanded products with maximum visual impact on the contemporaneous audience. These works' imposing size, elaborate execution, and enormous production efforts made them largely unsuitable for display in private surroundings.[1] Frequently, they ended up in public collections. Many of them are exhibited in museums throughout the world. And, as I already pointed out, these same works are also customarily found in our art history textbooks. Rarely, however, is the deliberate market orientation of these paintings discussed nor the fascinating reasons for its development. The history of late eighteenth and nineteenth-century painting is filled with examples of artists' pragmatic economic thinking and insight into their audience.

All the emphatically different art products created nowadays—some great and breathtaking, others not so much—are indebted to an art market that was deliberately constructed during the last two centuries. Intense competition for attention drove artists to be different, unique, revolutionary, transformational, controversial, disruptive, provocative, poetic, lyrical, incomprehensible, outrageous, brilliant, clever, political, apolitical, environmental, conceptual, monumental, bizarre, vulgar, grotesque.

More adjectives could be added, but these few should make the point. Without a laissez-faire art market with low entry barrier and no restrictions on product design, save the all-important demand for novelty, the art produced over the last 150 years would be exceedingly dull and uniform. The 1917 Armory Show at which Marcel Duchamp introduced his 'Fountain' to a stunned public would have looked very differently, indeed. The urinal would have been displayed in the men's toilet.

One-Man Shows

The establishment of the Royal Academy triggered a seismic shift in the art world's economy, transforming not only the type of paintings created but also how artists perceived the monetary value of their work. The Academy's financial model, which distributed exhibition proceeds equally among members, proved flawed. This system failed to account for the disproportionate revenue generated by individual artworks that stirred the public's enthusiasm.

As a result, artists who invested months or even years in creating monumental works, which became the main draw of an exhibition, received no additional compensation. This imbalance between effort and reward was unsustainable. Resourceful artists soon devised strategies to capitalize on their popular works. One solution was the one-man show, where an artist would showcase a star attraction—neo-Baroque sensations—alongside other works for sale and retaining all the profits.

Shouldering the responsibilities of sole exhibitor, organizer, financier, and promoter added to the artists' already demanding workload. Nevertheless, they demonstrated remarkable flair and effectiveness in managing these new demands. Like their modern counterparts, eighteenth-century artists were adept at generating publicity. As the art world continued to evolve, artists would become increasingly savvy in promoting their work, albeit with still slightly more restraint, and capitalizing on their success. The days of Pietro Manzoni and Jeff Koons were two centuries away.

[Piero Manzoni (b. 1933–1963) Merde d'Artists (1961) consists of ninety tin cans filled with the artist's own feces. Influenced by Duchamp's 'Readymades', i.e., ordinary objects transformed into art through an artist's action, the Italian artist applied this concept to the product of his digestive tract and signed every tin can. This provocative work garnered tremendous publicity for Manzoni and is housed in the Tate Museum, London.]

There is a particularly amusing and somewhat famous precedent for one-man shows that reaches far into the future. In 1775, Nathaniel Hone (1718–1784), an Irish painter working in London, had sent his painting, *The Conjurer*, to the Royal Academy's hanging committee to be considered for the upcoming 1775 annual exhibition. The Hanging Committee accepted it for display. Unfortunately, anonymous rumors were immediately reported in the press, alleging that this painting depicted the image of a woman writhing nakedly while brandishing a smoking torch. This fact alone was already shocking. What made it even more outrageous was the claim that the naked woman represented none other than Angelica Kauffmann (1741–1807), an eminently proper, married lady and one of the two women among the founding members of the otherwise very manly Royal Academy. (Mary Moser (1744–1819) was the second one.) Such outrageous gossip was utterly intolerable. The Hanging Committee saw no other choice but to remove this vile canvas and have it returned in due haste to its painter. This rejection utterly ruined Nathaniel's chances to show his great opus to the London public. Accounts of this scandal were published in various dailies. Although the artist denied any such described unseemliness, he still went to great length to apologize to his violated female colleague in a well-publicized letter.

The painter took the rejection in good stride. There was publicity value in notoriety. In record time and with remarkable organizational skill, he produced a catalogue, rented showrooms, and mounted an exhibition of some 30 of his works. The star attraction? None other than the scandalous and, by now very infamous, canvas. The entry fee to see Madame Angelica contorting in the buff was 1 shilling. Of course, the press jumped on it. What an impressive display of entrepreneurial zeal and organizational know-how! One might be permitted to wonder who was behind the rumor. The obvious beneficiary was the painter. As all of us know, anonymous calls to the press for self-promotion are still as popular as ever (Figs. 7.1, 7.2, and 7.3).[2]

The upper left-hand corner of the sketch shows the objectionable scene. The finished work is owned by the National Gallery of Ireland, Dublin. In the final version, this section of the painting was reworked.

I don't know if the resourceful Irish artist sold any of the works shown at his exhibition. Most likely, he wasn't concerned about it. He made out rather well with entrance tickets. However, the use of such exhibitions specifically for selling art works on display directly to the public was ready and waiting in the wings. This new business model entered center stage only a few years after *The Conjurer* scandal, with the lead role performed by another enterprising painter, this time an American from Boston. A seemingly innocuous organizational tweak turned into one of those trigger incidents in history that only later come to be recognized as seminal events. In this case, I can state without hyperbole that it dramatically and fundamentally changed the entire future history of the art market.

Art Exhibitions as Sales Events: The Middleman Rises

The lead role in the first staging of a public exhibition for the singular purpose of selling art went to the above-mentioned American painter, John Singleton Copley (1738–1815) when he decided, in 1781, to organize such a one-man event and see how it would play out. The rebellious and entrepreneurial Bostonian was already prominent in London and thought it was worth the risk to withhold his already much-hyped ten-foot-wide dramatic opus, *The Death of Chatham*, from the annual summer

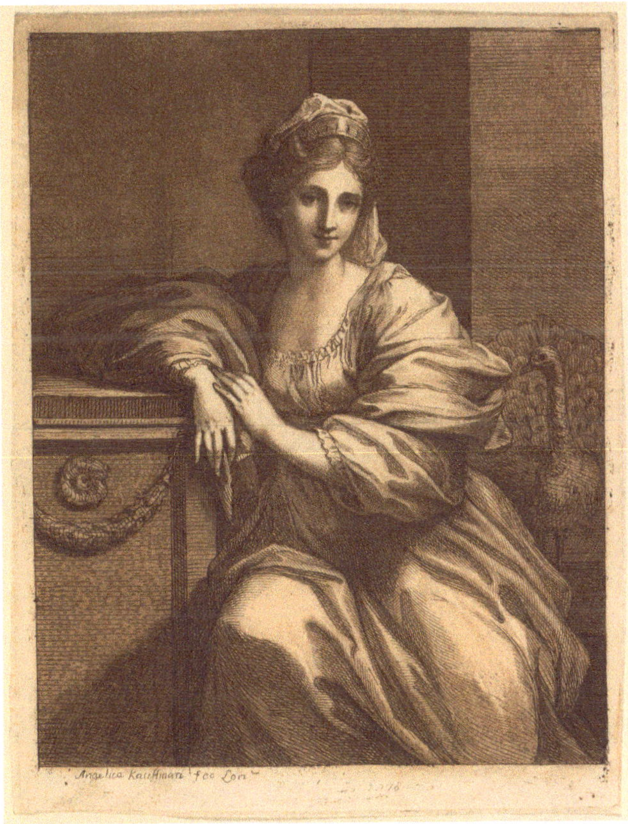

Fig. 7.1 Angelica Kauffmann (1741–1807), Angelica Kauffmann

exhibition at the Royal Academy and try something different. Monetarily, all he had to lose was the paltry share he would have gotten from the proceeds of the ticket sales at the Academy. His plan was to make this spectacular visual drama the center attraction of a special exhibition at Spring Gardens, a one-artist-one-work exhibition or, described differently, a deliberate middle finger at the Royal Academy, the most powerful organization in the British art milieu. When considering venues for this event, Copley may have remembered that this was the same location where Hogarth and his groups had their first public exhibition nearly fifty years prior. Or was it just one of these wonderful historical coincidences?

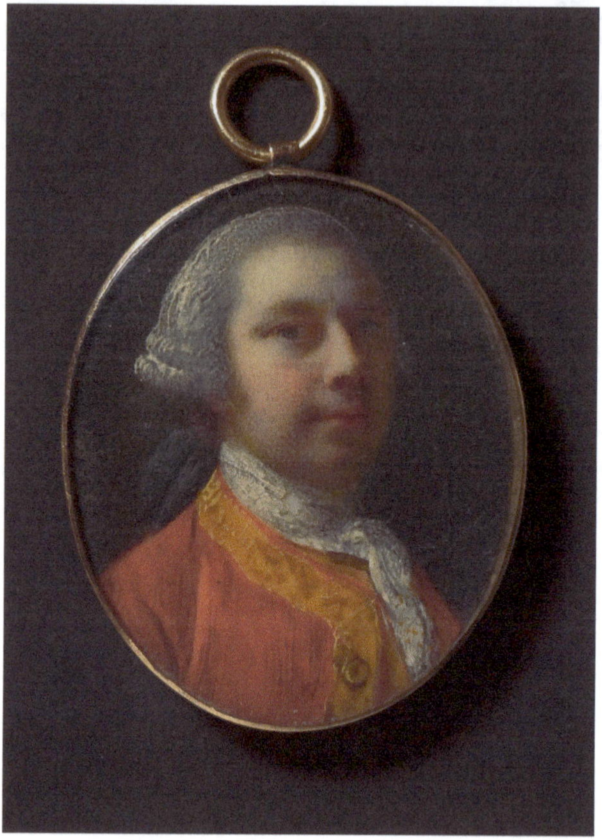

Fig. 7.2 Nathaniel Hone (1718–1784), Self-Portrait of the Artist

The painting he had chosen was perfect for the job—a gigantic scene of an intensely dramatic event that had occurred in Parliament some three years earlier. Copley had given it his all. It was a stunning display of his extraordinary skill as a painter, his depth of erudition, his intimate knowledge of classical composition, and his inspired creativity, heavy with allegory and symbolism. He had deliberately created a work that had all the accoutrements of a pictorial sensation. So how would he monetize this effort? He had invested over two years of labor!

Copley introduced two new and critical factors to the usual entry fee. One was a revenue-generating product, the other a partner. He planned

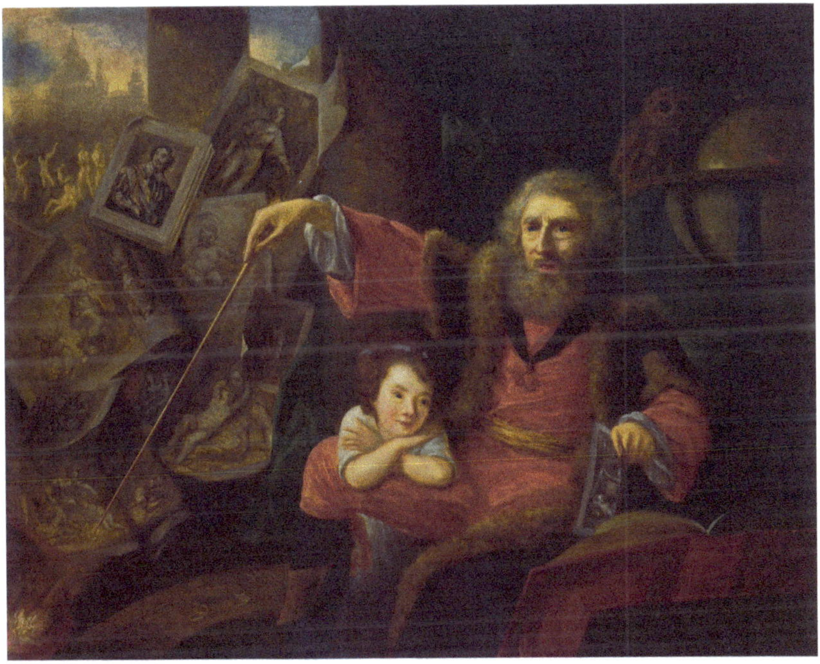

Fig. 7.3 Nathaniel Hone, The Conjurer

to sell inexpensive paper reproductions of his famous painting at the exhibition; and he partnered with the printer, entrepreneur, and influential politician, John Boydell (1720–1804), to manage production, logistics, promotion, and sales. It was not the first time that reproductive prints were sold to the public. Hogarth, and many others, had been involved in that business. The vital role of the eighteenth-century print in the history of the art market will be discussed in greater detail later under its own heading. For now, it suffices to point out that the critical difference between earlier print publications and Copley's project was the size and sensational character of the original work and the scope of the enterprise. It far exceeded the level that one person could undertake alone. It needed professional management. This was a high-risk venture with a lot of moving parts. It required upfront money for arranging and setting up the exhibition space as well as paying for a manually engraved reproduction of the painting on a steel plate and mass-produce inexpensive prints by the thousands. Moreover, advertisement had to be designed and paid for, and the logistics for collecting entrance fees and selling the print to exhibition visitors had to be organized.

Copley's business model effectively separated his original painting into three distinct products that could be monetized individually. One: he could sell the original work; two: he could charge entrance fees to its exhibition; and three: he could generate further revenue through sales of a cheap derivative product—the engraving. Copley calculated that the combined revenue from entry fees and high-volume print sales would not just offset the substantial investment of time and money he had made in this project, but it would also leave him and his partner with a tidy profit.

His enterprise made national and international news,[3] and the underlying economics—revenue from the sales of cheap derivative products—were copied almost immediately, and they are still being used today. The artist Christo (1935–2020), for example, who gained international fame in the second half of the twentieth century, frequently raised funding for his complex and expensive wrapping projects of architectural landmarks with publications of prints after original preparatory drawings related to a specific wrap.

Copley reaped a veritable fortune with his daring enterprise. In terms of present-day buying power, it easily exceeded several million pounds, dollars, or Euros. No artist in history had even remotely come close to such earnings from just one single painting. Moreover, his rebellion against the authority of the Royal Academy also bore fruit. Copley's exhibition event was responsible for a drop of over 30% in that year's attendance of the crown jewel among the London art events, the all-important annual exhibition at the Royal Academy (Fig. 7.4).[4]

Death of Chatham depicts a highly dramatic moment that occurred on April 7, 1778, when William Pitt, 1st Earl of Chatham, collapsed in the House of Lords.

In the history of the modern art market, the London exhibition of Copley's *Death of Chatham* is a symbolic milestone. It marks the point where product design, revenue method, middleman opportunity, and audience demand fully synergized. Other painters, like Thomas Gainsborough, James Berry, and Benjamin West undertook similar projects within a span of three years. This combination laid the foundation for the full commercialization of art exhibitions.[5]

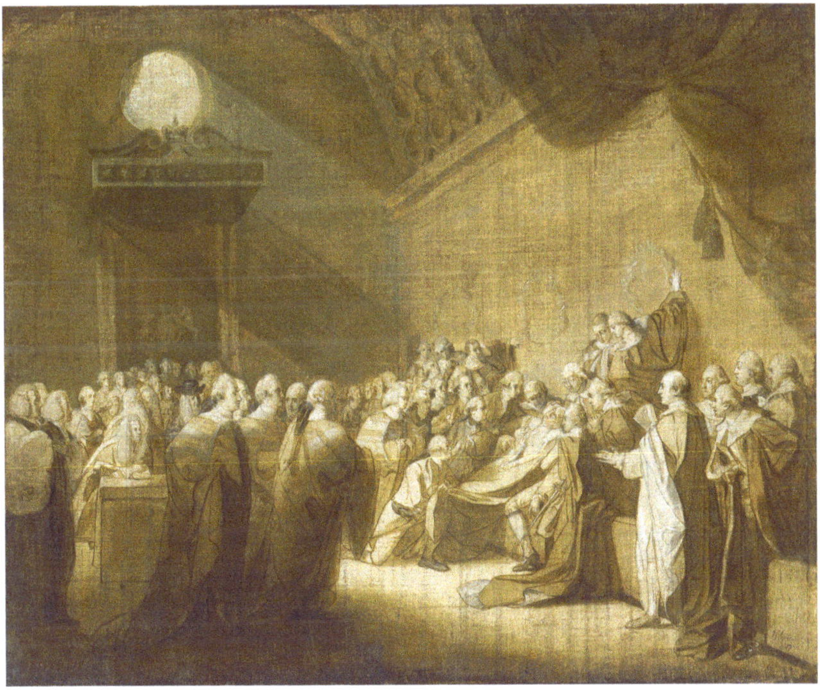

Fig. 7.4 John Singleton Copley (1738–1818), The Death of the Earl oChatham, 1779

Soon, there were subtle organizational and content innovations. One example is *The Shakespeare Gallery*, started in London in 1786 by Copley's former partner, John Boydell. The idea was the same, but with a twist—a unifying theme: an exhibition of different interpretations of a variety of Shakespearian subjects commissioned from different painters. Copying Copley's business model, entrance fees were charged, and prints were offered for sale. A similar project was *The Poets Gallery*, started in 1787 by a competitor, Thomas Macklin (1752–1800), a print publisher and dealer.[6] Around the same time, an exclusively Milton-themed exhibition was organized by the painter/entrepreneur Henry Fuseli. A similar event, featuring patriotic themes of English history, was put together by the miniature painter and print publisher, Robert Bowyer.

The theme show was born.[7] The idea proved to be very successful, if we take longevity and ubiquity as measures. Museums, university art galleries, and commercial art galleries worldwide all have adopted this business model ever since it was introduced, tested, and refined in eighteenth-century Britain. I can confidently predict that wherever Leonardo's *Salvator Mundi* will be displayed when it comes out of hiding, there will be inexpensive postcards and posters available for sale, likely even t-shirts, puzzles, mugs, and keychains.

[John Boydell (1719–1804) was a publisher, print seller, Lord Mayor of London, and art market entrepreneur. Henri Fuseli (1741–1826) was a founding member of the Royal Academy, painter and art market entrepreneur who founded the Milton Gallery where works based on Shakespeare and Milton were exhibited. Robert Bowyer (1758–1834) founded the Historical Gallery in London which showcased paintings and prints of historical themes by contemporary artists. His two major enterprises were an illustrated edition of the Bible and David Hume's The History of England.]

The size of these enterprises can be appreciated best by the Parliamentary appraisal of John Boydell's inventory when he filed for bankruptcy in 1804. The Napoleonic Wars had caused the loss of the firm's vital export market and financially ruined him. His stock was valued at 350,000 pounds. Depending on the conversion method, this amounts to well over 100 million pounds today.[8]

Copley's project and the others that followed his also signify the merger of two important interests, those of artists and art dealers. The developing union between artists and the emerging group of professional dealers/promoters/showmen received a lot of attention from the press and contributed to an unprecedented growth in the general consumption of pictures during the nineteenth century. Graphing overall auction market growth during this period and the number of dealers active in it show that the expansion of the art market was causally associated with the rise of dealers.[9] As middlemen, their financial interest was directly coupled with expanding both, consumption and production. They became the conduit through which art flowed. In economic terms, as middlemen, dealers were aligned with artists. Without this all-important alliance, the history of art of the modern period would surely have been written differently. The synergies inherent in any successful relationship between producer and middleman tend to modify (commoditize) the behavior of the involved parties towards achieving the best possible outcome for both.

Notes

1. This observation was made by Hogarth. Quoted by Richard Redgrave, A Century of British Painters (New York: Cornell University Press, 1981): 2.
2. For more details on Hone's painting, see, Martin Butlin, 'An Eighteenth Century Scandal: Nathaniel Hone's "The Conjurer"', Connoisseur, CLXXIV (1970): 1–9; also Richard Altick, The Shows of London (Cambridge: Harvard University Press, 1978): 104; Walter Koch, Die Kunstaustellung (Berlein: Walter de Gruyter & Co., 1967): 215; William Whitley, Artists and Their Friends in England 1700–1790, 2 vols. (London & Boston: The Medici Society, 1938), vol. 2: 266.
3. I found over twenty individual mentions in London papers dating from May 1 to June 21, 1781, of this event in the collection of art-related press clippings kept at the Mellon Centre in London.
4. Public Advertiser (June 2, 1781): 2.
5. On Copley's enterprises see Joseph Farington, The Farington Diaries, 1793–1817, 2 vols., J. Greig, ed. (London: Hutchison, 1922–1928), vol. 1: 48, vol. 2: 76; Hugh Amory, John Singleton Copley, R.A. (New York: Houghton, Mifflin and Co., 1982), ch. 5; Altick: 105; Koch: 215–216; Whitley, vol. 2: 137–140; on Boydell see Herbert Bruntjen, John Boydell (1719–1804): A Study of Art Patronage and Publishing in Georgian London (New York: Garland Publishing, 1985).
6. Gallery of poets, Pall-Mall and Fleet Street (April 2, 1790); catalogue of the third exhibition of pictures painted for Mr. Macklin by the artists of Britain (London: Printed by T. Bensley, Bolt Court, Fleet Street, 1790).
7. For an extensive discussion of these and similar events, see Altick.
8. John Pye, Patronage of British Art, A Historical Sketch (London: Longman, Browm, Green, and Longman, 1845): 253, n. 62.
9. Bayer/Page data.

CHAPTER 8

The Market Coming of Age

Inevitably, the rapid expansion of the art market and the increasing competition fueled a demand for ever more diversification in all areas—among artists, art dealers, art products, the press, and art theories. This need for specialization and innovation was the main driver of the extraordinary explosion of styles, unprecedented in the history of art, that began during the last third of the nineteenth century and continues to this day. It is a manifestation of the ongoing commoditization process of the arts environment that I have pointed out earlier on several occasions. The contemporary art market never saturates. By design it always has room for something new, it attracts innovation. Continuous renewal is the art market's only constant.

The examples I described in the preceding chapter set the scene for the nineteenth century when the professionalization of art dealing came into full bloom. The combination of sensational visual spectacles, dramatic subjects, and inexpensive mass-produced derivatives, all enthusiastically promoted by the press, was an irresistible marketing *tour-de-force*. It thrust the earning potential of contemporary artists to dizzying heights and putting fortunes into their and their dealers' pockets.

Yet, as with most remarkable success stories, luck also had a hand in it. In the case of English painters, *Fortuna* took on the shape of a short Corsican dressed in the cloak of war. Artists benefitted from a market condition economists describe as a 'lemon problem'. In the aftermath of the

T. M. Bayer, *The Genesis of the Modern Art Market in London, 1700–1900*, https://doi.org/10.1007/978-3-032-00594-6_8

Napoleonic Wars (1803–1816), extraordinary treasures from Continental collections, looted or rightfully bought, found their way to England where enterprising dealers turned them into ready cash, attesting to art's capacity to store transportable value.[1] Unfortunately, along with masterpieces came untold fakes that were unceremoniously dumped on the market.[2] The unavoidable 'lemon problem' that resulted from this flood of phonies turned into an enormous advantage for contemporary painters.[3]

[Box: George Akerlof's seminal 1970 study of the used car market may seem an unorthodox comparison, but the art market reacts similarly to the problem of information asymmetry. The prevalence of questionable authenticity and age in the market for Old Masters can cause its collapse. Buyers shy away and owners of authentic works are equally reluctant to sell for fear that they won't get good prices.[4]]

When faced with reluctant demand for dubious 'old masters' from ambiguous places on the Continent, the trade—as the art dealing industry is often called—turned to the next best thing, a close substitute: contemporary paintings.[5] Just like old pictures, they were nice to look at, just younger. And they had an incontestable advantage over old paintings when it came to authenticity: the individuals who had painted them were still around and could vouch for their genuineness.[6]

There was another benefit to contemporary paintings, although a less obvious one. Boydell's spectacular bankruptcy occurred as a result of the collapse of the market for print reproductions on the war-torn Continent.[7] The last thing one thinks about when cannon balls are crashing through the roof is what lovely print to hang on a wall that may collapse at any moment. The loss of this formerly very lucrative market seriously hurt English painters, engravers, print publishers, print dealers, glassmakers, and framers. The biggest publisher had gone broke. As a result, demand for commissions for artists to do original paintings for reproduction dried up, the engraving industry went into a slump, and print dealers suffered from a lack of fresh merchandize to offer to their customers.

But many of the smaller print publishers and dealers, well below the size of Boydell's or Bowyer's vast enterprises, jumped at the chance to display contemporary paintings to improve the much-reduced inventory of prints in their shops. Others joined in. Event promoters and ambitious wheeler-dealers all wanted to try their hand at trading in this new, exciting, and, frankly, classy stuff. Few had any deeper knowledge of art. But they all shared a keen sense for a lucrative business opportunity when they saw it. There was no shortage of contemporary paintings, and, even better, there were always more. Auction records show that by the 1830s, dealers were increasingly trading in contemporary paintings.[8]

Out of this mélange, by mid-nineteenth century, a retail gallery system came into being in London that has been the norm for the worldwide art market ever since.[9] It was these Victorian professional dealers in contemporary art who first organized the informal collaborative networks that to this day help regulate and protect the mechanism that turns the different interests of the market's main players into money—lots of money. Everyone was only too happy to play along: artists, publishers, the media, art writers, collectors, nascent public collections, auction houses, and, of course, the dealers themselves. Art's asset quality would not exist without them. For anything to become a storage for value, the stakeholders must have access to an exchange mechanism—a market—that allows them to trade their asset class for other asset classes, be that fiat currency, crypto currency, shares, real estate, etc. Art dealers were and remain an existential and defining part of the art environment's exchange mechanism.

Among painters, the need to attract attention was now greater than ever. But so were the potential rewards. Again, the artists displayed remarkable imagination, creativity, entrepreneurship, and market savvy to compete in this rapidly expanding and increasingly profitable market. They investigated every conceivable—and respectable—way to show that their work was different from that of their fellow artist competitors. The market's inherent demand for continuous innovation gave all of them more opportunity and more freedom to experiment and to explore new ways of pictorial expression, and, frankly, to show off.

To make sure that they would be recognized, they had their own bag of tricks. 'Style' is a more conventional term, or one might call it 'brand', to use a currently in vogue description. An excellent example is England's perhaps greatest master, Joseph Mallord William Turner (1775–1851). A brilliant, exceptionally skilled, and incredibly fast painter, he has been described as an early action painter, an '1830s Jackson Pollock, ferocious sometimes' (Fig. 8.1).[10]

He employed his extraordinary technical talent and speed, together with his daring use of brush and colors, to add final, masterful, and conspicuous touches to his Royal Academy exhibition paintings. To gain an

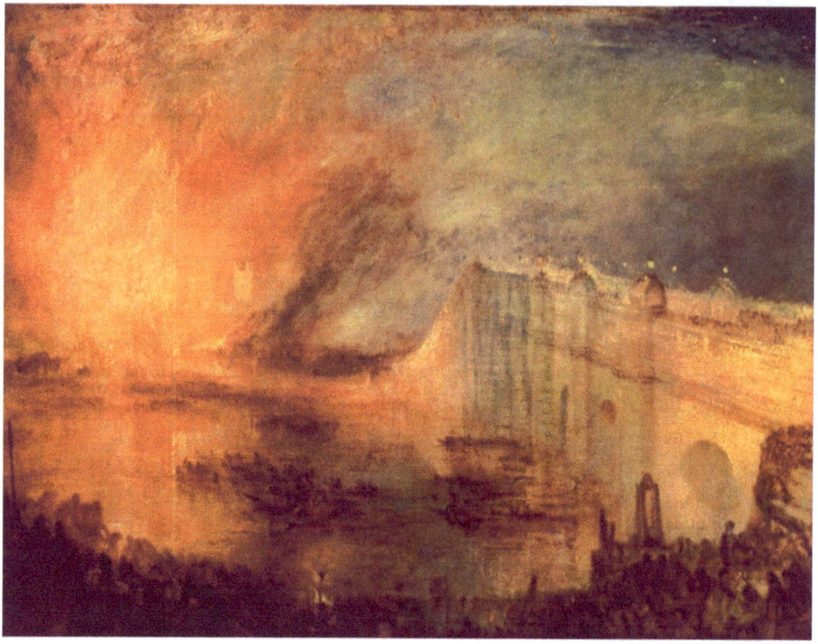

Fig. 8.1 Joseph Mallord William. Turner (1775–1851), The Burning of the Houses of Parliament

edge over the competition, Turner would wait until he had had the opportunity during 'Varnishing Day' to look at the finished works of all his competitors and then do his magic. His canvasses literally outshined all the others. Once, in 1832, Turner, peeved about the colors and flags of Constable's *Opening of Waterloo Bridge*, grabbed his brush, and painted a small red dot on the foreground of his seascape *Helvoetsluys* to indicate a buoy floating in the water and then later varnished the addition. When Constable came by, he supposedly said: 'He has been here and fired a gun'.[11] The anecdote is wonderfully presented in the 2014 feature film, *Mister Turner*, directed by Mike Leigh.

['Varnishing Day' at the Royal Academy is the day when artists were allowed to add finishing touches and apply varnish to their paintings before the exhibition opened to the public. The word vernissage—varnishing—is still widely used today to describe the opening of an art exhibition.]

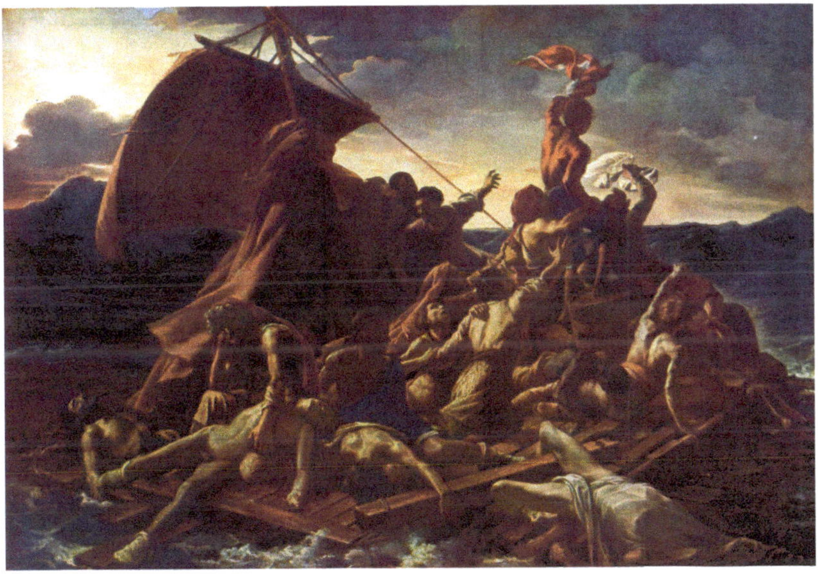

Fig. 8.2 Théodore Géricault (1791–1824), The Raft of Medusa

In this contest, it was not just about color; size also mattered. Some paintings, like the French painter Theodore Gericault's *Raft of Medusa*, were so big—16.1 feet x 23.5 feet (490 cm x 716), they dwarfed the viewer and required special exhibition accommodation when it was publicly shown to enthusiastic crowds in 1822 at the Egyptian Hall in London (Fig. 8.2).[12]

In 1820, Theodore Gericault's (1791–1824) Raft of Medusa (1819) went on an exhibition tour to London and Dublin organized by the artist in partnership with an English promoter, William Bullock.

Apocalyptic events that could put the fear of God into viewers' hearts were great attention getters, too. Depiction of biblical spectacles of epic proportions were also popular crowd-pleasers (Fig. 8.3).

Heroic military charges would fire up manly courage and patriotism like Thomas Jones Barker's (1815–1882) epic Charge of the Light Brigade. The monumental canvas shows Lord Cardigan in the center surrounded by Russian guns with the 13th Light Dragoons and 17th Lancers during the Battle of Balaclava in the Crimean War (1853–1856). It can be admired today in its fitting location in the Defence Academy of the UK in Shrivenham, Oxfordshire.

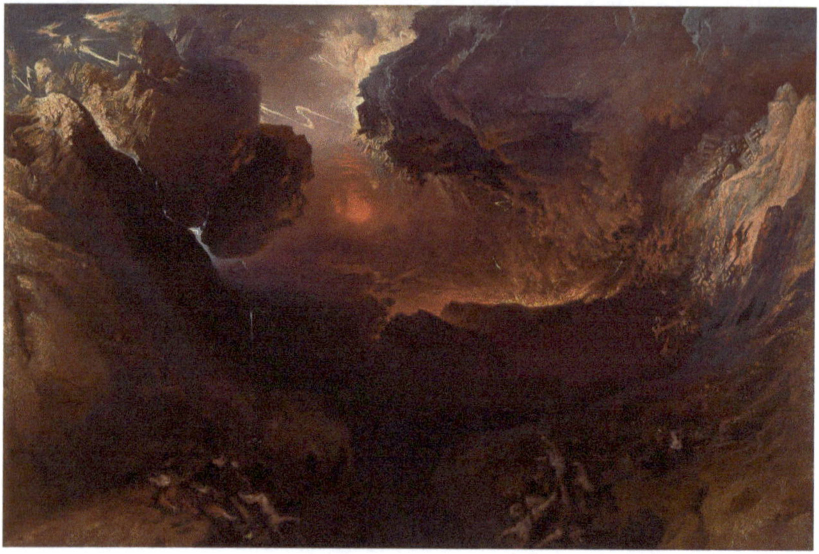

Fig. 8.3 John 'Mad' Martin (1789–1854), The Great Day of His Wrath

But terrifying images were not restricted to military campaigns. Near life-sized stampeding cattle, snot and foam flying, also were crowd pleasers as evidenced by Henry William Banks Davis' (1797–1876) five meter-wide canvas, *A Panic* (1830) currently in the Beverley Art Gallery.

[I bought a slightly smaller engraver's version (175 x 375 cm or 69 in x 148) painted by the artist of this enormous painting (200 cm x 500 cm or 79 in. x 196 in) in London at auction in the late 1980s. Competition for 12 feet of very realistically painted stampeding cattle was negligible despite the work's fame and quality. Understandably, for European dealers in old paintings, this was a non-seller. It took up valuable wall space in a gallery. It would cost a fortune to crate and ship. Then who would buy it? Who has a room in their house that could accommodate this 12-feet canvas? Subject and size made this superbly painted work commercially unappealing. But I had a client in Montana, a rancher with enough land to match the size of Luxembourg and a proportionally sized house with the right room, the right wall, and the right light. He also loved his cattle and had the appreciation for the subject. It was a perfect fit and still hangs in the family home.]

Ghost, goblins, and fairies; ancient gods; mythologies; knights in shining armor; great moments in history—nothing was off limit to a painter eager to create a brand identity for him—and, by now, herself (Figs. 8.4, 8.5, 8.6, and 8.7).

As testimony to the tenacity of labor-based valuation in art, meticulous detail and conspicuous time-consuming labor were equally regarded. There should be plenty of evidence of months, and months, and more months of hard labor, ideally involving some level of personal sacrifice, even a hint of danger. Holman Hunt's (1827–1910) stories of personal suffering and acute dangers while painting his *Scapegoat* quasi in situ in the Holy Land were great fodder for a sensation-hungry press.[13] The reports lent a sacralized aura to the original painting that also embraced its mass-produced engravings (Fig. 8.8).

Other crowd-pleasers were authentic-looking scenes of everyday life in ancient Rome. These provided painters with countless opportunities to include their versions of the ever popular 'wet drapery' look: gorgeous, slim-figured teenage girls wrapped in revealing transparent togas showing pink nipples and rosy bottoms. Fairytales or scenes of oriental splendor with pashas surrounded by scantily clad harem girls also offered themselves for similar risqué treatment. And nudes, of course. Just because

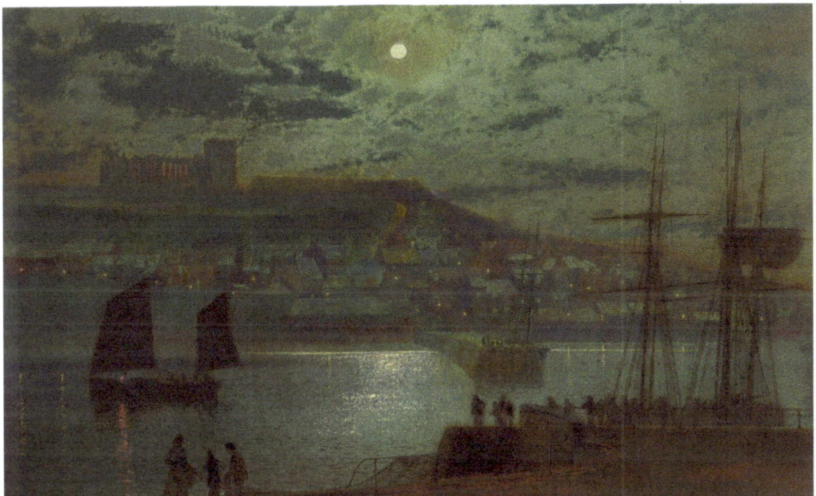

Fig. 8.4 John Atkinson Grimshaw (1836–1893), Whitby Harbor

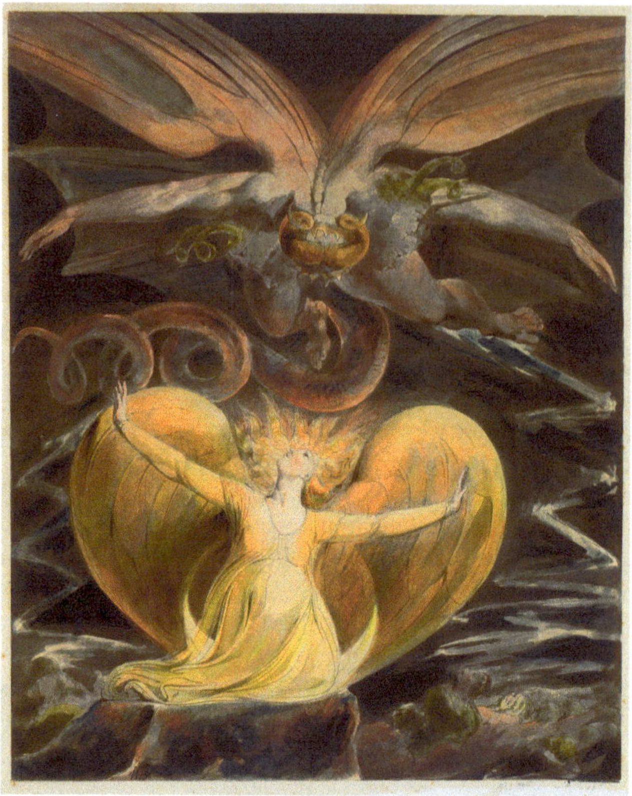

Fig. 8.5 William Blake (1757–1827), The Great Red Dragon and the Woman Clothed with the Sun

this period is called the 'Victorian' Age should not suggest that soft-core erotica was not appreciated. Public exhibitions of the hardcore variety, however, had to wait until 1990. And it took place in Italy, in Venice at the Biennale, not on the British Isles (Figs. 8.9, 8.10, 8.11, and 8.12).

It also paid off to paint crowds, very, very large crowds. Hundreds of people doing perfectly ordinary things. A packed railroad station, a busy day at the races, or a crowded beach were perfect subjects and big hits with the public. Allegedly, Daniel Marlise's gigantic canvas of the medieval wedding attended by countless guests, even dead ones, had to be roped off to protect it from the surging masses of enthusiastic spectators. All

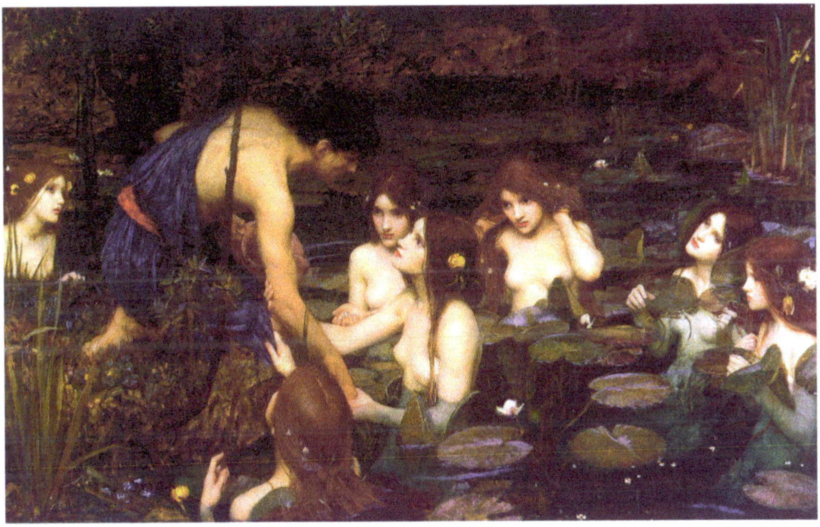

Fig. 8.6 John William Waterhouse (1849–1917, Hylas and the Nymphs

these paintings were evidence of their respective painter's hard work (Fig. 8.13).

These types of paintings produced staggering incomes for their artists. Victorian sensation pictures were phenomenal work horses. They maximized Copley's business model of generating revenue for their owners through direct sale, entrance fees from exhibitions, and sale of inexpensive mass-produced reproductions. The amounts paid to painters for these epic money-makers reflected their earning potential. It would take until 1980 before any living painter's work—the Yorkshireman, David Hockney's 1972 *Pool with two Figures*—would command such prices.

Membership in an artists' organization—like the famous Pre-Raphaelite Brotherhood (PRB) founded under a cloak of secrecy in 1848—was another useful marketing device for painters.[14] The Brotherhood was championed by the great arbiter of taste, John Ruskin (1819–1900). More about him later.

Artists formed other interest groups and exhibition societies—not quite as cryptic as the Brotherhood—to compete with the sovereignty of the Royal Academy. Membership in these groups and participation in their

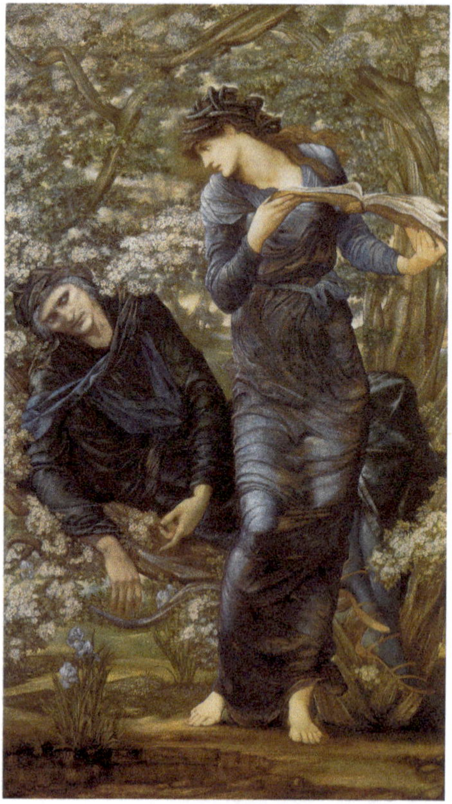

Fig. 8.7 Edward Burne-Jones (1833–1898), Beguiling of Merlin

vetted exhibitions were considered peer-approval stamps and were—and continue to be—useful marketing devices (Figs. 8.14 and 8.15).

There are thousands of other examples of painters' increasing differentiation from one another. A quick look through Christopher Wood's *Dictionary of Victorian Painters*, still the standard reverence work for this period, is ample evidence of artists' responses to the dictates of the market.[15] Emphasis on personal interpretation, diversification in subject, and manner of execution became the hallmarks of the age.

Artists recognized the market's ever-present need for innovation and kept expanding the boundaries. The proverbial explosion of painting styles that started during the last quarter of the nineteenth century is as much a response to changing market conditions as it is a rejection of tired

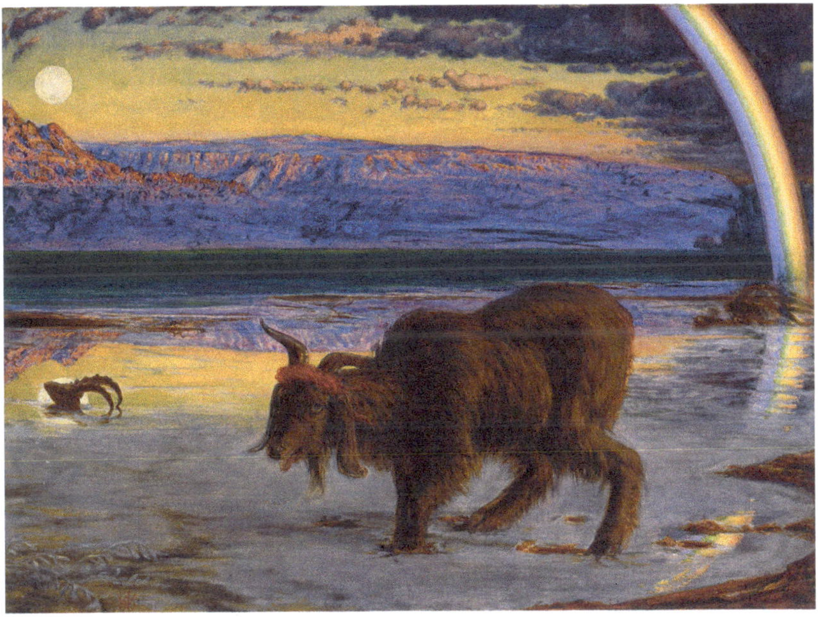

Fig. 8.8 William Holman Hunt (1827–1910), Scapegoat

aesthetic doctrines imposed by domineering art institutions like the Royal Academy in London or the Salon in Paris. In France, the rebellious artists were dubbed the *Intransigeants* for that reason.

Painters also accommodated the recently established retail gallery system. Display space is a critical aspect in the operation of a retail establishment. In addition to location, it is among the factors that determine rents for such premises. Conveniently, and, I would argue, not coincidentally, interior design during the Victorian period was afflicted by a pronounced '*horror vacui*', a fear of empty space. The manner in which paintings were displayed in galleries, hung at home, or in private clubs reflected this fear. Every suitable wall space had to be covered with pictures. This fashion was most opportune for gallery owners. It gave them the pretext to exhibit the maximum amount of works for sale in a way that echoed paintings' decorative arrangements in domestic settings. Since it had been established that art is good for society, crowding one's home with art must, of course, be good for the family. And, let's not forget, it was also a most enjoyable demonstration of sophisticated patriotism (Fig. 8.16).

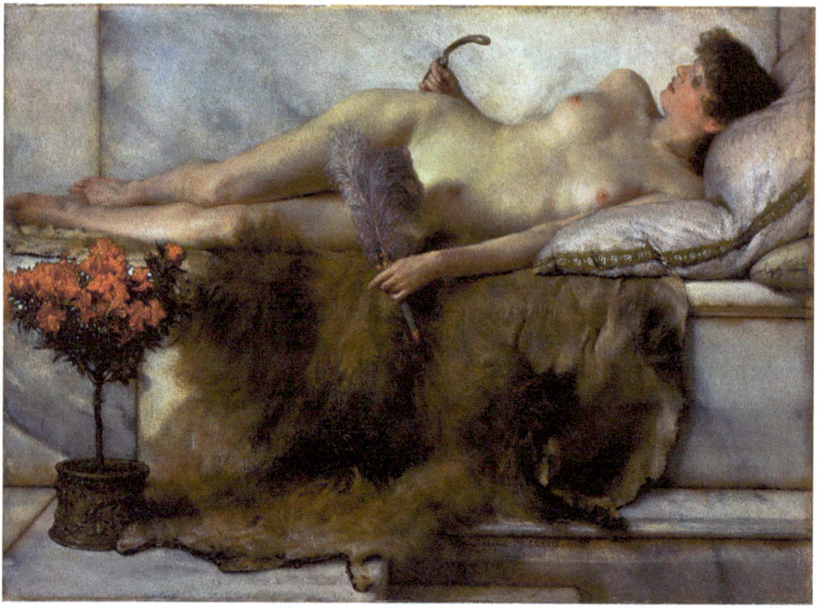

Fig. 8.9 Lawrence Alma-Tadema (1836–1912), Tepidarium

Artists and gallery owners collaborated to promote this style of interior design and cash in on the opportunities it offered. Auction records show that during this coming-of-age period of the market, aside from the huge sizes of "Sensation Pictures", contemporary paintings became, on average, smaller.[16] This is not surprising. Galleries could improve their sales by displaying larger numbers of smaller paintings, offering customers a wider range of choice at affordable prices. The most common canvas sizes, according to these sales records, were 18 x 24 inches and 24 x 36 inches—still known today in the trade as 'sofa-size'. 'Sensation' pictures, of course, were the exception. The daunting dimensions were part of their product character. But the bread and butter of the art market were the millions of oils and watercolors that were painted to beautify English homes.

Style and subject were not the only way for artists to differentiate themselves. Certain painters deliberately constructed distinguishing personal images. The public persona of Lord Frederick Leighton (1830–1896), for example, and his custom-built London home were an integral part of his branding strategy. The image of someone who exists outside conventional

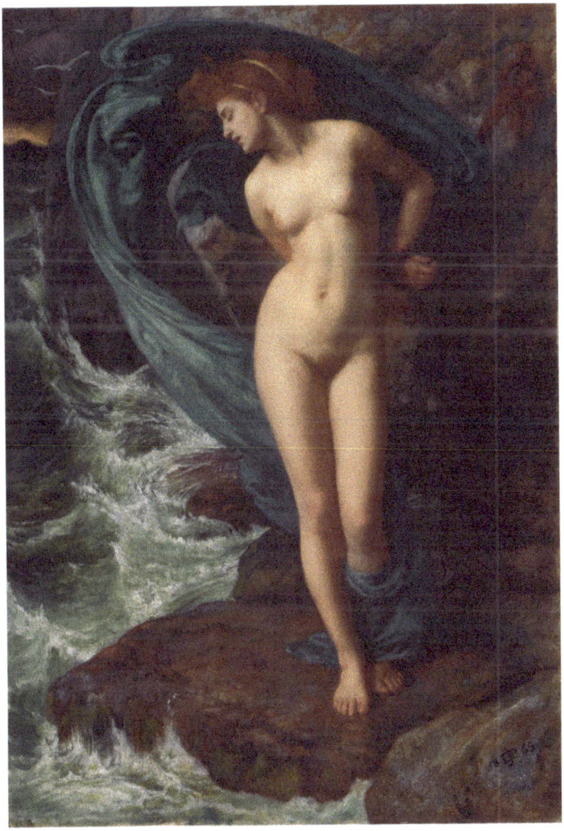

Fig. 8.10 SIR Edward John Poynter (1836–1919), Andromeda

norms was cultivated and became an integral part of artists' personal aura to the point that it is expected now. Who wants an artist friend who is 'normal'? This aspect of artistic freedom has brought out talented showmen and creative self-promoters who would seek out, even create, opportunities to be in the limelight. Outrageousness is monetizable. What else is left to feed a market ever hungry for sensation and innovation in a society with elastic norms? (Fig. 8.17)

Leighton House, his custom designed mansion in Holland Park, London, now open to the public as a museum, housed Lord Leighton's extensive

Fig. 8.11 John William Godward (1861–1922), The Mirror

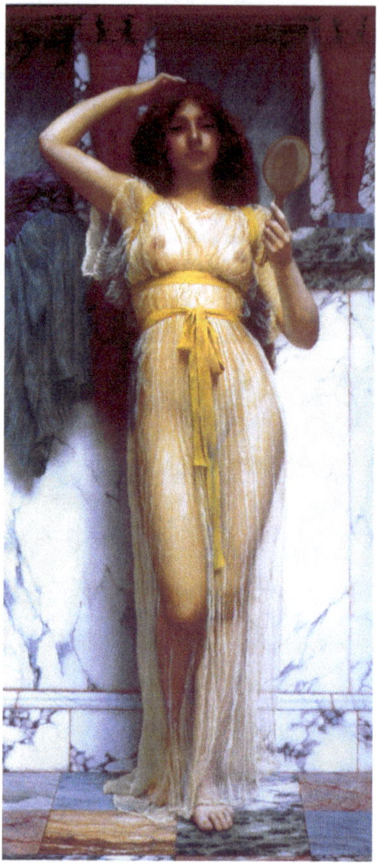

collection of art and artifacts. The house resembles a fantasy mixture of Victorian and Middle Eastern styles.

Just like today, tabloid-type gossip helped keep names in people's conversations. Reports about a possible marriage between Rosa Bonheur and Sir Edwin Landseer (1802–1873), the two most successful animal painters of the age—she, a French woman who scandalously wore man's trousers in public; he, a knighted British gentleman and favorite painter of the Queen—circulated for years. The chatter kept both painters in the limelight, journalists busy and the public titillated. All this publicity helped sales.

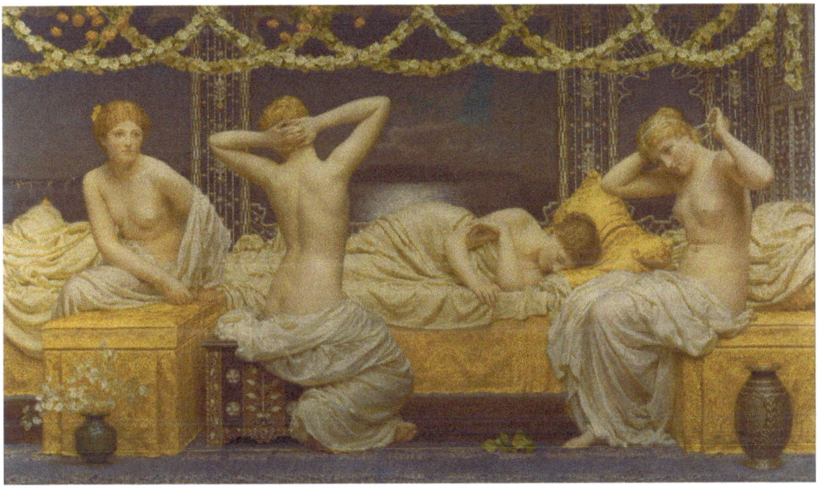

Fig. 8.12 Albert Joseph Moore (1841–1893), A Summer Night

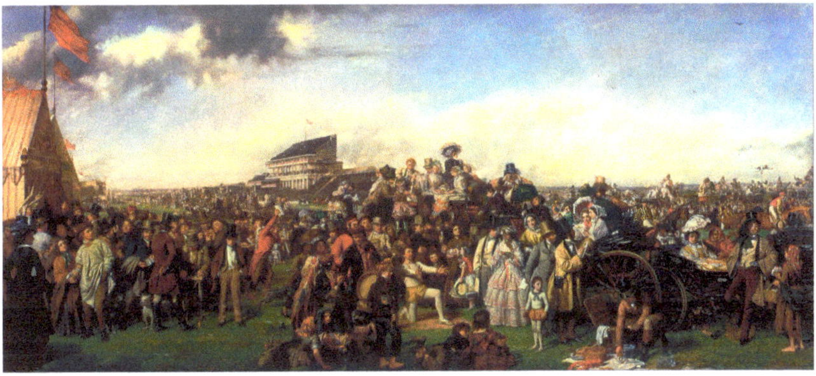

Fig. 8.13 William Powell Frith (1819–1909), Derby Day

Royal patronage yielded similar marketing benefits. It made painters' careers and money for dealers too. It was a much-envied coup to have your work chosen for the Queen's collection, even if it had to be given to her or sold at cost. In today's art market, we see the monetary value of provenance extending beyond royalty to certain private individuals and collections, including public museums, whose reputations in the arts

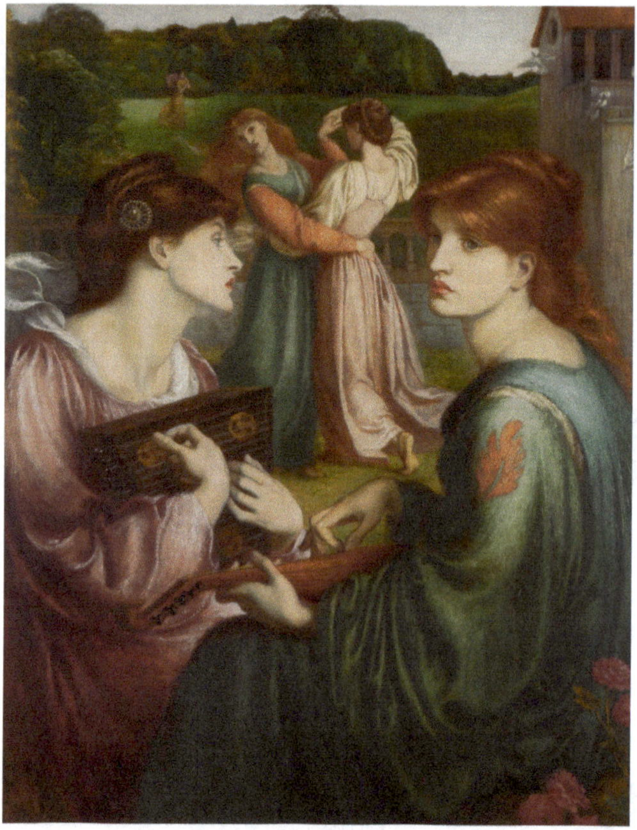

Fig. 8.14 Dante Gabriel Rossetti (1828–1882), The Bower Meadow

environment yield financial benefits to artworks and artists. To have any of their art added to the permanent collections of, say, the Beyeler Foundation, the Whitney, MoMA, or the Tate Modern is a huge boost to the monetary value of any contemporary artist's brand. Savvy painters have even sent portraits of heads of state to their offices for the sole purpose of being able to claim that their work is at this prestigious location.

[W. P. Frith had sold his painting Life at the Seaside to a dealer named Lloyd who sold it at cost to Queen Victoria. The dealer retained the rights for the engraving. The market potential of an engraving of a painting owned by the Queen explains his patriotic spirit.][17]

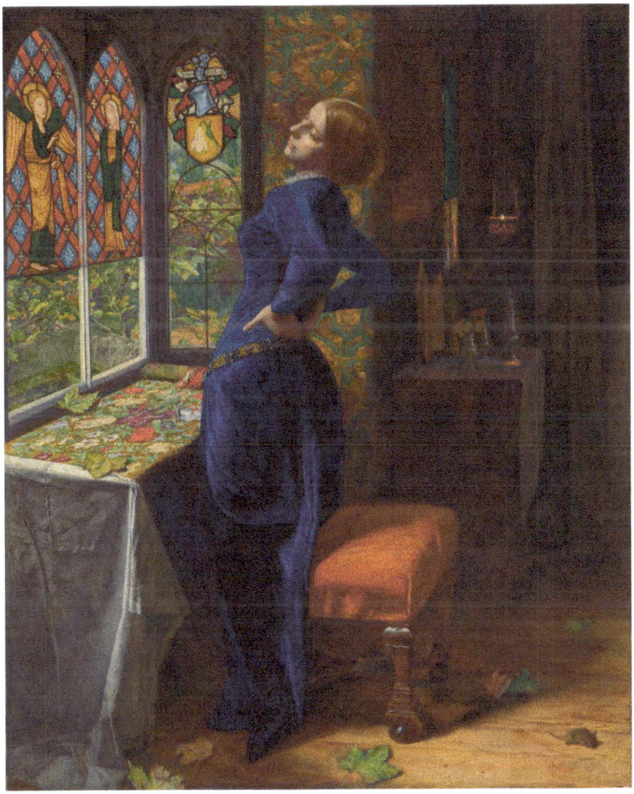

Fig. 8.15 John Everett Millais (1829–1896), Mariana

The Golden Age

By middle of the nineteenth century, the coalition of dealers, auctioneers, artists, and the media had, to a large extent, become what it is today. Painters not only designed their art works to suit the new retail gallery system and the mass market for popular reproductions; they also practiced market intervention by conspicuously and publicly supporting the prices of their artworks.

The great J. M. W. Turner, as auction records show, would regularly bid on his paintings when they came up for sale. He even paid record sums. Instead of accusing the great man of manipulating his own market,

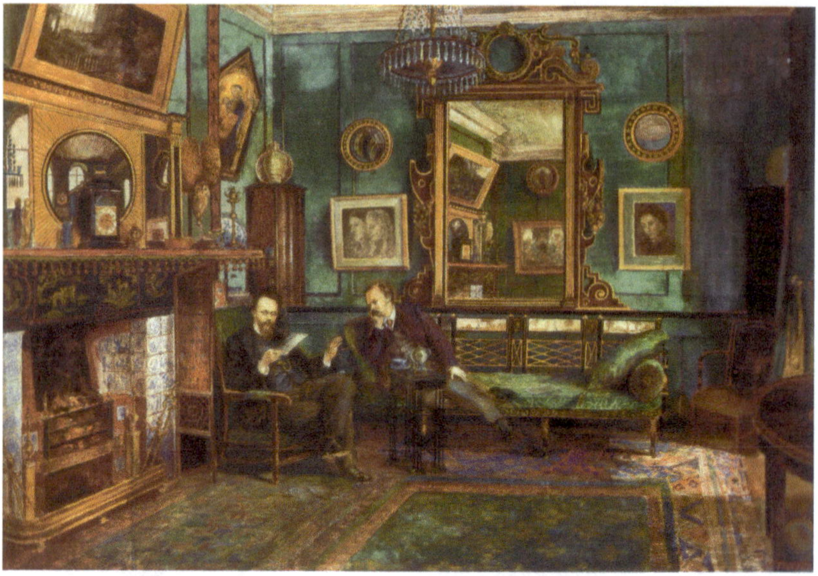

Fig. 8.16 Henry Treffry Dunn (1838–1899), Henry Treffry Dunn Rossetti and Dunton at 16 Cheyne Walk

the press, in fact, praised Turner for personally protecting the steep price level to which his paintings had risen.[18] Today, this type of price manipulation is frowned upon. Nonetheless, it is still used when warranted, albeit inconspicuously. The over-the-top promoted auction sale in 2007 of Damien Hirst's diamond-encrusted sculpture, gracing this book's cover, to himself and a group of investors for $100 million is a good example of such producer-centered protective market intervention. The event is so rich in allegory, metaphor, and irony that it will surely provide many future doctoral aspirants in art history or marketing with much to contemplate.[19]

Turner's bequest of 300 oils, 300 sketchbooks, and 30,000 sketches and watercolors to the National Gallery in London in 1856 after his death, accompanied by specific instructions for display, apotheosized simultaneously the artist as well as his body of work. According to a scene in the film *Turner*, the painter, in 1845, turned down an offer of 100,000 pounds—an absolutely staggering sum—from Joseph Gillot, a mega-collector and pen nib manufacturing millionaire, for his collection. If true—I have not

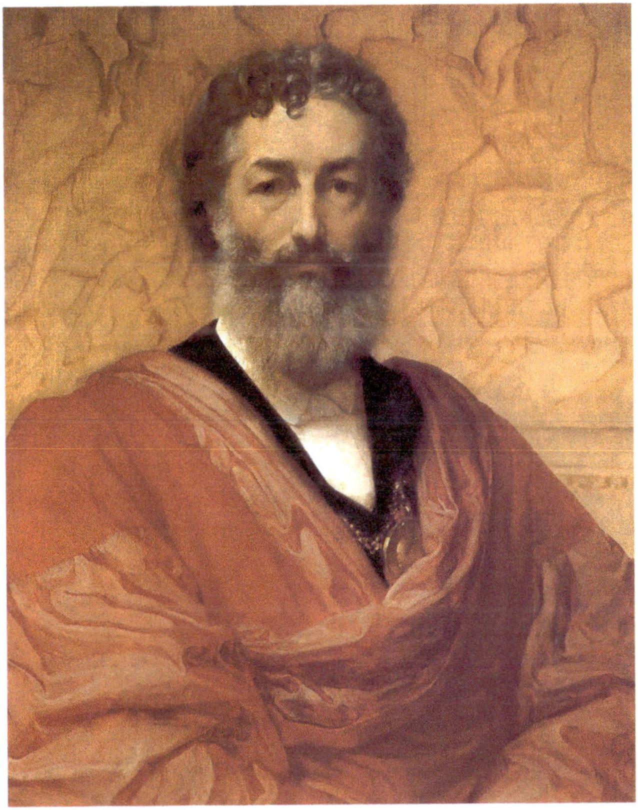

Fig. 8.17 Frederic Leighton (1827–1876), Self Portrait

found a reliable source for this story—it certainly would have been a persuasive signal to the market. Turner collectors felt reassured in the value of their possessions and continued buying more at steadily rising prices that are still increasing to this day. A fine Turner is, as ever, a beautiful and safe asset to have.

The press played a role, too. Whenever the opportunity existed, newspaper reports on art auctions listed prices paid in previous sales for paintings that had just sold. Since the earlier amounts were always considerably lower, the public's perception of the art market was one of remarkable profitability.[20]

Dealers performed their part as well. Auction data show numerous instances of dealer-to-dealer sales via auctions rather than privately transacting business with one another, away from the limelight. There were obvious advantages in the publicity garnered by a public sale.[21] The high prices they paid made headlines, and dealers were praised for their steadfast commitment to the market. These reports, too, promoted the impression of a thriving art market in which you could make money.[22]

None of this could have happened without the enthusiastic participation of the public. Owning art had become part of English identity, built upon a century-old philosophy that buying such art works was a demonstration of patriotic sentiments. No longer the preserve of an aristocratic elite and the upper middle class, art consumption had become a great democratizer. The rich patronized the superstars; the well-to-do bought in the middle ranges, and there were thousands of artists painting countless, inexpensive oils and watercolors for the less affluent. There even existed subscription schemes managed by working men's clubs that made owning cheap engravings possible for the working class.[23]

It was a Golden Age, indeed!

Notes

1. William Buchanan, Memoirs of Painting, 2 vols., J. Greig, ed. (London: Ackerman, 1824), vol. 1: xiii.

   John Pye, Patronage of British Art, A Historical Sketch (London: Lomgman, Brown, Green, and Longman, 1845): 279; Thomas Winstanley, Observations on the Arts (Liverpool: W. Wales, 1828):3–6.
2. Samuel Carter Hall, Retrospective of A Long Life from 1815–1883 (N. Y.: D. Appleton & Co., 1883): 200. Hall provides no source.
3. Hall: 197.
4. Georg Akerlof, "The Market for 'Lemons': Quality Uncertainty and the Market Mechanism," An economic theorist's book of tales (Cambridge: Cambridge University Press, 1970): 7–22.
5. Jeremy Maas, Gambart (London: Barrie Jenkins, 1975): 43 quoting this letter written on July 4, 1850, by Rought without providing a source. According to Rupert Maas, this letter could have been part of his father's extensive collection of art-related correspondence from the Victorian period.
6. Wilkie Collins, A Rogue's Life (London: Richard Benleyt & Son, 1879): 46–47.
7. Pye: 253.
8. Bayer/Page data.

9. Thomas Bayer, John Page, The Development of the Art Market in England (London: Pickering & Chatto, 2011): 81–98.
10. Lawrence Gowing, The Essence of Turner, Turner: Imagination and Reality, exhibition catalogue (N.Y.: Museum of Modern Art, 1966):163–185, 171.
11. Michael Rosenthal, 'Turner Fires a Gun', in David Solkin, ed., Art on the Line (London and New Haven: Yale University Press, 2001): 145–155.
12. Lorenz Eitner, Géricault's Raft of Medusa (London: Phaidon, 1972), Eitner, Géricault, his Life and Work (London: Orbis Publishing, 1983): 209–121; Elizabeth G. Holt, Triumph of Art for the Public (Washington, D.C.: Decatur House Press, 1980): 206–210; S. Lodge, 'Géricault in England', Burlington Magazine, CVII (December 1965): 616–627; Lee Johnson, 'The Raft of Medusa in Great Britain,' Burlington Magazine, XCVI (August 1954): 249–254; a review of the event can be found in the London Literary Gazette and Journal of better Letters, 180 (July 1, 1820): 427.
13. Holman Hunt, Pre-Raphaelitism and the Pre-Raphaelite Brotherhood, 2 vols. (London: Macmillan, 1905), vol. 2: 335–344.
14. Many books have been written about the Pre-Raphaelite Brotherhood since William Michael Rossetti's The Germ: Thoughts towards the Nature in Poetry, Literature and Art in 1850 and Holman Hunt's, Pre-Raphaelism, published in 1905. Christopher Wood's Preraphaelites (London: Weidenfeld and Nicholson, 1981) was the first post-WWII publication.
15. Christopher Wood, Dictionary of Victorian Painters (London: Antique Collector's Club, 1978). Christopher Wood was one of my good friends and colleagues during my art-dealing time, as well as the London representative of The International Fine Arts Association from 1979 until his untimely death in 2000. Together with Jeremy Maas, Christopher was responsible for the revival of interest in Victorian art. Sotheby's, London, even opened a new location in London's fashionable district of Belgravia especially for auctioning off works from this era.
16. Bayer/Page data.
17. William Powell Frith, A Victorian Canvas: The Memories of W. P. Frith, RA, N. Wallis, ed. (London: Geoffrey Bles, 1957):84–85.
18. Morning Chronicle (June 15th, 1829), reported in the review of the George Hibbert sale at Christie's of June 13, 1829, that Turner's 'Abingdon' (National Gallery # 485) was purchased by the artists himself, 'who, very prudently … always attends sales to keep up the price of his work'. William Whiteley, Art of England, 2 vols. (New York: Hacker Art Books, 1973): 167.
19. https://news.artnet.com/art-world/damien-hirst-skull-storage-2064567 (Last accessed March 2025).

20. Art Journal (June 1863):121–122; Frith, My Autobiography and Reminiscences, 2 vols. (New York: Harper and Brothers, 1888), vol. 1: 30, vol. 2: 143.
21. Bayer/Page data.
22. Bayer and Page, The Development of the Art Market in England: 100–117 and notes.
23. Geoffrey Agnew, Agnew's, (London: The Bradbury Agnew Press, Ltd., 1967): 65.

CHAPTER 9

Interlude. The Etching Revival: A Case Study in Branding

Before moving on, I want to share a story about the creation of a new art product, about the process of art branding and about Clio, the Muse of Creativity, in a mercenary mantle.

Years ago, while researching the nineteenth-century print trade in England, an old book, published in 1868, caught my eye. It was titled *Etchers and Etching*, and written by Philip Gilbert Hamerton (1834–1894), a name hitherto unfamiliar to me. I leafed through the book and learned that the author had been a principal figure in a campaign that came to be known as the 'Etching Revival'. It focused on original etchings, an art product that had been demoted to the background during the bullish days of sensation pictures and reproductive engravings.[1]

This sparked my curiosity. What I discovered should be of particular interest to artists, but also to others trying to understand the creative process of brand building. I learned about a campaign that explicitly focused on creating a new category of art product—a new brand—specifically designed in response to changing market conditions. Madison Avenue-style P.R. and branding campaigns were still decades away, but Edward Bernays, the great guru of public opinion influencing, could not have done a better job.[2] It is a superb step-by-step example of creative artistic genius applied to commercial branding and marketing, one that should be included in marketing courses' curricula.

T. M. Bayer, *The Genesis of the Modern Art Market in London, 1700–1900*, https://doi.org/10.1007/978-3-032-00594-6_9

Painters, dealers, engravers, framers, glass makers, and printers all depended for much of their income on the publication and sale of millions of inexpensive reproductions of commercially suitable original works. Any change in that market would affect the entire art industry. These publishing ventures had become the most profitable sector of all art-related commerce with a customer base that ranged from members of workingmen's clubs to the social elite.

But as all vogues, this one, too, ran its course. The appeal of reproductive engravings had dropped by the last quarter of the nineteenth century. Much of it had to do with photographic piracy and cheaper graphic reproduction methods. Compounding the problem was the 1897 law that stated that copyrights were the property of the respective paintings owner and no longer could be sold separately. The old cash cow was also getting worn out. Crowds weren't paying anymore to see sensation pictures, and unsold engravings were stacking up in warehouses and shops.[3]

The loss of the market's main revenue source had the expected devastating impact. It slowed down and, ultimately, almost entirely stopped the production of a genre that had come to define, in art historical terms, Victorian painting as well as the art of the Continent. For the time being, Sensation Paintings, as a genre, became a thing of the past. Instead of enthralling admiring throngs of spectators, they gathered dust in storage rooms.

The declining demand for reproductive engravings made room for other graphic products that had been consigned to the basement during the heydays of the engraving market. One of them was the original etching. Recognizing their chance, practitioners of the art orchestrated a rebranding campaign in England known as the 'Etching Revival'.

Using the term 'revival' was the first step. Although the skill of etching had never died out on the island, it had been relegated to quasi amateur status with a noticeably 'feminine' aura—nothing for Victorian manly men. Such pejorative terms separated the macho 'revival' etchers from their 'effeminate' predecessors.[4]

A further step in this brand building venture was the construction of a legitimizing provenance to validate etchings as an established art product. The campaign rhetoric, therefore, discussed etchings as a medium within a broad historical context going back over 200 years, to Rembrandt and his contemporaries. Revivalist etchers had no qualms about describing themselves as modern-day 'disciples of Rembrandt', the 'great representative of etchers of all time'.[5] Appropriating Rembrandt as their patron saint was timely, since the great master's work as an etcher had received a huge publicity boost from the 1867 auction sale of his *Hundred Guilder Print*

(*Christ Healing the Sick*) for the incredible sum of 1180 pounds, or nearly sixty times the average annual earning of a laborer. The record price made worldwide news. The artist's own image even received a do-over. He had been described as someone who prostituted his art for a life of debauchery and wealth; but now he was spoken of as an inspired, if misunderstood, heroic artistic ancestor.[6]

A very important part of the branding strategy was the creation of a special aura for this unassuming medium. Revivalist etchings, therefore, were portrayed as a unique, intellectual art created by enlightened artists, skilled in the ancient art, and collected by a sophisticated elite distinct from the crass consumers of machine-made and mass-produced prints. This strategically worded rhetoric suggested specific associations to potential customers. Etching was not an art for ordinary individuals. Such folks were just too uncouth to recognize, never mind appreciate, the refinements and subtleties of fine etchings. Culture, taste, erudition, and sophisticated intellect were prerequisites for the appreciation of etchings' true nature. Collecting etchings was proof of high culture.[7]

One writer proclaimed that the enlightened connoisseur of etchings could elaborate on the qualities of different papers the same way as the afficionado of Bordeaux wines talks of Pontet Canets and Pichon Longuevilles.[8] Using an established brand, like expensive fine wines, as a reference point further cemented the aura of class and culture.

The goal of this PR campaign was to evoke an image of intimate, refined, even sensual, leisure, the pursuit of which was, naturally, expensive. But the real objective for charging a high price was not crass money. The true reason for the high price asking price—twelve to sixteen guineas—½ year's wages for a laborer—for a sheet of printed paper was to convey the impression that these were very precious things, indeed. Priciness was turned into a branding tool. Paying high for the priceless is still cheap, as the dealer, Duveen, would say. Birkin bags, Patek Philippe or Rolex watches, and other well-known luxury products have followed the same strategy. Some of them have even succeeded in establishing a secondary market and, imitating art, strive to establish their bona fides as transferrable value storage, i.e., investment quality assets.

This aura of exclusivity was further enhanced by contrasting the rarity of original prints with the ubiquity of reproductive ones. Unlike the mechanically produced engravings, revival etchings were usually printed either by the artists personally or under their immediate supervision. These artist-printed proofs were promoted as the rarest of the rare, the finest of the fine, the unspoiled and purest physical manifestation of genius.[9] The direct involvement of artists in the creation of their prints conveyed a sense of intimacy shared between creator and beholder. Different from the mass-produced and mass-consumed reproductive engraving, each original etching was special—and by extension, so was its owner.[10]

To promote this scarcity further, the campaigners adopted one of the primary marketing devices of the reproductive print industry—issuing limited editions. Unlike the edition sizes of mechanical reproductions which numbered in the hundreds, even thousands of prints, the much smaller editions of original etchings were typically well below a hundred sheets. To maintain rarity, etchers advocated for the destruction of the plate after a specific number of copies, regardless of the condition of the plate.[11] The famous American painter and etcher, James M. Whistler, a prominent participant in the Revival, wrote in The Pall Mall Gazette in 1890 that the refined collector of etchings 'hates the common crowd and will only have etchings that are rare. It is easy to gratify him by keeping the supply down'.[12] The purpose of limited editions couldn't be stated any clearer.

In addition to a new artistic pedigree, intentional product scarcity and elitist consumer prestige, the rebranded etchings were also given a new aesthetic in deliberate opposition to the hegemonic doctrine of high finish, detail, realistic rendering, easily discernible narrative content, and, especially, the clear evidence of time-consuming labor.

Undaunted by the immensity of this feat, P. G. Hamerton launched a head-on offensive against the very template used for assessing the quality of High Victorian painting. Here is what he wrote: '[t]he uninformed spectator admires execution for itself, as handicraft, with little reference to its meaning; the true judge calls that the best execution which expresses the most'. Visible evidence of physical effort, one of the bedrocks of the aesthetic doctrine he attacked, was also rejected as objectionable. 'Too minute renderings in matters of art is bad', he proclaimed, because it would 'weaken the primary ideas and conceptions of the artist'. Speed of execution was vital for the artist to transform these 'primary ideas and conceptions' into visual expressions, unblemished by off-putting and obviously laborious 'toil and trouble'. This could only be achieved by 'spend[ing] a great deal of time in looking, and having decided upon the strokes to be laid, lay[ing] them at once and leav[ing] them'. Intuitive speed of execution was given market value by framing it as the brilliant finale of the profound introspection and heroic physical action needed to express artistic ideas in their purest, most 'honest' form.[13]

If these words ring familiar, it is for a reason: they articulate the principles of Abstract Expressionism's aesthetic theory. The superhuman effort demanded by the creative process required to produce such works is illusive and personal. Hamerton is describing Jackson Pollock eighty years before Action Painting was born.

Rather shrewdly, instead of dismissing the Victorian credo of labor/exchange value entirely, this strategy appropriated it by placing the labor involved in the production process into the intangible realm, evident to the sophisticated connoisseur by the apparent absence of labored exertion.

This deliberate construction of a new identity for etchings was an unconcealed challenge to the entire market model of the reproductive engravings industry. Its downfall made way for the introduction of a diametrically opposed aesthetic that appreciated physical effort in art making by its noticeable absence and put stylistic control, once again, back into the hands of the artist in open rebellion against established orthodoxy.

It takes a lot of entrepreneurial gumption to demand to get paid for the conspicuous lack of work, rather than for the visible evidence of it.

Many years ago, I received the cutout of a cartoon that depicted two men in a gallery interior looking at a large empty canvas. The cartoon was done in the typical New Yorker Magazine style. One man, displaying the obvious trappings of wealth, said to the other, dressed in elegant art dealer attire: 'This is the most profound statement I have ever seen on a blank canvas'. Nowadays, artistic creativity does not even require any physical evidence. In 2009, the Swedish artist, Nils Gustafson, was awarded a grant by the Swedish Arts Council. But rather than presenting physical evidence for artistic work, he pocketed the money and pronounced that the absence of the artwork is his actual artwork. A direct line can be drawn from Hamerton to Duchamp to Gustafson: from Hamerton promoting the reduction of evidence of apparent physical effort to Duchamp's Readymades which became art merely by the artist's declaration to Gustafson's no-artwork. What will be the next novelty?

Further branding efforts went into an outpouring of books, articles, and the publication of journals, like *The Portfolio*, *The Etcher*, or *English Etching*, that promoted the new etchings.[14]

The last step in this campaign was the establishment of an organization to lobby for the new brand's interests. To that end, in 1880, the Society of Painter-Etchers was founded to institutionalize the position of etchers as a distinct specialization among professional artists.

The construction of the brand was now complete. That notwithstanding, its success still had to be validated in the market. Regardless how ingeniously packaged and designed, no product can become a success without distribution. It is doubtful that the rapidly growing popularity of etchings would have continued without several of the prominent dealers in London, like Colnaghi, Agnew, and, particularly, The Fine Arts Society, who began offering original etchings besides the usual paintings, drawings, and reproductive engravings. It made economic sense. Already in the early 1870s, alarm about declining attendance of single picture exhibitions was voiced. Trying out a newly branded product was sound business. It added to the gallery's selection at insignificant cost, and the small size of the etchings made them easy to display. Most likely, the artists offered excellent terms to the dealers. Since the etchers needed visibility, they were motivated to bargain.

It was the right decision. By the end of the decade, the *Magazine of Art* reported that 'there is no branch of art which is more rapidly forcing its way into the notice of the English art-loving world, than etching'.[15]

Finally, at the beginning of the 1880s, The Rembrandt Gallery was established. It was the first gallery specializing in original etchings. Fittingly, a large shop sign conspicuously featured a portrait of Rembrandt. Symbolically and factually, this marks the conclusion of this astonishing campaign to create a new 'brand' of art.

The Etching Revival stands as a textbook example of producer agency faced with opportunity. Participants engaged in niche marketing, embarked on a complex, multi-faceted campaign to re-brand their product, took control over it and monetized the resulting competitive advantage.

The path navigated by the Etching Revival was not unique; other artists had traveled on their own roads for decades in their search for creative autonomy. It is a path of limitless innovation on all levels: challenging prevailing dogma, creating new aesthetics, new forms of visual expression and new ways to monetize them. The art market's demand for perpetual novelty correspondingly tests society's definition of what art is. An inevitable byproduct is increasing ambiguity.

There are several noteworthy aspects to this campaign, besides the proposal to pay for invisible labor. The language used in the Etching Revival was deliberately elitist. Its word choice described an aesthetic opposed to the mainstream character of much of the art produced during the preceding 100 years. It had come full circle. At the start of this survey of artists' agency in the art market, the patronizing Earl of Shaftesbury maintained that painters should be no more than illustrators of noble ideas fed to them by their social superiors. Artists rebelled against such snobbish presumption. In due course, they succeeded in taking ownership of the design of their paintings and found new ways to expand their audience by deliberately making their art to appeal to the masses, rather than the social elite. Ironically, as we have seen, this conscious anti- Shaftesburyanism yielded them social acceptance among the very elites whose dictates they opposed. Etching Revival proponents turned this on its head and adopted a deliberate rhetoric that rejected this populist orientation. In contrast, it defined its audience as a highly refined and educated Shaftesburyian-type elite that could afford to indulge in intellectual contemplations and sensual delights inspired by a printed piece of paper (Fig. 9.1).

A twentieth-century example of art branding is, for example, Andre Breton's *Manifesto of Surrealism* published by the self-appointed father of the movement in 1924. A talented and dictatorial brander, he delineated

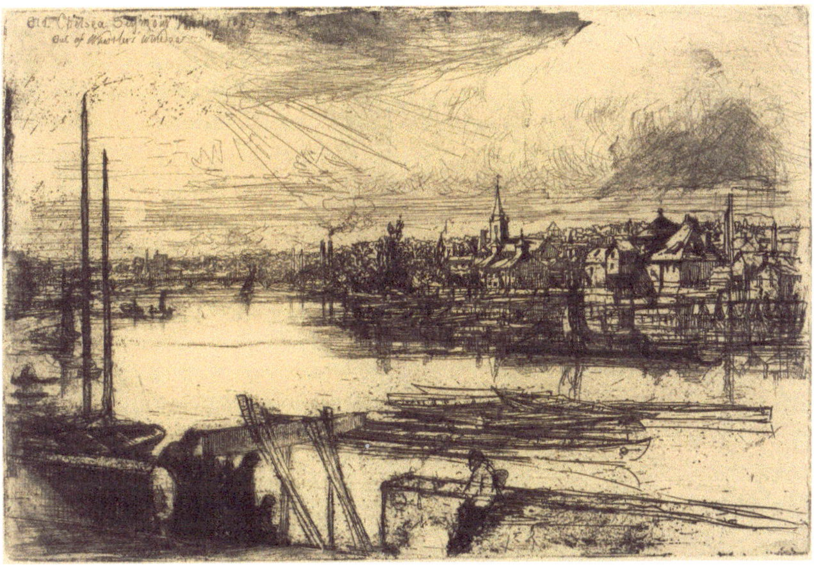

Fig. 9.1 Francis Seymour Haden (1818–1910). Battersea Reach, 1863; uses of parliament

strict parameters for what constitutes Surrealism in art. Much of it had to do with the processes and sources of artistic expression. According to Breton, it was the unconscious element of the mind (Echoes of Reynold's IX discourse?), the 'Id', to use a Freudian term, that was to be given full reign to express itself freely, unencumbered by conscious thought. He referred to this as 'automatism'. His ideas caught on worldwide. Exploring the mysteries of the mind was in vogue. Sigmund Freud's and Carl Jung's investigations of the subconscious and the world of dreams were hot topics among the artists and intellectuals of the time. The chance to express freely personal sexual obsessions, haunting nightmares, and dark repressions—our mysterious inner landscapes, rather than the world around us—offered artists new and near limitless themes. Picasso, Miro, De Chirico, Magritte, Dali, Kahlo, and many more explored this realm. Hallucinogenics, alcohol, hashish, cocaine, etc.—just about anything that would induce an altered state of consciousness—were often used to make the journey to the inside. Breton encapsulated these ideas in his Manifesto—a term that was quite fashionable at the time for any booklet with avantgarde, anti-bourgeois content—and created a new brand of art: Surrealism.

Other artists have succeeded in creating distinct brands that function as umbrellas beneath which followers can gather. Cubism, Performance Art, Conceptual art, transitory art, or 'die Brucke', 'Wiener Schule+, 'Action Painting', etc., are familiar examples. There are many more, and countless new ones are yet to come.

End of Interlude.

Notes

1. Philip Hamerton, Etching and Etchers (London: Macmillan and Co., Ltd., 1868).
2. Edward Bednays, Crystallizing Public Opinion (N.Y.: Boni and Liveright, 1923), provides a pragmatic, no-nonsense introduction to the manipulation of public opinion.
3. Geoffrey Agnew, Agnew's, 1817–1967 (London: Bradbury Agnew Press, 1967): 27; Jeremy Maas, Gambart (London: Barrie & Jenkins, 1975): 209; on photographic piracy, see The Atheneum (20 August, 1864): 250, and The Times (3 November 1862).

4. Hamerton, 'Modern Etching in France', The Fine Arts Quarterly Review 2 (1864): 96; Henry Alken, The Art and Practice of Etching (London, 1849): 7.
5. Frederick Keppel, 'Modern Disciples of Rembrandt', The Art Review, 2 (September-November 1887):145–149, quote:145.
6. Frederick Wedmore (ed.), Rembrandt: His Life, His work and His Time (London: Heinemann, 1894).
7. Hamerton, 'Modern Etching In France': 69; and his Etching and Etchers (London, Macmillan and Co., Ltd.): 28, 29.
8. Wedmore, 'My Few Things', The Art Journal 46 (January 1894): 7.
9. Martin Hardie, Frederick Goulding: Master Printer of Copper Plates (Sterling: Eneas Mackay, 1910): 83.
10. Ibid., 83.
11. Hubert Herkomer, The Atheneum, (April 1893): 478.
12. 'Mr. Whistler's New Etchings: A Chat with the Master' The Pall Mall Gazette (4 March 1890): 2.
13. Hamerton, Etching and Etchers: 60–62.
14. Martha P Tedeschi, How Prints Work Reproductions, Originals, and their Markets in England: 1840_1900, Ph.D. dissertation (Evanston: Northwestern University 1994), ch. 3 lists additional examples of promotional on original etchings.
15. Marcus B. Huish, Étching in England', Magazine of Art (1878), I: 146.

CHAPTER 10

Art Dealing: The Early Days

Dealers in precious objects have been around since the dawn of humankind. There is no doubt that middlemen have left an impact on design, workmanship, size, and subject, i.e., the physical make-up of the art works in which they traded. Customers choose from middlemen; middlemen communicate customers' choices to suppliers by buying from them according to their customers' preferences; middlemen modify this relationship to benefit their own interests.

Due to the richness and granularity of data, the London art scene offers a particularly good and rare opportunity to probe this issue in greater detail. That fact is among the chief reason this book is about the English art market rather than the art markets of other countries. To be sure, there were similar developments in other locales on the Continent, foremost in Paris and Rome, but the documentation is sparse by comparison. I am not aware of a data set similar in size and detail to the one I use for the English market. For good reason, the British were called a nation of shopkeepers. Shopkeepers keep records. And what are art galleries but shops for art?

We start this survey of art dealing in the early eighteenth century, when dealing in art was in the hands of fearless merchant adventurers who risked all they had, including their lives, to forage the Continent for paintings and other precious objects to transport back to England with the intent of selling them there for a profit. It was about as dangerous and risky of a business as one can imagine. Banditry was widespread, large sums of

T. M. Bayer, *The Genesis of the Modern Art Market in London, 1700–1900*, https://doi.org/10.1007/978-3-032-00594-6_10

money had to be carried physically, the roads were deplorable, and the goods bulky and fragile. While these intrepid gentlemen were motivated by profit—I assume—they were inadvertently responsible for the dispersal of many of the great works of art throughout the United Kingdom. And who knows if any of these precious objects would have survived the destructive conflicts that swept the Continent had they not been removed out of harm's way?

From there, the discussion moves to a considerably less adventurous one and a less perilous business model: the first derivative mass product of the modern art market—the reproductive print. It was dealers who turned these printed sheets of paper into the venerable cash cow for an entire industry. And it was dealers who fed this cow, distributed the cash it produced, and created fortunes for themselves, the artists, and a host of others—paper manufacturers, engravers, framers, retailers, etc.—with whom they collaborated.

Then there was a tectonic shift in the arts industry, this one resulting from the Napoleonic Wars and their aftermath. The European-wide conflict interrupted the rise of the reproductive print while, at the same time, offering new, if time-limited, opportunities in the Old Master market. The misfortune of some were the good fortune of others. Then, once again, the focus of the art industry shifted, away from Old Masters to paintings by still living artists. These were the heydays of the art business in the nineteenth century, the 'Golden Days'. The innovations of the preceding hundred years were refined and further commoditized, ultimately concluding the modern art market's developmental phase—its genesis. The size and scope of the projects this first generation of 'uber' dealers pulled off were truly astonishing. They introduced the world to what can be likened to Hollywood-type blockbuster releases, only then it involved modern paintings and the reproductive print, the market's reliable cash cow.

Not for the Faint of Heart: The Merchant Adventurers of the Art Trade

A first measure of the extent of dealers' influence over the art of a given period is their market presence. Auction records show that between 1710 and 1760, up to 40% of recorded picture sales at auctions was organized by dealers to sell their inventory.[1] The available information on these dealer-organized sales, although thin, suggests that these events may indeed be responsible for noticeable ups and downs in the London art market in general: it was slack without dealers' inventory sales and buoyant because of them.

What were they selling? Records show that they offered mainly inexpensive original imported pictures, or copies made by English artists of such original works. While many of the cheaper works frequently had rather fanciful attributions to Raphael, Leonardo, Titian, Rembrandt, etc., their low prices indicate that most of them were copies or of doubtful authorship.[2] It seems that the most reliable way for dealers to earn money was by supplying inexpensive works to a modestly wealthy, yet large, customer base. The fact that dealers hired contemporary painters—English or Continental—as copyists indicates that there existed a limited and unreliable supply of good original works.[3]

However, at the time, import duty in England was charged on an ad valorem basis. Therefore, to save on this tax, export documents at times were falsified, and real masterpieces were imported with intentionally understated value.[4] The history of Caravaggio's *Taking of Christ* (c.1602) found in a religious house in Dublin after having 'disappeared' for nearly two centuries is a good example. The painting's trail from Italy via Scotland to Dublin became only apparent after two young Italian art historians realized that the original export license issued many years ago in Italy for this canvas listed the name of a much lesser-known painter and only a fraction of the actual work's value (Fig. 10.1).[5]

To get one's hands on good quality original works was a demanding and adventurous enterprise three hundred years ago. It required putting up a great deal of money, not just one's own, but often also that of others. And then one had to crisscross the Continent, loaded up with cash for extended periods of time, traveling on rough, muddy, and bandit-infested roads, staying in inns of dubious quality, unsanitary conditions, and little safety. If you managed to stay alive and were lucky enough to find anything that might turn a profit, you had to have ready money to pay for it. But that was not all. Experienced and honest packers had to be hired to pack the art works for transport to London via perilous seas or land routes at tremendous expense. There was no certainty that along the way the art would not be stolen, damaged, or end up on the bottom of the ocean. Cargo insurance existed, but it was not uniformly available. Assuming all worked out, and the dealer with the purchased art made it safely to London, he still had to secure a suitable location, advertise, organize, and conduct a sale as well as collect payments before there was any return on

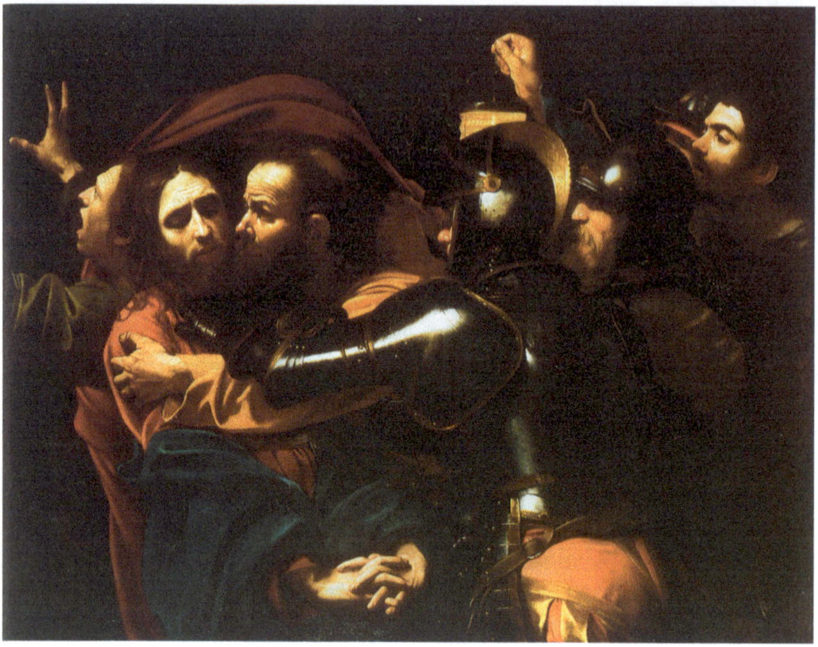

Fig. 10.1 Caravaggio (1571–1610), The Taking of Christ

the investment. Under the best of conditions, this was an ultra-high-risk (ad)venture.

The successful operation of these enormous undertakings, particularly in the eighteenth century, was a financially extremely speculative and logistically complex project fraught with high personal dangers. Arrangements with international merchant banking houses—Fagniani in Rome, for example—may have helped in some cases to arrange payments and reduce the acute physical risks that come with hauling large sums of money around. Still, safety of the cargo during inclement weather, times of war, civil unrest, and widespread lawlessness must have been a constant worry. The art had to sell at a considerable amount over the original sum these intrepid merchants of culture originally paid just to re-coup the enormous investment of money, time, and personal safety they had made.[6]

Obviously, this kind of adventurous and hazardous business attracted particularly hardy types. Only the strong could survive. One of the early success stories of these entrepreneur-adventurers of the first half of the century was a tough and fearless Scotsman and sometimes painter, named Andrew Hay (1690–1754).[7] A quick-thinking and shrewd negotiator with a keen eye for profit, Hay focused primarily on France and Italy to buy his supply of art. Apparently with his own capital—I have no information to the contrary—he bought extensively during numerous trips and then sold these goods at auctions sales he conducted back in England. Between 1725 and his retirement in 1745, Hay travelled to Italy six times, twice on foot, and fourteen times to France—twenty trips in total over as many years. Anyone familiar with long-distance walking will fully appreciate Hay's astonishing feats. It takes a lot of stamina.

I can attest personally that the art business is quite different these days. I could stay in a nice hotel and not have to worry about lice, fleas, or bandits. I could inspect the condition of a painting or sculpture in comfortable and safe locations with a UV light, a magnifying glass, and loupe. I consulted with experts on specific artist and had time to verify provenance, a process that is not without complications and can take time. I paid by wire transfer, hired well-established and reliable logistics companies that would pick up the art, pack it securely, complete the necessary paperwork, and then ship it, fully insured, to wherever I asked them. Compared to my heroic and death-defying predecessors in the trade, I was on a proverbial 'walk in the park'. There is no doubt that the danger and general challenges of the business must have kept the number of dealers well in check. The difference between the size of the aspirant pool versus those who succeeded must have been enormous.

Another dealer who operated similarly, but less successfully, was Samuel Paris. He had a somewhat chaotic business style and, apparently, an unorthodox attitude towards fiscal responsibility that required him to stay clear of England for nearly fifteen years. At some point, however, Paris found a way to resolve his troubles and make it back to the island. According to auction records, he subsequently organized at least seven auctions between 1738 and 1745. Such titles as *Virgins and Saints* painted by none other than Leonardo, Raphael, Correggio, and Giorgione as well as mythologies and biblical subjects by the great Rubens and Rembrandt.[8] Who, in fact, painted these pictures is anyone's guess.

From the early 1740s to the late 1750s, Robert Bragge (1700–1777) dominated the Old Master trade. Apparently a rather colorful gentleman who was not averse to personal aggrandizement and pretension, he took to introducing himself as 'Doctor' Bragge and assumed the airs of a gentleman-connoisseur to avoid being confused with an ordinary merchant. However, the good doctor and gentleman-connoisseur had a particularly finely tuned knack for marketing. His sales catalogues stood out among those of his competitors for their consumer focus. The individual listings of lots included noticeably more descriptive details as well as better, i.e., more credible, provenances. Bragge must have learned somewhere that information asymmetry stands in the way of sales or, conversely, more information leads to more sales and higher prices. Any modern auction catalogue of an important sale—Old Masters, modern or contemporary—is ample proof that Doctor Bragge was on the right track. His practice has been adopted by today's higher-end commercial galleries, attesting to the validity of Akerloff's earlier-mentioned study of the used car market. The importance of each work appears to correspond directly with the number of pages dedicated to its related information. Comparisons with great artistic predecessors—as the Etching Revivalists had adopted—are frequently used. I remember reading about a young female artist who had been selling her paintings on an East Coast beach for very modest prices but was later compared to Botticelli after her association with a very major dealer. Her prices, unsurprisingly, shot up stratospherically. A cynical commentator might suggest that all this information is nothing more than marketing gimmickry designed to embellish the merits of the artwork in question—or obscure their absence. While such skepticism is not entirely off the mark, it needs to be emphasized that Doctor Bragge's example led to better due diligence, research, and scholarship. This development in the quality and accessibility of information continues to improve art collectors' knowledge about what they consider for purchase, expand the market and, of course, justify higher prices (Fig. 10.2).[9]

At the same time when Doctor Bragge boosted his business with newly designed sales catalogues, the dealer and portraitist, Arthur Pond (c.1705–1758), conceived of another brainchild that would also become firmly established in the modern art market as Bragge's approach to information asymmetry. Just as the doctor's new catalogue content, Arthur Pond's innovation was also focused on improving consumer confidence to increase sales and prices. His business was on a smaller scale than Bragge's, but Pond's idea was nevertheless equally influential. He was the originator of written guarantees of authenticity to deal proactively with the ubiquity of fakes in the market. In Pond's days, this authentication was a far cry from the multi-page, detailed expert reports of today. He would simply inscribe the word 'true' and his signature on the back of paintings he offered for sale as his personal product warranty.[10] Arthur Pond's eye

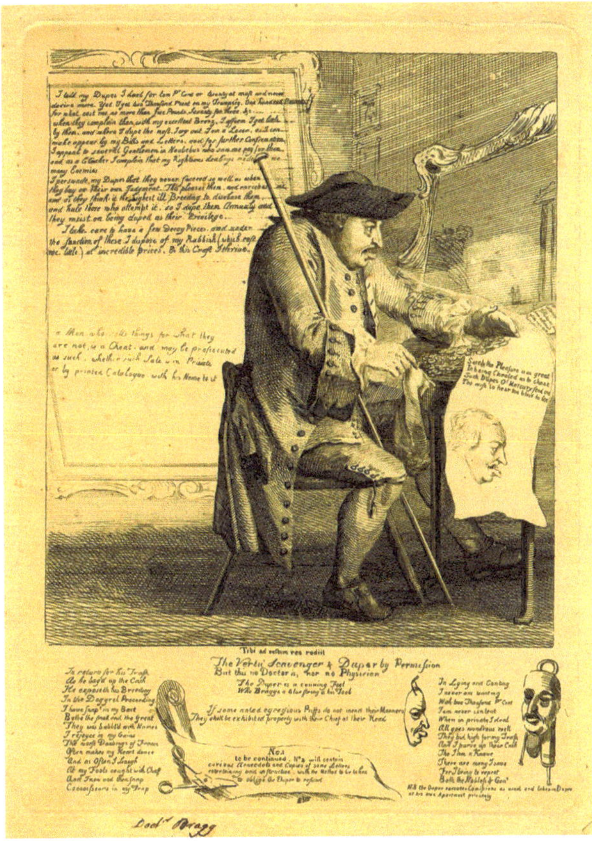

Fig. 10.2 Unknown, The Vertù Scavenger and Duper (Dr. Bragge)

passed the test of time. The dealer used to own Rembrandt's famous *Woman Bathing* (c. 1654), now on view in the National Gallery in London, as well as a number of other important paintings that bear his authentication and are now housed in different public collections. Providing an explicit written personal assurance of authenticity as part of a sale was a brilliant move, given the fact that today's art market includes an entire separate industry that grew out of Arthur Pond's clever brainchild. Written expert opinions on questions of authenticity have become a crucial cornerstone of the valuation and sales process of art works. The extraordinary jump in value of *Salvator Mundi* from its sale in New Orleans for $ 1175 in 2005 to its subsequent purchase for $ 127.5 million by the Russian collector, Dmitry Rybolovlev, in 2013 was strictly because a critical mass of experts had opined that the panel had indeed been painted by Leonardo, at least partially.

These early dealers were no small-time operators. The sizes of some of their sales were truly remarkable. An impressive example is an auction sale that took place in the spring of 1770, at which the dealer Goodall offered a group of over one thousand imported old paintings. It must have been a logistical nightmare. Other than his last name, unfortunately, I know nothing else about him.

An equally large group of old masters was assembled by the mega dealer, Gerard Vandergucht (1697–1776), and put under the hammer at Christie's in London at a sale that lasted three days, from March 6–8, 1777. He then sold another similar collection, again through Christie's, on March 14 and 15, 1788, a little over a year before the start of the French Revolution. Typically, both sales included vast numbers of paintings supposedly by the great masters of the Renaissance and the Baroque. The eleven years' time span between these two events could be an indication of the difficulties involved in assembling more than a thousand different paintings that were worth bringing to London to sell. By the end of the 1780s, the Continent had been the grazing ground for British dealers for a century. Auction records show that another eight years later, in 1796, Christie's sold the dealer's entire inventory.[11] The records also indicate that by that time the auction firm had established a near complete hegemony over the art auction business in England.[12] Dealers loved the fact that they no longer had to organize their own sales. Instead, they could rely on an experienced, professional, and well-connected auctioneering firm, to handle all that. This arrangement freed them to direct their energies and resources on procuring more stock to sell. The social and political problems on the Continent were getting worse, and there were a lot of opportunities for dealers with ready cash.

Auction records of this period also reveal the activities of yet another dealer, French-born Noel Desanfans (1741–1807). Well-educated and with an air of Continental sophistication, he was among the first to commercialize sales by private treaty as an alternative to auctions.[13] The core of the Dulwich Picture Gallery collection in London consists of a large group of pictures originally assembled by this dealer and his partner, Sir Francis Bourgeois (1753–1811), for His Majesty, Stanislav Augustus,

King of the Polish-Lithuanian Commonwealth. In 1795, after they had crisscrossed Europe for over five years looking for worthwhile pictures, unfortunately, their client's Commonwealth and thus his source of funds ceased to exist. There was, and still is, a tremendous risk associated with such high-level art dealing. The dealers were unable to sell most of pictures elsewhere, and Sir Francis Bourgeois, who had inherited his partner's share after the latter's death in 1809, bequeathed the remaining collection upon his own death two years later, to the foundation that supported the Dulwich school, College of God's Gift (Figs. 10.3 and 10.4).[14]

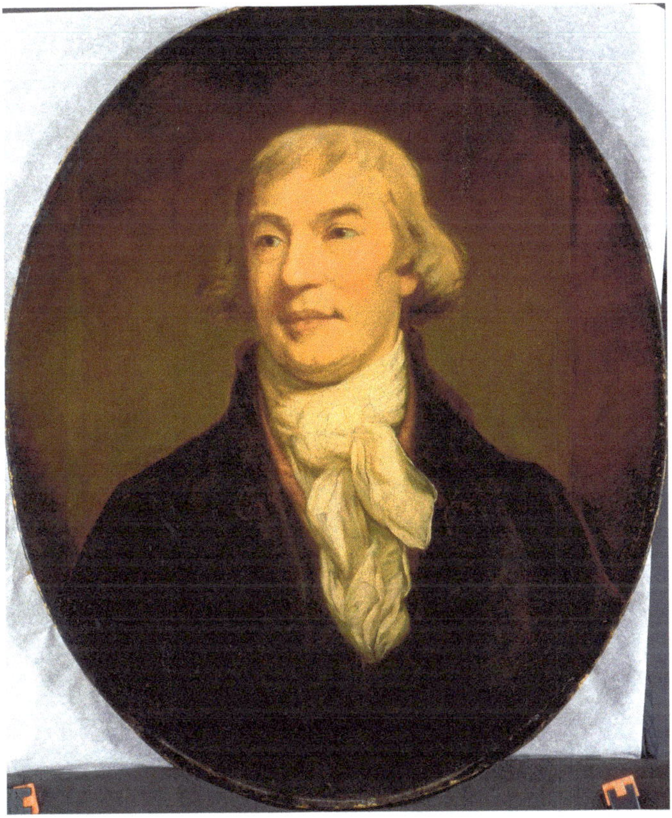

Fig. 10.3 James Northcote (1746–1831), Noel Joseph Desenfans

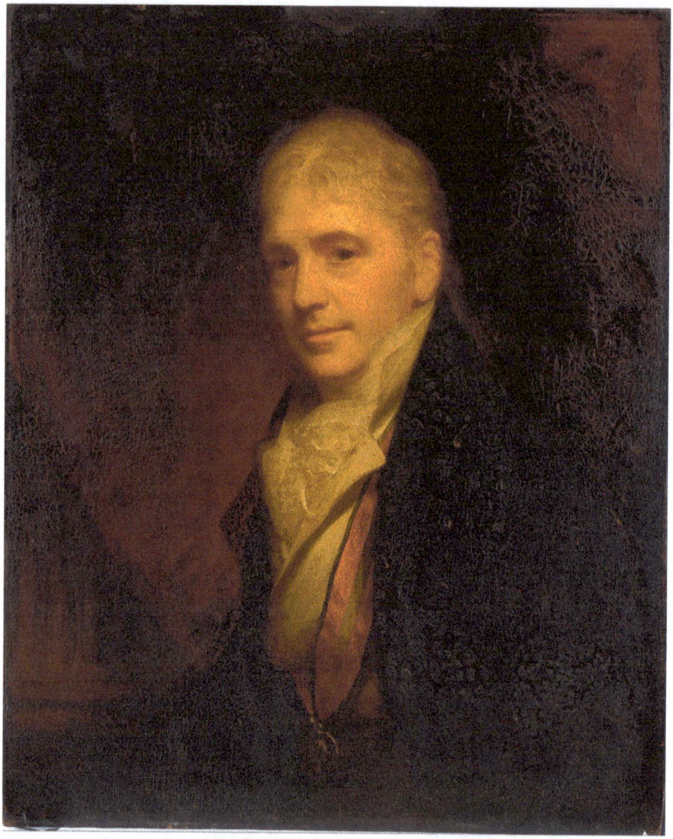

Fig. 10.4 Sir William Beechey (1753–1839), Sir Francis Bourgeois

Today, private treaty sales are a norm in the art market. There, the real money is made, discreetly and away from the public's eye. The little Leonardo panel was involved in two private treaty sales. The first one earned the individuals who had bought the picture in New Orleans the difference between $1.175.00 and $83 million minus sundry expenses. The second sale netted the dealer who had bought it for $ 83 million a profit of roughly $40 million when he sold it to the Russian oligarch for $127.5 million. The latter deal incurred no significant cost or risk to the gentleman in the middle: apparently the buyer had agreed to the purchase before the seller paid for it.

[The 'Bouvier Affair', as this series of transactions has been called, was not without consequences. In 2017, legal actions were initiated by the Russian billionaire, Dmitri Rybolovlev, against his good friend, Yves Bouvier, a Swiss art dealer and Sotheby's, the largest international auction house. The point of contention was the amount of profit—alleged to be over one billion dollars—Mr. Bouvier, who also owned a Geneva-based art warehousing facility, had made on two billion dollars-worth of art sales to Mr. Rybolovlev. The Leonardo panel was among them. The Russian multi-billionaire argued that Ives, his good friend, was working for him as his agent and, therefore, was not entitled to such a profit. The Swiss gentleman, however, countered that he was an independent businessman and could charge as much as he wanted for the art he sold. The suits were dismissed by the courts. I suspect that the judges considered the fact that Mr. Rybolovlev sold one of the paintings—the Salvator Mundi—for which he had paid Mr. Bouvier $ 127,000,000 in 2013 for $ 400,000,000 at Christie's in 2017. Making a gross profit of $ 273,000,000 on a piece of art and then claiming to have been ripped off by the man who sold it to him, apparently was not convincing to the eminent jurists. One can't help wondering what da Vinci would have thought. Who knows? At least, he could have told us if he, indeed, had painted the piece. A detailed account of the relationship between Yves Bouvier and Dimitri Rybolovlev, 'Yves Bouvier: The Art World's Most Notorious Middleman', by Rebecca D. O'Brian and Tom Metcalf was published in Bloomberg online, March 18, 2015. I last checked the link early March 2025. Two months later, it no longer worked.[15]]

Contemporaneous with Noel Desanfans, Michael Bryan (1757–1821) made his first appearance on the international art dealing scene. His name will forever be remembered for two accomplishments. He wrote the now outdated *Biographical and Critical Dictionary of Painters and Engravers*, first published in London in 1813–1816; and he was instrumental in putting together the biggest art deal of the period, even topping the spectacular sale of the Walpole collection to Czarina Catherine the Great in 1779. Bryan's coup consisted of a joint venture that culminated in the exhibition and sale of an immense collection of over 500 paintings, that had been assembled by Philippe d'Orleans, the duke of Orleans between 1700 and his death in 1723.[16]

The legendary Orleans Collection was opened to the public on December 26, 1798, and received nearly non-stop press coverage during the six months it was on view. As usual, the public was invited for a 1 shilling entrance fee per person. But this event was different. It did not feature one reproductive engraving for sale together with its original painting, as was the case with Copley's *Death of Chatham*, or engravings of original works by different artists, like the Shakespeare Gallery offered. Instead, this exhibition afforded visitors the opportunity to see in person a truly legendary royal collection of some of the greatest paintings ever done. And if one was so inclined financially, any of the paintings gracing the walls could be acquired. The press was all over this unprecedented exhibition, providing free publicity. And art writers were able to produce thousands of words about every conceivable tangent related to the art on display.

In his memoirs, the dealer William Buchanan (1777–1864) offered some insight into the business end of this event.[17] To get his hands on this magnificent collection, Michael Bryan had taken on the Duke of Bridgwater, Lord Carlisle, and Lord Gower as investors in a joint venture. Their agreement entitled them to select a number of paintings for their own use with the remainder to be sold at a specifically organized exhibition, rather than at auction. Bryan's Orleans Collection project turned out to be very profitable and ranks among the watershed art market events of the period. The investors had acquired the entire collection for 43,500 pounds (approximately 8,000,000 pounds today, although the actual buying power of that sum was significantly greater). Buchanan writes that the exhibition and sale of the 211 pictures passed up by the aristocratic financiers realized around 42,500 guineas—more than enough to pay for the 94 paintings, separately valued at 31,000 guineas, they kept for themselves. Several of these works are still in the possession of the descendants of these owners, while others are in famous public collections, like the National Gallery of Scotland and the National Gallery in London. In today's market, many of these paintings, Correggio's (1489–1534 *Io* (1531/1532), just as one example, would individually command prices likely ten times as much as the original cost of the entire collection.

Many of the personalities who made their living by trading in art works, like the landscape painter-turned-dealer, Thomas Manby (1769–1834), had started out as artists or professional antiquaries before venturing into the business. James Irving (1736–1795), George A. Wallis (1761–1847), and Jacob More (1740–1793), all well-known dealers of the period, are others who made their appearance on the auction scene. The dealer and later auctioneer, John Greenwood 1739–1799), also started out as a painter and engraver. Even fashionable portraitists like Thomas Hudson (1701–1779) or John Closterman (1660–1711) dealt in paintings done by other artists.[18]

There were also certain 'virtuosi' and 'connoisseurs' who augmented their personal collecting through dealing. Auction records list numerous sellers of whose identity I know nothing but a name. Many of them could have ostensibly done business in this manner. Alternatively, they may have profited from purchasing paintings for other private collectors on a commission basis or by adding a fixed surcharge for their services. The antiquary, John Talman (1677–1726), for example, had such an arrangement with Lord Somers (1651–1716) in the acquisition of the exquisite drawing collection of Padre Sebastiano Resta (1635–1714).[19]

John Talman's well-known collection played a large role in the popularity in England of drawing by Italian masters of the Baroque period, introducing works by Guido Reni, Annibale Caracci, Antonio Correggio, and others.[20]

Working as a runner or scout for professional dealers was another option. It was less prestigious but could be quite profitable. There were also diplomats, bankers, and political exiles who dabbled in the business of art. Dr. Hickman, the associate of the Duke of Kingston in Paris, and the Parisian banker, Mr. Selwin, doubled as art dealers.[21] Even secret agents, like the infamous Scottish spy, John Macky (d.1726), occasionally dealt in art as a cover for their clandestine work.[22] Hollywood is not so far off the target in its various depictions of art dealers' inconspicuous side.

A similar kaleidoscope of characters still exists today. This assorted fringe of the art trade is indicative of an early stage in the development of a market. But at the same time, it characterizes an unregulated business without standardized professional pre-requisites. Such low barriers were among the engines of growth in a nineteenth-century business environment that still wrestled with its restrictive past. Even in present-day art dealing, this fringe performs a vital function. The art trade is still unregulated and still lacks uniform standards. Anyone can become an art dealer, and the fringe is a good place to start and learn. There is no formal apprenticeship or university degree for art dealing. This is unlikely to change despite the well-intentioned efforts of various trade organizations to introduce norms to the business of art. In the context of the market, the function of these groups is mainly to enhance consumer confidence, rather than enforce professional standards internally. Auction houses have started to offer courses in art dealing and the art market from which students are graduated. These courses teach practical information about the prevailing modus operandi, but little about the entrepreneurial aspects and larger social role of art dealing.

In today's mature art market, below the level of professional dealers, there still is a great number of semi-professionals like their 'ancestors' in the eighteenth century and equally as colorful. Most established professional galleries and private dealers rely to varying degrees on loose networks of individuals below the radar, away from the publicly projected sophisticated image of the art business. These can be estate lawyers, accountants, academics, museum professionals, restorers, appraisers, and the socially well-connected members of old-world aristocratic families. During my four decades of art dealing, I relied heavily on a network of usefully connected individuals. They included an Austrian Baron, a British Lord; a former member of the French Secret Service; the director of one of the largest US museums; a wealthy Parisian lady with a 45-meter houseboat on the Seine in Neuilly on which she entertained Paris' social elite; a famous film star; a Moroccan model, and others. We worked together for years and became good friends. While the expansion of the market called for the firm entrenchment of the professional picture dealer, it did not do away with the 'proto-professional' roles from which this occupation evolved and on which it still relies.

However, something stuck out. Auction records show that, in contrast to today, in the eighteenth century those dealers whose identities are known rarely appeared as *buyers* of paintings at auction. Instead, they used auctions predominantly to sell their own inventories.[23] This experience taught them a few useful things. One of them, a very important one, was how to influence auction results.

Auction records reveal that this traditional modus operandi of dealers in the auction market changed fundamentally during the next century. From being dominant sellers at auctions during the eighteenth century, dealers would become the principal buyers, while their role as consignors appreciably diminished.[24] The discovery of this change of middlemen from being predominantly sellers to becoming the dominant buyer group was among the most significant revelations resulting from the analyses of auction data. This switch would fundamentally transform the workings of the art market. Dealers became market makers.

Buying at art auctions was to remain almost exclusively the domain of middlemen well into the last third of the twentieth century. Of course, experienced private collectors would also attend auctions, but they were the exception. However, by the beginning of the 1970s, there was another seismic shift in the market. The 'retailization', or to be more precise, the 're-retailization', of the auction market started. The term describes an intentional recalibration of the auction industry's marketing strategy to increasing the participation of private collectors at their sales. This calculated effort to sell directly to the end consumers was a deliberate gauntlet thrown at the feet of the retail art dealing industry. I will elaborate on the implications of this momentous change in greater detail later.

In addition to new information on different individuals about whose activities in the art market little or even nothing was previously known, auction data also show that a high degree of specialization was practiced quite early among London art dealers.[25] In fact, this information made it possible to predict with a high degree of accuracy who among the London dealers would most likely attend a specific sale, bid on this work or that, and how much they would likely pay.

Thus far, this account has focused on the trade in imported old paintings by dead artists. The market was remarkably buoyant, and opportunities for the plucky and adventurous were there for the taking. These early dealers were like a funnel that sucked up the great cultural riches of the Continent and spilled them out onto the London market for redistribution across the island and, later, across the world. The resulting Europeanization of former national treasures left a permanent imprint on the cultural landscape.

But what about dealers in *contemporary* paintings? How did they come into existence? Obviously, dealing in paintings whose artists were still alive and producing has different parameters and dynamics. Two important factors played decisive roles as midwives in the birth of this new profession: the reproductive print I already mentioned earlier and, again, the familiar Napoleonic wars and their aftermath.

Notes

1. Bayer/Page data.
2. Iain Pears, The Discovery of Painting (New Haven & London: Yale University Press, 1988): 102, 166; Bayer/Page data.
3. Carol Gibson Wood, "Picture Consumption in England at the End of the Seventeenth Century," Art Bulletin, 84 (2002): 496.
4. Pears: 51–55, and n. 20.
5. https://www.nationalgallery.ie/art-and-artists/exhibitions/past-exhibitions/caravaggio-25-years-display/caravaggio-celebrating/how (last accessed March 2025).
6. Pears: 51–55.
7. https://www.academia.edu/97611560/Chronology_for_Andrew_Hay_art_dealer_1690_1754_ (last accessed March 2025).
8. Bayer/Page data.
9. Louise Lippincott, Selling Art in Georgian London (New Haven & London: Yale University Press, 1983): 77–96 and notes, offer in addition to her discussion of Arthur Pond, also accounts of several of the individuals discussed in this section. For a chronology of Hay, see https://www.academia.edu/97611560/Chronology_for_Andrew_Hay_art_dealer_1690_1754_ (Last accessed March 2025); Frank Simpson, "Dutch Paintings in England before 1760," Burlington Magazine, XCV (February 1953): 39–42, mentions Peter A. Mottaux, Samuel Paris, and Robert Bragge. Also, Herman Bruntjen, John Boydell (1719–1804)A Study of Art Patronage and Publishing in Georgian London (N.Y.: Garland Publishing, 1985): 89, and William Whitley, Artists and Their Friends in England 1700–1790, 2 vols. (London & Boston: The Medici Society, 1938), vol. 1: 338, vol. 2: 76, 84, 87, 133; Noel Desanfans is mentioned by Frank Hermann, The English as Collectors (N.Y.: W. W. Norton & Co., 1972): 171–172 and Whitley, Artists and Their Friends in England 1700–1790, vol. 1: 109, 283, vol. 2: 10, 13, 32, 77, 88, 142, 190, and Whitley, Art in England, 2 vols. (N. Y: Hacker Art Books, 1973),vol. 1: 30–34. Desanfans published a pamphlet in 1799 promoting a "A Plan for improving the Arts in Britain."see, Joseph Farington, Diaries, 4 vols. (London: Hutchinson & Co, 1923), vol.4: pp. 1132–1133, entries for Jan. 11/12, 1799; George Vertue, Note Books, 6 vols. The Walpole Society, 32, vol. 3: 13–14, 125 (on Hay). Whitley, Artists and Their Friends in England 1700–1790, vol. 1: 75, 98, 109, 243 also discusses Hay, vol. 1: 18, 29, 31, 64, 124, 332, on Arthur Pond, vol. 2: 190, Michael Bryan, vol. I: 261, describes briefly the activities of the dealer Goodall.
10. For a comprehensive study of Arthur Pond, see Lippincott.
11. Bayer/Page data.

12. Bayer/Page data.
13. Bayer/Page data; also, Julia Armstrong-Totten, ¨Expand the Audience, Increase the Profits: Motivations Behind the Private Contract Sale,¨ La Circulation des Oeuvres d Árt 1789–1848, A. Panzanelli and M. Preti-Hamard, eds. (Rennes: Presses de Universitaire de Rennes Institute National de Histoire de l Árt, Getty Research Institute, 2007): 45–55.
14. On Desansans, https://www.dulwichpicturegallery.org.uk/about/our-history/#:~:text=Dulwich%20Picture%20Gallery%20sprung%20out,RA%20(1756%20%2D%201811), (last accessed March 2025.); Also, Noel Desanfans is mentioned by Hermann:171–172; Whitley, Artists and Their Friends in England 1700–1790, vol. 1:109, 283, vol. 2: 10, 13, 32, 77, 88, 142, 190 and Whitley, Art in England, 2 vols. (New York: Hacker Art Books, 1973), vol. 1: 30–34.
15. https://www.art-critique.com/en/2019/11/the-bouvier-affair-the-art-of-deception/ (last accessed March 2025)
16. The dealer Bryan is discussed in Armstrong-Totten, ¨The Rise and Fall of a British Connoisseur: the career of Michel Bryan (1757–1821), picture dealer *extraordinaire*¨ Auctions, Agents, and Dealers. The Mechanisms of the Art Market 1660–1830, Warren and Turpin, eds. (Oxford: The Beazley Archives and Archaeopress in association with the Wallace Collection, 2008): 141–150. For a discussion of the collection, see Inge Reist, ¨The Fate of the Palais Royal Collection: 1791–1800,¨ R. Panzanelli and M. Preti-Hamard, eds, La Circulation des Oeuvres d'Art 1789–1848: 27–44.
17. William Buchanan, Memoirs of Painting, 2 vols., J. Greig, ed. (London: Ackerman, 18245), vol. 1:1–219 and vol. 2: 18–19.
18. Buchanan: vol. 2: 96. Whitley, *Artists and Their Friends in England 1700–1790*, vol. 2: 200, 203, 325, 344 mentions an artist/picture dealer named James Irvine, most likely identical to the above James Irving. Jacob More is discussed in vol. 1: 350, and vol. 2: 199–203.
19. Genieve Warwick, ¨Gift Exchange and Art Collecting. Padre Sebastiano Pesta's Drawing Albums¨, Art Bulletin, 4 (December 1997): 644 and n. 108.
20. Pears, 'Patronage and Learning in the Virtuoso Republic: John Talman in Italy 1709–12', Oxford Art Journal, 5, no 1, (1982): 24–30.
21. British Museum, Add. MS 23724, ff. 14, 40, 60, 61, 62, 74, on Dr. Hickman, and 98, 103, 112, 129, 130, on Selwin, as cited by Lippincott: 114, ns. 32 and 33.
22. Wilmarth Lewis, Connoisseurs and Secret Agents in 18th Century Rome (London: Chatto & Windus, 1961), John Macky, Memoirs of the Secret Services of John Macky, Esq. (London 1733).
23. Bayer/Page data.
24. Bayer/Page data.
25. Bayer/Page data.

CHAPTER 11

The Institutionalization of Art Dealing

Copley's earlier mentioned *Death Of Chatham* enterprise shows that the eighteenth-century print was the main catalyst for the sweeping transformation of the contemporary painting business and the associated birth of the dealer in contemporary art. The reproductive print, as I pointed out, also marks the beginning of the development of merchandizing in the art market in the form of inexpensive derivatives to subsidize the high cost of blockbuster and sensational original work and, of course, to produce additional income. Nowadays, this is a well-established practice. Most museum giftshops, large and small, usually offer some type of inexpensive merchandize of something in their collection for sale to bring in extra income.

Prints were all the rage during the eighteenth century. Not just among consumers, but also with artists. The ever-insightful Hogarth had mused, 'this (he means prints) I found was most likely to answer my purpose, provided I could strike the passions, and by small sums from many, by the sale of prints which I would engrave from my own pictures, thus secure my property to myself'. He was spot on. Prints cost much less than original paintings, they were smaller and cheaper to frame and, certainly in the case of Hogarth, much more entertaining. His first set of prints attracted over 1200 subscribers, solidly establishing the artist's reputation. Since he often engraved personally, Hogarth also controlled the production process.[1] A comment by the artist in his *Autobiographical Notes* shows how much economics were on his mind. He explains that '... neither great

T. M. Bayer, *The Genesis of the Modern Art Market in London, 1700–1900*, https://doi.org/10.1007/978-3-032-00594-6_11

correctness of drawing or fine Engraving were at all necessary but on the contrary would set the price of them out of the reach of those for whome [sic] they were chiefly intended'.[2] Monetary consumer-oriented consideration directly impacted the design of the artist's work. I am confident that Hogarth was not the first and only artist to fashion their work based on their perception of consumer behavior. Nor the last. Inevitably, products created under modern consumer market conditions reflect the interplay of supply and demand.

The industry grew quickly. Prior to 1733, there were only two shops selling prints in London; by the end of the century, such shops existed in every major town.[3] To fuel this growth, the engraving trade refined production and marketing and deliberately took a populist approach in choosing subjects for reproduction.

Prior to specialized print shops, print publishers had relied for their distribution—the key to the success of selling mass products—as well as their marketing methods, on an extant infrastructure of booksellers. Since authors and booksellers/publishers often used engravers as illustrators, bibliophiles were already familiar with prints. This early collaboration also gave print publishers some familiarity with the book publishing trade's well-established production, financing, and marketing methods.

This relationship between the book selling industry and the dissemination of contemporary art through reproductive engravings had another, especially far-reaching, impact that went beyond marketing and distribution. I mentioned earlier that most of the major publishing ventures of the last decades of the eighteenth century involved themes chosen from English literature familiar to most of those who patronized bookstores. As a result, the first popular introduction of contemporary English paintings via reproductive engravings had a distinctly literary and narrative character. These were qualities, I pointed out, that were conveniently favorable to writers and made for easy conversations about art. As a result, these prints sold very well and greatly influenced popular taste.[4]

By the last quarter of the eighteenth century, the print trade had grown from a cottage industry into a huge commercial enterprise. An engraver testifying before the Select Committee of the House of Commons on the Arts commented that 'by the graver's art, … copper has been turned into gold.'[5]

The 'philosopher's stone' quality to which this observation alluded had a far-reaching effect. The spread of retail print shops whose owners had experience in dealing in art products coupled with the great popularity of literary and narrative scenes were part of the seedbed on which professional art dealers specializing in contemporary art would grow in the next century.

Like Copley, many other artists partnered with dealers to produce and sell prints. The huge undertakings of the leading art dealing/publishing entrepreneurs of the period, Boydell or Macklin, presented contemporary English—and Continental—painters with an appealing income possibility and paved the way for other entrepreneurs to try similar, smaller ventures. This was the time when the 'theme show' I described earlier, was introduced. These and similar enterprises provided an ideal training ground for entrepreneurial individuals keen to learn about new business prospects in the arts.

These were heady days for art lovers. Between the beginning of July and the first week of August 1799 alone, advertisements in various newspapers announced the exhibition of over 300 paintings from the famous Orleans collection in the gallery of the dealer Michael Bryan; Fuseli's exhibition of his Milton inspired series in the Royal Academy; William Elmer's show of Sportsman's Pictures, and the publication of views of London by Noah Black—four different major exhibitions spread across as many weeks.[6]

Unfortunately, progress in the commercial collaboration between artists, print publishers, and retailers slowed during the last quarter of the eighteenth century. The chief reason was the vast quantity of old paintings that came on the market because of the widespread disruptions caused by the Napoleonic wars. Just at the time when the contemporary art market had evolved to a point that offered promising commercial opportunities from an alliance between producers of art and professional art dealers, the competition stemming from imported old master paintings from the war-torn Continent delayed the full realization and exploitation of this merger. Dealers zeroed in on these new opportunities. As a result, it took nearly half a century before a significant recovery in the economic conditions of contemporary painters materialized.

The conflict delayed the commercial alliance between artists and dealers until well past the beginning of Queen Victoria's reign in 1837. The effects of the Napoleonic conflicts on the British art market in general and its specific impact on the development of contemporary painting in England are among the most persuasive examples of the influence of dealers' resource allocations on the arts environment.

William Buchanan, the Old Master dealer, wrote in 1824 that 'the last thirty years have produced events in the history of Europe which … forced from their ancient sanctuaries those treasures of Science and of Art, that had long been the pride and glory of the states to which they belonged'.[7] England benefited economically from the damage and general disruption this drawn-out conflict caused France, its main trading competitors. Britain's own infrastructure was left unscathed. Apparently, such times of mass slaughter and suffering were useful not just for providing heroic and gruesome themes for art, but also for the art market. Another dealer of the time Thomas Winstanley (1768–1845) noted in his memoires for the late 1820s that 'the immense fortunes which have been made by individuals during the late war…is another cause of the great prices now to be obtained for articles of high taste and virtu … Paintings are universally acknowledged to be objects worthy of possession …'.

These two factors, the increased supply Buchanan mentioned and the parallel growth in demand referred to by Winstanley, substantially enlarged the market for old paintings and, at the same time, increased dealers' opportunities to turn a profit. The pivotal phrase is Winstanley's comment: '[P]aintings are universally acknowledged to be objects worthy of possession …'. This statement, self-evident to us today, marks an inflection point. Winstanley, a dealer, auctioneer, and keen observer of the art trade, declared that paintings were now *universally* considered to hold value for their owners. This observation was based on his personal knowledge of how art works performed as movable storage of value on an international scale in times of crisis.

This special commodity characteristic of art was the reason for the magnificent private collections that formed the core of the National Gallery in London founded in 1824, barely a decade after the Battle of Waterloo. Again Winstanley:

> … agents are employed not only in this country but in every part of Europe, to purchase, at almost unlimited prices, Pictures of the highest class. Large prices have been paid by… Dealers … it is not uncommon to find that they are outbid at public sales abroad and meet with formidable rivals at home in the agents of Foreign Amateurs and Dealers, who every season visit London for the purpose of purchasing as well as of selling.

He adds, '[i]t is well known that since the termination of the late continental war, every corner of Europe has been searched – and, as it were, hunted for Pictures, both by the Collector and Dealer … Eminent dealers have sought for Paintings in every city, town, and almost every village in

Holland, Flanders, and Germany, to satisfy the cravings of their English customers. Accordingly, the number of pictures consigned to England became astonishingly great … when the storm of the French Revolution burst over the different countries of Europe …'.[8]

In addition to the importation of old pictures, there was also money to be made with well-known Old Master collections already in England. These private treasures were coming on the market because their owners liked the excellent prices they could realistically expect for them. Pure speculators likely also played the market during this time. Unfortunately, I am unable to identify any by name.

[Among the better-known examples are the Trumbull collection sold by Christie's over several days in February 1797; the pictures owned by Baron Fagel, the Dutch Secretary of State, sold at Coxe on May 23 and 24, 1801; and the superb collection of Dutch paintings owned by the Countess of Holderness on the block at Christie's on March 6, 1802.]

Dealers loved this buoyant market. The established firms profited from their existing connections, and aspiring new ones sought out opportunities to get into the market. Auction records reveal numerous new names among the many dealers trading on the London auction exchange who are only vaguely, if at all, familiar today.[9]

It's an old maxim in business that resources should be allocated to where they produce the best returns. Art dealers were well-aware of this rule and focused on the obviously profitable importation and sale of dead Old Masters. This was disadvantageous to still living painters. Here is Winstanley once more:

> … many Pictures, purchased even at the best sales of the most valuable Collections have been resold at a very large advance … *It is then only natural that all those engaged in the traffic of Pictures, commonly called Picture Dealers, will uphold the value of the works of the old Masters in which they have probably embarked their fortunes*, and to obtain the possession of which they have exerted all their skills, industry, and enterprise.[10] [*italics* are mine]

This statement marks the second inflection point. Winstanley's remark is the first explicit acknowledgement of market intervention by dealers to support the prices of the art in which they traded. Together, these two points—universal acceptance and market making—are characteristics of movable and tradable assets that store value. Auction records support Winstanley's statements: there are many specific examples of this type of price support by stake-holding middlemen.[11] Not surprisingly, this practice of market-making took root, and it has become a core function of art dealers ever since.

No tradeable asset can store value without an exchange mechanism, i.e., a market infrastructure. And someone has to manage that market. At a certain stage in its history, when a critical mass of the England's population had surplus, i.e., more than they needed for basic survival, the country's socio-economy introduced a market for certain types of art—in this case Old Master paintings—that functioned like a bourse.

The Napoleonic Wars presented the opportunity to owners of artworks to showcase the exceptional qualities of their possessions as a highly mobile and liquid asset. The London art market offered itself as the ideal place where these assets could be turned back into cash. Since then, price manipulation and other market-making activities have become one of the foundation stones that support art's qualifications as a financial asset. They are a *sine qua non* of today's art market.

Price protection in the market for Old Master paintings by dealers went hand in hand with their malicious attacks on contemporary paintings. One art milieu insider, the painter and Royal Academician, Joseph Farington (1747–1821), remembered a friend's claim that dealers in old pictures 'have at present prejudiced Lord Grosvenor's mind so far against the merit of modern art as to interrupt his design of making a Collection of modern pictures ...'.[12]

What made matters even worse for the market in contemporary paintings was the near disappearance of the overseas trade in reproductive engravings I described earlier. The market on the Continent for these inexpensive mass-produced consumer goods had largely collapsed with the onset of hostilities there. So had the income of contemporary English painters from supplying the original works. Over a period of roughly 20 years, Continental Europeans had more pressing matters on their mind than buying charming wall décor, survival being chiefly among them. As we know, Boydell's huge publishing house had gone bankrupt as a result.

There was also a money issue. The buoyancy of the pre-war art economy had spoiled artists. According to Thomas Winstanley, contemporary painters in England had such extravagant price expectations for their works that they 'preclude[d] them from becoming anything like an article of commerce'. Even one of their own, the above-mentioned Royal Academician Joseph Farington thought that prices were so 'extravagant even to be ridiculous'.[13] If artists asked prices for their works that were too high for middlemen to make a profit, then why should they bother buying any?

Not just esoteric questions of taste and reputation of artist, but simple, self-interested economic and business decisions played decisive roles in the changing arts environment of this developmental stage of the modern art market. It made economic sense for dealers to take advantage of opportunities to make money by trading in old pictures. The market was buoyant, and for the time being paintings by dead artists turned a better profit than pictures painted by living ones.

The upswing in the old painting market, however, was only temporary. In many ways the boom bred its own demise. After decades of harvesting pictures on the Continent, there was little good art left. The generally mediocre quality of the overwhelming majority of imported old paintings, their sole distinction being that they were from the Continent, came back to haunt the market. In the words of Winstanley, these dregs were dumped on the English by dealers of 'less eminence… who have no other feeling for the Works of Art but as they produce profit'.[14]

This deluge of inferior-quality art was, to an extent, exacerbated by governmental policy: the earlier described reduction of the *ad valorem* tax in 1826 to five shillings per painting with an additional one shilling for each square foot of size. This tariff had unintended and unfortunate results. 'In reducing the duties from almost an exorbitant to a nominal charge', a July 1839 editorial in the *Art Union* argued, 'Government could not have contemplated the mischief that resulted from the change – an influx of worthless and injurious copies …'. The English market was effectively flooded with 'canvases that had never been seen by the artists to whom they were attributed'. The essay's author, Samuel Carter Hall, founder of the *Art Journal*, maintained that less than 25% of the pictures imported into England since the tariff reduction were indeed painted by the artists to whom they were ascribed.[15]

Consumer trust in the market for old paintings suffered further because of a home-based mass-production of forgeries. There existed entire 'manufactories' where recently painted 'Old Masters' were carefully aged and then flogged to the unsuspecting public. One 'manufactory' in Richmond was known as the 'Canaletti Manufactory', because of its mass-production of forgeries of the Italian painter Antonio Canaletto's works that were all the rage at the time. Even today, the Canaletto market is still plagued by the effects of these forgeries. Another such 'factory' run by a Mr. Zachary on Adelphi Terrace near the Strand treated freshly painted pictures with heat and smoke. This 'baking' would essentially convert a recently finished work into an old one. The heat would create craquelure, while the smoke produced the required darkened appearance of the canvas. Varnish would be applied subsequently to prevent detection through smell and/or rubbing off the soot. Clearly, the demand for old paintings was larger than the available supply of legitimate works could satisfy.[16]

By the 1830s, the ubiquity of the 'lemon problem' in the market for old paintings had created a situation pregnant with change. Indeed, as soon as the market signaled that business conditions were changing in favor of contemporary paintings, all hostilities between the camps were forgiven and forgotten. Dealers jumped at the new opportunities, and artists welcomed them with open arms. By mid-century, dealers in contemporary paintings were well established in London.

An excellent example of early dealers' agency in an artist's career, as well as their role in larger cultural crosscurrents, involves the landscape painter John Constable (1776–1837) and two dealers, John Arrowsmith (1790–1873) and Claude Schroth (n.d.). The two gentlemen had decided to introduce Constable's paintings to French audiences as part of a monumental promotional and marketing event known as the 'British Salon', organized in Paris in 1824—only two years after the defeat of Napoleon at Waterloo.[17] Aside from marking a notable instance of cultural diplomacy, the relationship with these two dealers affected not just Constable as an individual, but it also had a historic impact on the very future of the art of painting. Within only two years, by the summer of 1826, when the French connection, Monsieur Schroth, discontinued his business relationship with the artist, more than twenty of Constable's exquisite canvases had made their way to France, ultimately changing the course of the history of painting forever.[18] His energetically painted landscapes with their windswept vistas, dramatic clouds, magnificent skies, and rich and vibrant colors seemingly effortlessly applied blew away the French art lovers and, more importantly, French painters. They had never seen this type of free and untamed representation of nature. One could almost smell the trees,

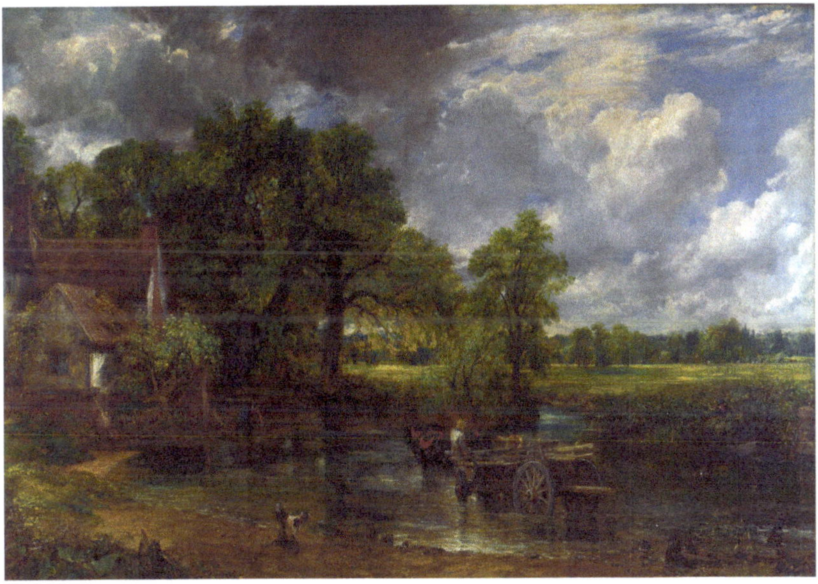

Fig. 11.1 John Constable (1776–1837), The Hay Wain

hear the creeks and brooks, and feel the sun and wind on your skin. Constable's canvases made a profound impact and planted the first seeds of Impressionism in painters' heads. While the artist would achieve international fame, very little credit is given to the two dealers for their part in affecting the radical change of style that resulted from their introduction of Constable's work to French audiences (Fig. 11.1).

The time for dealers had finally arrived. Over the preceding half century, they had gathered valuable experience, developed marketing and promotional skills, and understood how the art market can be managed to the best of their interests. Vauxhall, the Foundling Hospital, artist- organized group exhibitions, private sales, and single 'sensation picture' shows were crucial milestones on this path to the convergence of interests of artists and middlemen—the professional art dealer.

Notes

1. George Vertue, *Notebooks*, 6 vols. (London: The Walpole Society, 22, 1934), vol. 3: 281–283; Horace Walpole, Anecdotes of Painting in England, 3 vols. (London: Henry C. Bohn, 1849), vol. 3: 728.
2. Hogarth is cited in Artists on Art, R. Goldwater and M. Treves, eds. (New York: Pantheon Books, 1945):179; Walpole, vol. 3: 986.
3. Jean Rouquet, The State of the Arts in England (London: J. Nourse, 1755): 28; John Pye, Patronage of British Art, A Historical Sketch (London: Longman, Brown, Green and Longman, 1845): 243.
4. James Raven, "The Book Trades," Books and Their Readers in Eighteenth-century England: new Essays, I. Rivers, ed. (London and N.Y.: Leister University Press, 2001): 1–34. Ronald Paulson, Hogarth: His Life, Art, and Times, 2 vols. (New Haven and London: Yale University Press), vol 1: 280, for data on seventeenth-century book publications by subscription. On the same topic see Alexandre Beljame, Men of Letters and the English Public in the 18th Century (London: K. Paul, Trench, Truber, 1948): 363. For profit figures of books published by subscription see George Sherburn, The Early Career of Alexander Pope (Oxford: Clarendon Press, 1934): 188, 253–259.
5. Mentioned by Pye: 211, without providing a date.
6. Fuseli's enterprise is discussed in detail by Gert Schiff, Johann Heinrich Fuesslis Milton Galerie (Zurich: Fretz & Wasmuth, 1963); also, Luisa Cale, Fuseli's Milton Gallery: Turning Readers into Spectators (Oxford: Clarendon Press, 2006).
7. William Buchanan, Memoirs of Painting, 2 vols., J. Greig, ed. (London: Ackerman, 1824), vol. 1: xiii.
8. Thomas Winstanley, Observations on the Arts (Liverpool: W. Wales, 1828): 3–6.
9. Bayer/Page data.
10. Winstanley: 38.
11. Bayer/Page data.
12. Joseph Farington, The Farington Diary, 6 vols. (London: Hutchinson & Co., 1923), vol. 1: 99, entry for May 17, 1795, vol. 4: 177, entry for July 15, 1807.
13. Winstanley: 8; Farington, vol. 5: 172, entry for May 24, 1809; vol. 1: 15, entry for Nov. 13, 1793, 201, entry for July 3, 1809, respectively.
14. Winstanley: 5–6.
15. Samuel Carter Hall, Retrospective of A Long Life from 1815–1883 (N.Y.: D. Appleton & Co., 1883): 197 and 200.
16. Hall: 199–200; Art Union, 7 (1845): 121–122; Art Journal, May 1 (1852): 151–152. For an account of some of these practices and the indi-

viduals involved, see Wilkie Collins, A Rogue's Life (London: Richard Bentley & Son, 1879): 39–41ff.

17. For more on this topic see P. Noon, *Crossing the Channel, British and French Painting in the Age of Romanticism* with contributions by S. Bann, D. B. Brown, R. Meredith, C. Riding and M. Watteau (New York and London: The Metropolitan Museum of Art in association with Tate Publishing, 2003).
18. Patrick Noon, 'Colour and Effect, Anglo-French Painting in London and Paris', Crossing the Channel, British and French Painting in the Age of Romanticism (London: Tate Publishing, 2003): 27.

CHAPTER 12

Victorian Picture Dealing: The Big Times

In December of 1871, the editor of the influential *Art Journal*, Samuel Carter Hall, reported that dealers have 'taken the place of the patron, and to him has been owing, to a great extent, the immense increase in the price of modern pictures'.[1] Hall's observation about the impact of dealers on the art market is verified by auction records of this period.[2]

'Fame' has been an intriguing topic for many years, and investigations into the complexities of fame enjoy great popularity, particularly in the influencing market. How is fame achieved? How is it maintained? What are the prerequisites for achieving it? To what percentage is luck a factor? Fame is a product of human action. What human action does it take to achieve it?[3] Intriguingly, it seems that the most important factor is not talent, however it may be defined, but having a 'champion', someone who has faith in you, who carries your torch, who wants you to do well, and who energetically, passionately, and creatively pursues and guides your interests. This 'champion' can be an individual or a network/organization. And it was precisely this role that Victorian art dealers perfected during the nineteenth century with remarkable effectiveness. They defined professional art dealing in a consumer-oriented modern society. Dealers form the hub around which the art market turns. But they are more than champions of artists. Dealers are also principal drivers of the market-inherent commoditization process. Their job as art's champions is to

T. M. Bayer, *The Genesis of the Modern Art Market in London, 1700–1900*, https://doi.org/10.1007/978-3-032-00594-6_12

promote, facilitate, and improve the exchange of art products, and to modify/manage the exchange mechanism for those purposes.

Other champions of art and artists are art critics, museums, universities, kindergartens, teachers, and, of course, governments. We share an understanding that all of us who engage with art are also her champions. We don't think any more about the big issue of the eighteenth century: is art good for society? This debate has been replaced with an ongoing discussion about what *kind* of art is good for society. Consensus on this question requires first an agreement on the definition of what constitutes a 'good' for society. *Entartete Kunst* (degenerate Art), the classification given to art that was deemed not good for Nazi Germany's society, was assigned by dictate, not societal consent. The use of taxpayer money to champion the arts is a controversial dynamic.

The auction sales and other records I analyzed reveal previously unknown activities of dealers that show how market intervention was practiced. S. C. Hall's above comment was on target. Data confirm that, indeed, during this time a fundamental structural change had occurred that firmly entrenched dealers as the driving force in the operations of the art market. This hegemony of the trade was of profound consequence to the way the art market functions nowadays.[4]

I mentioned earlier that throughout the eighteenth and for the first few decades of the nineteenth century dealers rarely *bought* at auctions. Instead, they used this trading platform mainly to sell their inventory of old pictures. In general, their business in paintings by living artists was negligible. Then, from the 1840s on, this relationship between dealers and auctions changed fundamentally. Dealers largely stopped selling at auction and became the dominant *buyers* of both old and new pictures at these sales. The auction market for both types of paintings, old and new, was effectively under their control.

There was also a change in the Old Master market: It had run out of steam for the time being. The good things were largely gone, and major private collections sold directly through Christie's auction house rather than using dealers. Since auction prices were reported in the London press, it was difficult for local dealers to buy at auction and resell with a good profit unless they had overseas clients who were not privy to the auction results. Therefore, the stage was handed over to a cast of living artists and their new dealer-champions.

Contemporary observers were aware of this change. Modern pictures had become 'articles of commerce', wrote Wilkie Collins (1824–1889), the eldest son of the painter William Collins, in 1848. Along similar lines, the dealer Thomas Rought (1801–1872) mentioned in an 1850 letter to one of the leading collectors of the time, Joseph Gillott (1799–1872), that 'all the old dealers [were] in spite of themselves now going into the Modern ...'.[5]

[Joseph Gillott was an English collector and industrialist from Sheffield. Gillott used a press to produce steel pens and, as a result, revolutionizing the industry. His innovation made his pens almost as good as quills in elasticity. At its peak, his business produced over five tons of steel pens weekly, employing 450 people, GillottGillott also had a reputation for treating his workforce well. He was a major collector of paintings and musical instruments, including a Stradivarius violin. He frequently partnered with dealers like Gambart in print publishing enterprises and epitomizes a new type of collector/investor that entered the market. His collection was sold at Christie's in 1872, after his death. The instrument sale alone realized £4195 9s 6d, approximately £5 million today. His art collection was sold over six days and raised a total of £164,501, more than £165 million today.][6]

In many ways, painters had paved the road. Their success in creating innovative methods to sell directly to the public had familiarized English art-loving consumers with new ways of viewing and purchasing art. Established art dealers and other enterprising gentlemen from different walks of life saw their opportunities refined the now proven marketing methods pioneered by artists and added a few new tricks of their own.

Artists were conscious of this increasing influence of the trade. The famous painter Holman Hunt (1827–1910) claimed that 'affluent connoisseurs, whatever their independent instincts might be, did not in modern England decide upon art by their own judgment, but were guided by the voice of the majority and of dealers'. It was generally known that 'it is now in the rooms of the most eminent picture dealers that we must look for those productions of our painters ...'.[7]

Art consumers apparently did not mind paying a little extra to the gentlemen in the middle. 'So long as buyers would rather give five hundred pounds to a dealer for a picture than three hundred for the same picture to the artist, the dealer was necessary to the artist himself', P. C. Hamerton, the lead figure behind the Etching Revival, wrote in 1868.[8] *The Illustrated London News* commented in 1862 'surely these are the golden days for the picture dealers…'.[9] Finally, in December 1871, Samuel Carter Hall, the editor of the *Art Journal*, summed it up: 'The influence of the dealer is one of the chief characteristics of modern art'.[10] This fact has not changed since then.

A market for modern paintings had developed in London and on the Continent that was defined by middlemen. As a result, the competitiveness inherent to their business shaped the commodities in which they traded. Mass-appeal, 'sensation' potential, and ever-increasing product differentiation were manifestations of this dynamic. The rise of narrative and domestic-themed pictures, the surge of landscape painting, and the revival of dramatic, baroque-like visual epics followed by an unprecedented proliferation of styles, all signaled a fiercely competitive art market hinged to the activities of dealers. These trends were also indicators of the art market's continuous commoditization.

Market Intervention

The use of art works as portable assets traded in a market with advantageous characteristics spread steadily. For countless families on the war-torn Continent, the art they managed to get to London and offer for sale, with or without the involvement of a middleman, was among the few hard assets that were moveable and maintained liquidity. By mid-nineteenth century, this perception of art as a portable liquid asset, as Thomas Winstanley already observed much earlier, had taken root in the collective consciousness of not just England, but of all Europe. 'Investing' in art, rather than collecting it, became fashionable. The famous Leonardo panel would not have been sold for four hundred million dollars were it not for the fact that art works have a well-established track record going back centuries as a reliable storage for wealth.

'Investing' in something sounds so much smarter and more sophisticated as a rationale for spending money. Nowadays, consumers do not engage in such mundane activities as 'buying' something. We casually remark that we are thinking about 'investing' in a new car. Or we 'invest' in a new dress, suit, handbag, or even a pair of shoes. All these consumer goods have one thing in common: they are expensive, and they rapidly lose value the moment we have 'invested' our hard-earned money in them. As an investment strategy, this approach should have limited appeal. But apparently the opposite is true.

Let us return to the topic of market intervention. Auction data show that in apparent contradiction to the rules of arbitrage—buy low, sell high—the average amount dealers paid for paintings at auction was substantially higher than the sums spent by any other category of buyers, save museums and similar institutions that have the convenient privilege of spending other people's money.[11]

This is counterintuitive. Shouldn't middlemen, as arbitrageurs, purchase as cheaply and then sell as expensively as market conditions permit? Why pay more than just about anyone else? Were they competing amongst themselves for the best works? No, the data nixes this assumption. Dealers, in fact, largely pursued non-competitive buying strategies: each of the major trade buyers bought in their clearly defined 'stable' and rarely transgressed into someone else's territory.[12]

If it's not competition, what else could explain this puzzling buying strategy? In a business in which middlemen customarily purchased goods for inventory directly from artists, shouldn't paying more at auction—plus additional transaction costs—get you something extra in return?

Yes! And, indeed, it did. The art business is a for-profit affair, after all. A market controlled to such extents by middlemen commoditizes to meet the collective interests of its dominant participants. In this case, dealers simply paid a premium to take full advantage of the public nature of auctions and its associated publicity value. Press coverage of art auctions enjoyed great popularity and was featured not just in the specialized art press, but also in daily newspapers, such as *The Times*. Of course, the press focused on what readers wanted to read. Most reports on auctions, even those on the weekly routine sales, included prices. There was even a special column in London papers for auction sales reports. Art auctions, in general, were newsworthy events, just like they are today. Every opportunity was taken to show the increase in price of a recently sold work compared to what it had originally cost. As best as I can judge by the volume and type of media coverage, interest in the arts in general enjoyed similar widespread public appeal as it does at present.

Here is an example. In June of 1863, *The Art Journal* published a partial cost and benefit report of the sale of the collection of the wealthy shipping magnate, Elhanan Bicknell, at Christie's held two months earlier. The owner had originally spent £6810 for the twenty-six oils and nine watercolors, and the sale realized a total of £39,015. Without the purchasing dates of each work, it is impossible to calculate an annualized return. However, the gross return represents a 572% yield on Bicknell's initial investment. No doubt, the *The Art Journal's* coverage of such a staggering profit from an investment in contemporary British paintings contributed to the perception of profitability of art market speculation. Art as an investment asset had entered mainstream.

Auction prices were—and are—powerful signals to the public on the state of the market. It only made sense for dealers to pay on average noticeably more for paintings at these heavily publicized events to advertise a healthy state of the market.

Perpetuating this aura of profitability of private investments in contemporary paintings benefitted the interest of artists, middlemen, as well as consumers with a stake in the market. The famous painter W. P. Frith commented that 'investment, a love of display, and a spirit of speculation … are the guiding-star of many of the picture buyers of the present day'.[13] Note that 'Investment' leads his list. Turning Karel van Mander's comment of 300 years earlier (quoted at the beginning of this book) on its head, in this case money followed art for its rich rewards. The lure of profit was a rational incentive to express one's cultural aspirations through the purchase of art.

However, what the public may have perceived as an open competitive market was in fact a system of informal collusion and networking among dealers. This was not unknown to art market insiders. *The Art Journal* featured an entire expose on specific aspects of this trade collaboration in its August 1852 issue.[14] As the dealer Arthur Tooth's business records reveal, dealers constantly bought from, sold or consigned works to each other.[15] The London art dealing scene was quite small, and everyone knew one another either personally or indirectly. It did not need any clandestine formal agreement to engage in tacit cooperation. A 'nod and a wink' sufficed. It still does today.

[The term 'ring' is often used as an example of a type of collaboration at an auction. A ring serves the opposite purpose than the one I describe. It is formed when a group of buyers at an auction decides ahead of time to collaborate by refraining from bidding against one another on specific works to keep prices low. Whatever is bought at this sale is later sold at a private auction—'knock-out auction' in trade jargon—and the resulting profits are distributed among the individual members of the ring. Every now and then, with a little luck, it is possible to participate in a ring by feigning interest in a lot in which you have no interest whatsoever and cash in at the knock-out event. It should pay for the hotel room, at least.]

Here is an example. In a letter of June 27, 1862, barely four months after the sale of the estate of the mega-collector, Thomas Plint (1823–1861), who had died surprisingly at age 38, the celebrated painter J. E. Millais (1829–1896) made the perplexing remark that 'nearly all the picture sales we have seen in the papers have been false'.[16] What did he mean by 'false'? Plint's death had unexpectedly put over three hundred, mostly Pre-Raphaelite, works onto the block. The auction catalogues of the spring 1862 season at Christie's typically listed almost exclusively dealers' names as buyers. However, hidden from the public, the catalogues also recorded the first failures of works by such celebrated cornerstones of the English artists pantheon as Edwin Landseer and Rosa Bonheur to reach their reserve prices.

In the same letter Millais bemoaned the saturation of the market with contemporary paintings. '...[t]here are so many works by Phillip, Frith, Ansdell, and the lot in the hands of [the dealer] Gambart, that if they fail [at auction] they must be sold anyhow'. Millais was referring to dealer-owned paintings about to come up for auction, implying that if a work would fail to reach its reserve, the dealer, Ernest Gambart, will make sure that would be sold.

'Working the oracle' was how painters described the business ways of this dealer, undoubtedly, the greatest of the Victorian Age.[17] Under his management, contemporary paintings went on worldwide tours as far as the United States and Australia, earning vast sums of money for both him and their artists. In 1856, Rosa Bonheur's *The Horse Fair*, for example,

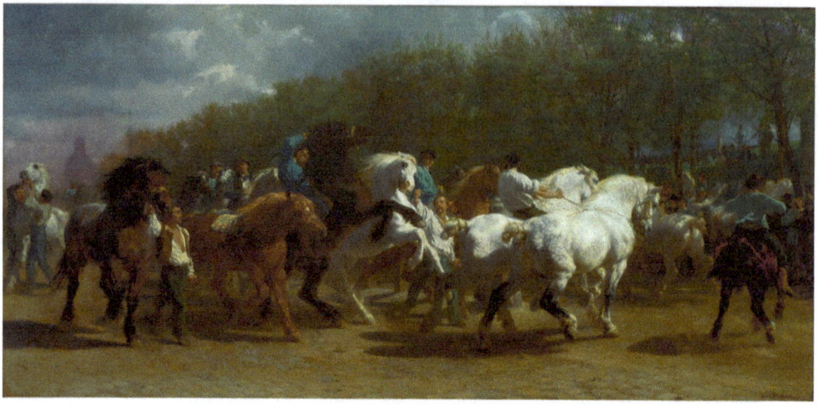

Fig. 12.1 Rosa Bonheur (1822–1899), Horse Fair

went on a six-year-long global exhibition tour and was henceforth dubbed 'circumnavigator'. This globe-trotting sensation picture is currently on view at the Metropolitan Museum in New York (Fig. 12.1).[18]

Such professionally organized, public launches of cultural products had even a moral dimension. Dealers were portrayed as missionaries who brought—at great effort and personal expense, mind you—the civilizing effects, i.e., public benefit, of art to the 'great unwashed'.[19] I can think of many present-day art dealers who would only be too pleased—perhaps even surprised—to be described in such an apostolic context. It was these devout crusaders of culture, the great Victorian art dealing champions, like Thomas Agnew, Victor Flatou, Arthur Tooth, Dominic Colnaghi, or Ernest Gambart, who, together with legions of small-time operators, set the modus operandi for international dealing in modern art that prevails to this day.

These dealer-champions were expected to take regulatory action to mitigate the negative effects of an unpredictable market by providing liquidity for the products in which they traded. This practice was not limited to dealers. Even the great master, J.M.W. Turner, as we have already observed, habitually and openly bid on his paintings, and occasionally even bought them back. The press lauded him for doing so.

Dealers publicly paid high prices not only to project market stability, but also to increase the values of works already in their inventory. As stakeholders, they created capital gains by market intervention. Think of it as publicly traded company buying its own stock.

Here is an example. Dealer X who used to represent a recently deceased artist and still owns a large inventory of works is planning a retrospective exhibition. X arranges with a business friend/collaborator Y to consign to auction, under Y's name, one of the artist's best pieces still in the dealer's storeroom. Then, at the auction, the dealer X bids conspicuously and aggressively so that everyone notices. Another friend Z who also has several nice works by the same artist agrees to step in as an underbidder. The purpose is to signal the public that the artist's dealer wants this piece for the planned exhibition at any cost, against any and all competition. After intense, head-turning competition, dealer X wins the battle for the work by paying a record-breaking price. The media reports the staggering amount the piece fetched and gives a description of the heated contest, perhaps even interviews the dealer, thus providing free publicity for the artist, the dealer, the auction house, and the upcoming exhibition.

A few weeks after the auction, this record price-making work is now prominently displayed in X's gallery exhibition for a price just modestly above the price paid at auction. This serves to counter the ugly rumor that art dealers are greedy. But, most importantly, collectors of the artist's work love the fact that prices are going up and their earlier investment in this artist's paintings is showing excellent results. This provides a perfect opportunity for the dealer to pitch to exhibition visitors that now is the time to buy more. The market for this artist's work is hot! The dealer's demonstrative support of the artist at auction positively affects overall market confidence. And since the dealer has raised the prices of all the other paintings in the exhibition in line with the newly established record level, the whole venture stands to make a tidy profit as a result. The cost of this maneuver is no more than the auction house's buyer's premium and seller's fee—which are negotiable—and, perhaps, a small charge for the color photo in the catalogue. These expenses are easily recouped with the first sale at the exhibition.

This use of auctions is also helpful for dealers to promote 'rediscovered' artists or certain niches, say, regional or ethnic art, stylistic commonalities, political or gender orientation, etc. It's a cost-effective pricing and publicity tool. The trick is knowing how to pull it off.

Auction data provide further evidence for the deliberate use of auctions' publicity potential in the form of dealer-to-dealer sales via auction. These sales happened so frequently that they could not have been coincidental. Over one-third of all paintings consigned by dealers during the second half of the nineteenth century were bought by other dealers.[20]

Why not save the transactions costs and just put the word out privately among your friends in the business? Perhaps the extra expense of selling through auction had a specific and more important benefit: to influence the public's perception of the state of the market for certain artists' works. In our current, mature, stage of the art market, this practice is an old hat.

By no means do I want to suggest an image of London picture dealers as unprincipled and deceitful. Of course, there existed fast-talking, slick wheeler-dealers who, as the editor of *The Art Journal*, warned 'trade in the most unscrupulous ways'.[21] In general, however, correspondence between artists, dealers, and collectors reflected noticeable high standards in their business activities.[22]

In today's art market, the choreographed high-end regulatory collaboration is largely performed on the stages of the world's leading auction houses. But the practice exists on all levels of the art market. The difference is only in the size of the stakes involved.

This cooperation is effective. There has never been a real crash in the art market. Interest and support change; yesterday's superstars are quietly forgotten, upstaged by the fanfares and hyperbole proclaiming new heroes. Novelty reigns supreme.

Such collaboration managed the re-appearance on the market of overpriced, often mediocre, works previously acquired by Japanese collectors in the early 1980s. Admirable team effort was also behind the handling of art sales during the financial crisis of 2008–2010.

Art dealing is a growth industry with no end in sight. *The Art Journal's* observation in 1871, quoted at the beginning of this section, that the art dealer 'has taken the place of the patron, and to him has been owing, to a great extent, the immense increase in the prices of modern pictures' turned out to be remarkably prophetic. These days, hardly anyone in the high-net-worth crowd is without their personal art dealer. No doubt, there are bundles of money to be made on Wall Street or the City. But there are also rich rewards in art dealing on the top level.

Of course, there are plenty of art lovers out there who simply make a living dealing in the art they love. It is fortunate that the art milieu is so rich in people driven by a sincere and deep passion for the art they trade in, rather than just by greed. But to be fair, a top dealer in contemporary art must be a rich dealer in contemporary art to do the job well. Market making requires money, and it is particularly important when major works or large collections of contemporary paintings unexpectedly come on the block and put pressure on existing demand. In an environment in which stability is very much a factor of the public's perception, appearance is more important than something akin to current price/earnings ratios. Prices of contemporary art exist in a quasi-bubble. 'Quasi', because until a bubble bursts, it is simply an expanding market. Since dealers create the primary market—the potential 'bubble'—it is essential that their financial support of artists' works extends to the secondary market to prevent it from bursting. The same conditions prevail in the old master market, save a fixed supply of works.

The undertakings of Victorian picture dealers were huge in terms of general scope and financial commitment. Erratic fluctuations of prices of publicly traded works would have undermined consumer confidence and led to panic selling with possibly devastating effects. The economic fate of countless individuals, from artists, printers, engravers, and large and small retailers to various types of collectors, some of whom had invested extraordinary amounts in contemporary paintings, depended on the perceived state of a market that was well integrated in the economic mainstream. Middlemen could, and did, intervene when they deemed it necessary. To that end, they developed strategies to create a relatively stable market environment for contemporary paintings and to promote their quality as a reliable storage of exchangeable value.

The business interests of dealers were the conduit for capital to become and remain the 'nurse and governess of art'. The regulatory measures taken by the industry were—and are—an indispensable ingredient to the establishment of art as a financial asset. They also helped chart the course for the unprecedented explosion of artistic and art collecting activity in Victorian Britain.

Despite this market intervention, *laissez-faire* still ruled. As soon as dealers' business interests shifted during the final decades of the nineteenth century away from contemporary works back to Old Masters and towards newly emerging styles, traditional Victorian paintings were consigned to the backstage. It would take nearly seventy years before they would again assume a place in the spotlight. Not surprisingly, their recovery was led in the 1970s by an excellent team of British dealers, scholars, and London-based auction houses. But that is a story for another day.

Notes

1. Art Journal, December (1871): 285.
2. Bayer/Page data.
3. Here is but a small selection of recent studies on this topic: Robert H. Frank "The Role of Talent and Luck in Achieving Fame", Journal of Economic Perspectives, 30(3) (2016): 71–86; Jo Piazza, "The Business of Fame: How Celebrities Create and Manage Their Brands", Journal of Brand Management, 26(1) (2019): 34–46; Sherwin Rosen, ¨The Economics of Superstars", American Economic Review, 71(5) (1981): 845–858; Ansgar Zerfass et al. "The Impact of Social Media on Achieving Fame", Journal of Communication Management, 21 (2017): 2–16.
4. Bayer/Page data; Thomas Bayer, ¨Arthur Tooth, A London Art Dealer in the Spotlight, 1870–71,¨Nineteenth-Century Art Worldwide, vol. 9, 1 (2010), https://www.19thc-artworldwide.org/spring10/arthur-tooth. (Last accessed March 2025.
5. Wilkie Collins, A Rogue's Life (London: Richard Bentley & Sons, 1879): 47; Jeremy Maas, Gambart (London: Barrie & Jenkins, 1975): 43, quoting this letter written on July 4, 1850, by Rought without providing a source. According to Rupert Maas, this letter may have been part of his father's extensive collection of art-related correspondence from the Victorian period.
6. Joshua Eversfield Jenkins, ¨Joseph Gillott and the Rise of the Collector - dealer¨, Edinburgh Research Archives (2023), https://era.ed.ac.uk/handle/1842/40821 (last accessed March 2025).
7. Holman Hunt, Pre-Raphaelitism and the Pre-Raphaelite Brotherhood, 2 vols. (London: Macmillan, 1905), vol. 1: 217.
8. Philip. G. Hamerton, Etchers and Etching (London: Macmillan, 1868): 74.
9. Illustrated London News, October 11 (1862): 7.
10. *Art Journal*, December 1871, p. 280,
11. Bayer/Page data.
12. Bayer/Page data sorted by dealers and picture type.
13. William P. Frith, *My Autobiography and Reminiscences*, vol 2 vols. (N. Y.: Harper & Brothers, 1888), vol.1: 30, vol. 2: 143.
14. Art Journal, August 1852, p. 246.
15. Bayer, ¨Arthur Tooth, A London Art Dealer in the Spotlight, 1870–71¨.
16. Letter to Effie of June 27, 1861. Pierpont Morgan Library, New York. Accession number: MA1485D, record identification: 132647.
17. William Bell Scott in a letter to James Leathart of 21 March, 1870. Leathart papers, Victoria and Albert Museum, London.
18. Maas: 75–76, 79, 92–93, 158.

19. Gerald Reitlinger, Economics of Taste: The Rise and Fall of Picture Prices, 1760–1960 (N.Y.: Hacker Art Books, 1982):143; Maas: 28.
20. Bayer/Page auction data sorted by dealers as buyers and sellers and title of work.
21. There are comprehensive accounts of two of the major dealers' activities, Agnew and Gambart. For the history of Agnew see, Geoffrey Agnew, Agnew's, 1817–1967 (London: Bradbury Agnew Press, Ltd., 1967); for Gambart see Maas.
22. The Life and Letters of Frederic Shields, E. Mills, ed. (London: Longmans, Green and Co., 1912): 74.

CHAPTER 13

Constructing the Trading Platform: Auctions and Auctioneers

I described earlier how dealers and, to some extent, also artists, creatively used auctions to their best advantage. Dealers were well ahead in this game. While English painters were deliberating over new ways to get their product to a wider public, dealers were busy getting familiar with this relatively new sales method. It had been introduced in England only recently, and learning how to use it effectively was paramount.

Sales by auctions are an ingenious way to sell or buy something that does not have a fixed market price but a value that is difficult to establish. Like art, for example. Who's to say what it is worth?

Selling by auction has been around for thousands of years. The word itself is ancient, rooted in the Latin term 'augere', meaning 'to increase' or 'to augment'. The custom even predates the Roman Empire. In ancient Babylon, for instance, the only legal way for a father to sell his daughter was by auction, as the grandfather of all historians Herodotus (c.484 BC–c. 425 BC) tells us.[1]

In theory, auctions are an impartial mechanism for different parties to transfer ownership rights. In that context, auctions should perform a similar function for paintings as the stock exchange does for certain financial products. The key phrase here is 'impartial'.

For bidders, there's no need to reveal their budget limit. They only need to outbid their competitors by a minimal margin. If all opposing bidders concede before reaching the winner's limit, the winner pays less than

T. M. Bayer, *The Genesis of the Modern Art Market in London, 1700–1900*, https://doi.org/10.1007/978-3-032-00594-6_13

their limit and saves money. But auctions also benefit sellers. Competitive bidding ensures they receive the highest possible price for each item on that specific day. This is the underlying principle of auctions. However, in reality, auction dynamics can deviate from this theoretical framework. Why?

To answer that question, let us look specifically at the origins of selling art by auction and how this method developed over time to become the international art market's primary reference point that it is today.

The first record of any art sold by auction in England dates to 1674.[2] It immediately caught on. Right from the start, auctions were hugely popular among the social elite as well as the nascent middle class. They all enjoyed buying at these events or attending as spectators for the fun of it. During the next decade or so, auctions became the established method for dealers to offer paintings for sale. Over 300 advertised sales took place in a span of only six years. This amounts to an average of one major painting auction a week. Estimations based on old catalogues suggest that as many as 90,000 paintings may have been offered on the block during that time.[3]

The extent of trading activity is truly extraordinary. We are looking at a 12-month average of over 15,000 pictures, or approximately 300 individual lots each week distributed over roughly 50 auctions each year. Unfortunately, I was unable to find sufficient information to determine what types of paintings were sold and for what price. Customs records indicate that very few paintings were imported at the time, and we can therefore assume that most of the pieces offered were already in England.[4] Beyond that, not much else is known. However, this astonishing volume of sales corroborates that 300 years ago selling paintings by auction was already a well-established custom in England. These numbers also attest to impressive amounts of surplus capital dispersed among a sizable number of consumers accustomed to purchasing something that had no obvious utility. Silver candelabras had a use, clocks had a use, silver flat ware and china had a use. But paintings? Besides filling an empty spot on a wall and providing visual pleasure, what use did pictures have? It is plausible that the high trading volume indicates that paintings were already then thought of as a storage of value. Auctioneers customarily drummed up business with promises of ready cash to owners of paintings.[5]

The romance with art auctions was contagious—and intentionally so. Auctions were a great opportunity, just as they are today, for the finer folks to get together, enjoy people-watching, to mingle, to gossip, to converse, affectedly or not, about connoisseurship and current erudite writings about art. In the absence of commercial galleries and museums, these auctions were the only opportunity the English public had to become familiar with paintings.

The events were also an ideal place to show off with class and style by conspicuously spending money. Auctions were there 'for the diversion and entertainment of the gentlemen and ladies', as one auctioneer advertised. Ladies were specifically targeted. One auctioneer went so far as to advertise specifically the 'convenience of galleries' set aside for 'ladies and gentlewomen' in the *London Gazette*.[6] While the business of art and the trade in paintings was still the preserve of men, the targeted consumer audience very much included women. They ruled the domestic sphere, and decisions over décor were their responsibility. Allegedly, budgetary decisions were still the man's domain, although reality may well have been different. In any case, these auctioneers certainly considered women to be important customers.

From all accounts, art auctions were all the rage as a new entertainment venue. Here is a poem of sorts written about these events.

> In curious paintings I'm exceeding nice
> and know their several beauties by their price.
> Auctions and Sales I constantly attend,
> But chose my pictures by a skillful friend.
> Originals and copies much the same,
> The picture's value is the painter's name.
> My taste in sculpture from my choice is seen,
> I buy no statues that are not obscene.[7]

I have no idea what the writer meant by the closing rhyme.

Evidently, at the time, consumer enthusiasm was not inhibited by the fact that these sales were riddled with obvious fakes. One commentator described them as 'a kind of gaming, where the knowing ones employ all the wiles and artifices imaginable to make dupes of the unwary; and too often they succeed'.[8] What a fine description of information asymmetry—apropos and still accurate today.

By the 1730s, auctions dominated the London art market, serving as the primary platform for buying and selling paintings. The thriving auction scene highlighted the artworks' desirable trait: liquidity. Auctioneers actively touted this benefit, emphasizing the ease with which these assets could be converted into cash.

Art auctions were taking place all over England. Provincial sales offered mainly qualitatively lower and much cheaper consignments than those in London. It only makes sense that London-based dealers, or knowledgeable amateurs, would also attend provincial sales, either in person or through a capable representative, looking for arbitrage opportunities.[9] As I mentioned in an earlier context, fanciful attributions of many of the offered paintings to well-known artists were rather indiscriminatingly and optimistically noted in the catalogues. But who knew what really hid under the darkened varnish and the grime of age? Was it worth making a low bid for it? Unfortunately, these early catalogues did not list prices, making it impossible to determine the quality of the lots offered at these provincial sales, or if, and to what extent, such arbitrage scenarios occurred. However, it makes business sense, and I feel on solid ground with the assumption that this bottom-feeding happened. Information asymmetry is common in the art market.

Even with today's far more symmetrical information distribution, dealers and private collectors still attend small sales of lower quality goods in secondary locations to look for the proverbial 'find'. The Leonardo panel is a good example. It sold at one of the small local auction houses in New Orleans, far away from the buzzling art capitals of the Western world, for a paltry US$ 1175.00. What a 'find'! And what great publicity for small provincial auction houses such stories are!

Already very early in this *menage a trois* romance of paintings, auctions and audience, the auction industry began to refine its ways. Contemporary commentators on the arts milieu explicitly emphasize the efficiency and consumer orientation of these sales.[10] The customer's needs were paramount. To enhance the sales process, policies and regulations were implemented to ensure efficient transactions and prompt payment for purchased items. Remarkably, these auction regulations established over 300 years ago remain largely unchanged today as testament to their enduring effectiveness.

One regulation is worth pointing out. It aimed to shield auctioneers from frivolous or fraudulent bidders. The existence of this rule highlights the auctions' vulnerability to manipulation. Auctioneers were clearly wary of shill bidders. However, history reveals that regulations often are but an invitation to find ways to circumvent them, thus undermining their intended purpose.

In the old days, registration before an auction was non-existent. Nowadays, even an ordinary visitor to one of these carefully choreographed tournaments must show identification or, in certain cases, even an invitation to be admitted. Bidders are required to provide additional financial references before being permitted to participate in one of these headline-making orchestrations.

There is no documentation for similar vetting processes during the early days of the auction business. However, marketing began to adapt to appeal specifically to the targeted audience. Several of the forward-thinking auctioneers started to pay writers to compose easily readable pamphlets on the appreciation of art. They used verbiage suitable for the audience and handed the brochures out to the attending crowd and elsewhere around town. These guides, available at various auctions, were by themselves already an audience attraction. And the auction catalogues also listed increasingly more reliable and useful information on individual lots. It was during this time that previous ownership, i.e., provenance, began to become part of an art work's valuation.[11]

Many of these early auctions initially were set up at coffee houses and taverns rather than in custom-designed spaces like they are today. Wherever there was room for people to gather was suitable.[12] By mid-eighteenth century, however, sales at fixed locations conducted by professional auctioneers had become standard.

[Auction records list Edward Millington, one of the earliest pioneers of the profession, who, already in 1692, was conducting regular sales at his location, 'The Vendu'; by 1694, James Cock's auction house started doing business and by 1697, Edward Davis][13]

Auctions of paintings, however, were not just opportunities for trading. They also fueled consumption. One contemporary observer commented that 'This sort of sales' [art auctions] 'have spread a pretty general taste for pictures in London; a taste which they not only excite but form; there you learn to know the different schools and different masters'.[14]

Occasionally, spectacular prices were achieved.[15] Auction data indicate that more affluent buyers tended to focus on one expensive picture—a 'centerpiece'—and then bought inexpensive pictures or copies to fill up the rest of their walls.[16] Unfortunately, this practice depressed the prices living painters could charge for copies or for their own original compositions. Nevertheless, from time to time, native artists used auction facilities to sell their works. They would stage their own sales or exhibit their works on the walls of established auction facilities. Occasionally, original paintings by contemporary painters would also appear on the block as part of large private collections that were put up for sale. Sometimes, the executors of estates of recently deceased artists would use auctions to liquidate studio contents.[17]

In the latter half of the century, a modest yet discernible rise occurred in the number of works by living artists sold at London auctions.[18] The outbreak of wars with Spain in 1739 and then France in 1744 likely contributed to this shift, as importation challenges forced the industry to rely more heavily on locally produced art, thereby increasing demand for works by domestic painters.

By the 1770s, London's auction houses were thriving, fueled by the Continent's unstable politics and looming wars. Wealthy collectors, forced to liquidate their assets, flocked to London, showcasing art's unique value in high-profile sales. Simultaneously, local estates were sold, featuring a mix of Continental and English works. London's auction industry solidified its position as Europe's largest art marketplace, with contemporary artists' works increasingly appearing. This trend would continue to grow to become a cornerstone of the mid-Victorian art market.

Throughout the eighteenth century, art auctions evolved to accommodate an expanding market. Initially, they focused on selling foreign collections brought to London by dealers. As the market grew, local entrepreneurs entered the scene, incorporating older local stock and newly produced works into their sales. Specialization followed, with professional auctioneers establishing fixed locations and dealers becoming retail gallery operators. Auctioneers bore minimal risk. Goods were sold on consignment, and the auction house earned a commission, usually around ten percent of the hammer price. Even when items were bought-in, i.e., failed to reach their reserve price, the auctioneer still received compensation, sometimes the same amount as if the lots had, in fact, sold.

During the eighteenth century's first half, the auction business diverged into two paths. Firms like Langford, Cock, Prestage, and Christie's catered to high-society clients, while another type of auctioneer, originating from the Upholders' Company, focused on selling second-hand household goods. These upholsterers-turned-auctioneers had been granted this right in the sixteenth century.

By 1770s, London auction houses were booming due to the progressively unstable political environment and the threat of revolution and war on the Continent. The city became the go-to place for the owners of many of the great collections of the Continent who were forced to turn their art assets into much-needed cash.

Once more, the special asset quality of art was conspicuously demonstrated in public and well-publicized events. At the same time, the auction rooms also profited from the sales of numerous private local estates that included a broad mixture of Continental and English works. By this time, London auction houses were firmly established as the largest clearing houses for art, both old and new. This trend was to increase steadily. During the subsequent nineteenth century, the use of auctions for trading in the works of living artists became a nexus of the mid- Victorian contemporary art market.

The eighteenth century also witnessed the first legal regulations of the auction business beyond the conditions of sale first created a hundred years earlier.[19] These laws dealt with licensing and the mechanics of conducting business, such as bidding up pictures by an accomplice. The fact that such laws were passed shows that this practice was not uncommon. The widely known problems of attribution, however, were ignored. *Caveat emptor* still prevailed, a fact that must have retarded overall market growth. However, this inefficiency of the auction market stimulated business for professional dealers on whose advice private buyers increasingly depended. Still, for the market to continue to expand, at some point, some type of consumer protection policies and/or guarantees of authenticity would be needed to reduce risk.

Nonetheless, despite the lack of such warranties, the earlier described improvements in consumer appeal and mechanisms of buying and selling yielded results. Their success is validated by the crucial role they played in the establishment of the auction market as the point of reference for the art market in general. By mid-nineteenth century, auction prices had become the price indices of the picture market. Reviews of sales took on the character of financial reports, a trend that has continued and grown in importance to this day. Maintaining the auction industry's hegemonic position required entrepreneurship, media-savvy, seductive glamour, theatrics, and wheeling-and-dealing. These skills are employed to provide skillful guidance of a synergy of interests that is fused together by a common focus on the management of the market for the most enjoyable wealth storage of all—art. Recent investigations of Christie's early auctions reveal remarkable success in achieving sales prices very much in line with presale estimates.[20] Clearly, James Christie knew how to deliver for his clients. Exactly how he accomplished this, however, is not disclosed in the records. It would be useful to know the identity of the buyers at these sales. Was Mr. Christie relying on dealers to help him produce results in line with his predictions?

Before art auctions changed from being mainly the territory of dealers to becoming, once again, the playground for private consumers, few warranties were offered by any leading auction houses. It was assumed that purchasers were aware of the risks and made their decisions based on personal knowledge and connoisseurship concerning questions of value, authenticity, and physical condition of the works for which they intended to bid.

However, starting in the 1970s, an industry-wide campaign began to target the less experienced, private buyers of art—the traditional customers of the art dealers. When I entered the business in 1974 at age 21, this transition was in progress, and presale views were increasingly attended by private individuals.

[I was fortunate to have been taught by dealers who had been in business for thirty or forty years. To inspect a painting at a presale viewing, I would often pull my suit jacket over my head to block out the light as much as possible and use a portable UV light and magnifying glass to inspect a canvas to check for evidence of restoration, or examine it from the side with the glare of overhead lights obfuscating the image but reflecting on the painted surface. One could usually notice the newcomers by their bewilderment at what I, and others too, were doing. Terms like 'flattened impasto', 'craquelure', 'alligatoring', or 'lining' meant nothing to them.]

Auction houses sought to tap into the profitable retail market dominated by professional dealers. They wanted to sell art directly to consumers, as they had done in the eighteenth and early nineteenth centuries. To achieve this 'retailization', auction firms created elaborate, detailed, and beautifully designed catalogues, highlighting the merits, history, and provenance of each lot. Additionally, they established 'Special Client

Services' to assist novice buyers with registration, credit references, and art-related queries, such as packing, insurance, and shipping. Auction staff would also gauge newcomers' interests and questions, providing personalized attention that both flattered potential buyers and helped determine their budgets. To sidestep potential conflicts of interest inherent in advice given by paid representatives of the seller, some collectors preferred to bring their own dealer or art advisor, leading to the emergence of independent buyer advisory services, such as the International Art Association, I founded in 1979.

To up the ante for customer service, certain auction companies began offering advances on consignments and financing of purchases through their newly set up 'Financial Services' departments. Private owners now could walk in off the street with a painting under their arm, and, with the help of the Special Clients office and the Financial Services Department, walk back out *sans* art, but with a check of up to 50% of the work's estimated pre-sale value. The auction houses, in other words, functioned as *de facto* banks specializing in loans on art. This practice is not without pitfalls. If the collateralized artwork does not meet the reserve price, and the owner cannot pay back the loan, the auction house is stuck with an asset stigmatized by a failed offering. In multiples, such scenarios can turn into a significant financial headache for the lender.

Furthermore, the auction house is no longer an impartial exchange agent, but a party of interest, a fact which changes the dynamics of the transaction. Due to the undisclosed nature of these arrangements, the currently in vogue quantitative analyses of the art auction market do not account for such scenarios and thus render their results questionable.[21] Recently, some of the auction houses are disclosing such ownership interests prior to selling a lot in which they hold a stake.

Offering financing on purchases is similarly wrought with difficulties. A classic example is the 1987 purchase at Sotheby's of Van Gogh's floral still life, *Irises* (1889) by the Australian brewing, media and property magnate, Alan Bond, for $ 53.9 million. At the time, this was the highest price ever paid at auction for any work of art. Today, this amount sounds modest compared to the $ 117 million paid for the artist's *Orchard with Cypresses* in 2022 or the nearly $180 million paid for Picasso's *The Women of Algiers (Version 0)* in 2015. To purchase the painting, Mr. Bond had taken out a loan of around $ 27 million from the auction house. Unfortunately, due to a series of financial reversals, Mr. Bond was unable to repay the loan. When the details of the deal became known, there were widespread concerns about artificial price inflation. Some three years later, Sotheby's sold the canvas to the Getty Museum in California for an undisclosed sum, rumored to be between $ 50 to $ 70 million. Luckily, this deal worked out at the end. It is unknown how many others have fared less well. Transparency is not among the pronounced characteristics of the art market.

More recently, auction firms are offering third-party guarantees to eliminate the risk of artworks failing to sell. Owners of particularly desirable works do not want the stigma of a failed offering negatively affect the reputation/value of their prized possessions. For this arrangement, one, or even more, private individuals or dealers contractually agree ahead of the actual auction to purchase the art in question for a specified sum should bidding not reach the reserve. If the lot would exceed the amount, they could, of course, bid themselves, if they so choose. They could also just sit back and wait for their compensation for the use of their money. Usually, it would be a percentage of the difference between the amount the auction house guaranteed and the final selling price. Some years ago, the owner of a particularly fine sculpture by Jacques Lipchitz had hired me to assist her in the auction sale of the piece. The remarkable quality and impeccable provenance of the work allowed me to negotiate a very favorable third-party guarantee. It worked out well for all parties involved.

But there are also occasions when there is simply no interest in an artwork, no third-party guarantee, no inquiries, nothing. Then, it might be the best strategy to withdraw the work just prior to the auction. Such a move avoids hurting the art works value with a very conspicuous failure to sell; it prevents the work being listed as bought-in in post-sale reports, and it can obfuscate a possible decline in an artist's popularity. The sudden withdrawal of Brice Marden's painting from Christie's major contemporary spring sale in May of 2024, estimated at $30–50 million, may have been such a case. The artist died the year before, and it appears that the anticipated post-mortem price increase was less than expected. 'It wasn't Brice's evening, and we're not willing to jeopardize the market of an artist like that', the sale's specialist explained.

Other enticements created by the auction industry were consumer protection measures designed to mollify the trepidations and insecurities of the uninformed. One of these risk-reducing methods took the form of detailed condition reports available upon inquiry. It eliminates the need to examine paintings personally and to acquire the knowledge of what to look for. Since these condition reports had to be requested from the auction house's staff, such an inquiry also revealed someone's curiosity about a specific lot. The resulting early identification of potential interest is a distinct advantage for the seller's agent, i.e., the auction house. Nowadays, it is rare to see someone at presale viewings, eyes close to the canvas, like I used to do, with a hand-held backlight, a magnifying glass, and a coat pulled over the head.

Further inducements were certificates of authenticity, a practice with a history as stellar as it is controversial, going back all the way to Arthur Pond in the eighteenth century.[22] In addition, auction houses offered their own warranties, usually described at the beginning of the sales catalogue. Degrees of certainty concerning authorship of specific pieces are distinguished by subtle differences in the listing of the name of the respective artists in the catalogue. All this deferred reliance on some other authority, unfortunately, negatively affected individual consumers' connoisseurship.

The value and trend-setting influence of auctions expanded further in the twenty-first century. Appraisals of paintings for income or estate tax purposes must now include comparable auction sales. In fact, a long-time former colleague collaborated with the Art Valuation section of the US Internal Revenue Service to streamline and codify the guidelines for valuations of art for tax purposes. The art market quickly adapts to these guidelines and intentionally manipulates the data needed to justify ever increasing deductions which, of course, benefit the high-net-worth crowd.

There exists a close and multi-dimensional relationship between public institutions, auction prices, and private collecting/donating. A record price at auction for a specific artist's work can trigger an increase in donations of comparable works to museums. The associated tax benefits are common knowledge. Museum exhibitions stimulate market activity and market/auction prices. In addition, works already in museum collections have a positive effect on the value of comparable works in private possession.

And so the wheel keeps turning. We must acknowledge the influence of financial considerations on the placement of works of art in the public domain. We should also be aware that these are precisely the objects which are commonly available to us for learning about the world of art, be that by visiting museums or attending art history lectures at school. We can quibble over the question if this is an accurate or curated representation of our visual culture.

Auction prices, as the art market's financial reference point, play an equally important role as a determinant of loan value in the increasing use of art as collateral. Art has been used in that manner for a long time. But, as of late, lending on art has become a growing niche for the banking industry. Major banks, Citi Private Bank or JPMorgan Private Bank, for example, provide loans collateralized with art to their high net-worth clients. I am confident that this is a growing niche. There is a lot of art around that can be monetized simply as collateral.

There is still more that relies on auction prices to provide reference points. Several boutique investment funds have recently been established that exclusively trade in art assets. To persuade investors, these funds' sales departments present auction performance data. The funds' managers also use this information to determine what and when to sell and what to buy. Treating the auction market as if it were the stock market, however, is fraught with problems. Individual shares of a company are identical, i.e. fungible, and can be graphed. An auction price graph of an individual artist's works, however, is inherently flawed because it does not reflect the fact that each price is the result of a sale of a unique item. This item might have been a good example of the artist's work, or a bad one; in bad condition; or sold for purposes other than liquidity; it could have been a shopped-around work, or a work in which the auction house had a financial stake. If during the period under observation, the majority of works of a given artist sold at auction were bad or mediocre, an auction price graph is an incorrect representation, a mere slice, of the artist's overall market performance.

A persuasive, if extreme, example for the misleading nature of auction price graphs is the Leonardo panel. A graph of Leonardo's auction prices from 2005 to 2020 would reflect a curve for which the incline is partially determined by a price of $ 1175 in 2005 and another price of $ 450,000,000 in 2017. An investor, ignorant of the working of the art auction market, would conclude that the auction market for Leonardo's work was extremely hot in those years, possibly the best performing artist during this period. Likewise, if a graph were created to show the auction market for Italian Renaissance paintings as a category and therefore include the Leonardo panel, it also would be skewed to the point of irrelevance.

In addition to funds investing in art, there are also instances where individual art works are being securitized. It is possible now to invest in a share of a specific work of art, which may translate into, say, 0.5 square inches of an original Basquiat. An old friend, a Catalan painter, acquired a 0.08% share in one of this artist's paintings. He sent me a photo of an enlarged minuscule section of the canvas, noting in the message in caps 'MINE'! The prospectus accompanying these deals are an amusing mixture of finance jargon, art history lingo, and disclaimer legalese. It is highly likely that the market will further commoditize, and the trading velocity will accelerate to take immediate advantage of buying or selling opportunities rather than depend on the physical auction stage as the only trading platform. Unfortunately, this ongoing commoditization of the art market is associated with increasing risk. The lessons of the 2008–2010 financial crisis and the fickle nature of derivatives should be remembered.

Auction prices are also reference points when an artwork is damaged or destroyed because of an insured-against event. Appraising works of art has become a lucrative pursuit. To satisfy the demand for higher standards, greater knowledge and professionalism are required—at a cost. Of course, no competent appraiser will rely on auction prices only. A credible estimation of the value of a work of art must take more than just recent auction sales into account. The appraiser also needs to research the dealer market and consider the currently available supply with regards to quality, asking price, and how long items have been on the market. In addition, the appraiser must have a level of connoisseurship and art historical knowledge to assess quality and relative importance. Moreover, a top-level appraiser also should know how to assess the art work's physical condition and degree of restauration. And to top it off, a professional appraiser is also personally liable for the accuracy of the appraisal. The sums of money at stake are rather intimidating, and for that reason, most professional appraisers carry a special liability insurance to protect themselves. The price for such high-level appraisal service is, understandably, high.

The story of certificates of authenticity follows a similar path. It has come a long way since the quaint method of the eighteenth-century artist/dealer, Arthur Pond. Simply writing the word 'true' on the back of a canvas with great airs of personal authority won't do anymore. Although this is not dissimilar to the habit of a venerated scholar and expert in the paintings of a particularly famous Flemish artist. Both are deceased and best remain anonymous. In *sotto voce* quivering with emotion, the revered academic would exclaim that he physically 'felt the presence of the Master' as a form of on-the-spot authentication.

It would be sensible to assume that the pre-requisites for issuing the all-important and much coveted Certificates of Authenticity should include a superior level of knowledge of the art object to be certified. But this is not the case. There are no international standards for 'art experts'.

This makes sense. With few exceptions, the art market is the deciding factor in the decision whether to accept some third party's subjective opinion about the authorship of a work of art or not. No degree or pedigree, no quivering voice or chest thumping should win the day, only the persuasiveness of the argument and the scholarship on which it is based. To be sure, the debates are intense and thorough. They are not casual exercises in jargon. Leonardo's *Salvator Mundi*, years after it was sold, is still a subject of heated debate among experts. The different arguments make fascinating reading.

Interestingly, in France, pedigree is, in fact, a factor in the issuance of authenticity certificates. By law, any direct relative of an artist, the closer the better, if designated as an heir, has the right to issue certificates of authenticity. Even artist's models and lovers have a claim under certain circumstances. Writing a voluminous catalogue raisonné is one way of staking such a claim.

Such a project might start by spreading the word of the intent to devote the next untold number of years to the pursuit of recording for posterity a great progenitor's contribution to the history of art—a *catalogue raisonne.* Anyone who has a work by the artist-ancestor is invited to send a high-quality photograph based on which the author of the catalogue will determine if it is worthy to be included in the great tome. Upon receiving the photograph, the owner is usually informed that a personal inspection is needed to assess reliably the merits of the submitted item. The hourly fee is such and such. If the physical examination has a positive outcome, the happy owner is advised that there is an additional fee for including this work in the catalogue. Printing costs, etc., etc.

The next opportunity to monetize such ancestry comes when this work goes to auction or is elsewhere offered for sale. The author/expert might receive a request from the seller or the seller's agent to write a letter that states that, indeed, the work shown in the photograph included in the request corresponds with the painting personally inspected by the author/expert and, furthermore, will be included in the still forthcoming oeuvre. The expert might even be asked for an official certificate of authenticity for which, naturally, there is also a charge. Sometimes, catalogue raisonné projects take a decade or more. I have had dealings with the elegant grandson of a great Post-Impressionist painter and with the charming former nude model of a famous sculptor. (She was dressed for our meeting.) But this scheme only works if the market accepts the expert's opinion. And the professionals in the market, I can confidently state, are very well informed the higher the values are.

Controlling the trading platform, i.e., the auction process is not primarily about earning commissions. It is about protecting and regulating the market. Sovereign Central Banks perform the same service for the market for which they are responsible. And we are generally happy about what they do, even if we might disagree with how they do their job. The only differences are that the art market can afford to take the longer view, and it is too small to cause economy-wide recessions. To maintain its qualifications as a sophisticated asset, art must be able to live up to the requirements of that task. Auctions play a fundamental part in this.

It makes, therefore, perfect sense that private ownership of the two leaders among international auction houses, Christie's, and Sotheby's has become such an appealing diversification for high-net-worth individuals. If one of them happens to own an array of famous luxury brands, this is a union made in heaven. No annoying shareholders and irritating transparency requirements make an already tough job even more difficult.

We currently have a duopolistic nexus prevailing in the auction industry. Christie's and Sotheby's, both now privately owned, have dominated the field for decades, even centuries. With branches in more than 40 different countries, they are the global powerhouses of the auction world. While there have been frequent attempts to break this duopolistic hegemony, none has succeeded so far.

For about 140 years, from the last two decades of the eighteenth century to the years between the two World Wars, Christie was the dominant player. Sotheby founded 22 years before Christie in 1744, initially specialized in books and only began selling art during the interwar years between WWI and WWII. Christie's hegemony was impressive. Auction data show that from around 1840 to 1900, as much as 90% of all major auction sales were in the hands of this firm.[23] An analysis of Christie's old bank records kept in the archives of Coutts might reveal evidence for payments of advances to secure important consignments as well as loans collateralized with works of art.

But there is the other side of the industry, the one away from the glittering spectacles of public sales. It is the responsibility of regulating the art market. Very deep pockets as well as a sophisticated understanding and appreciation of the uniqueness of art's asset characteristics are needed to choreograph the all-important headline making auction/publicity events. Furthermore, it requires the financial will, knowhow, and wherewithal to manage this market, and its associated liquidity needs simultaneously.

Notes

1. Herodotus, The Histories, (London: Penguin Publishing, 2003): chapter 196.
2. David Ormrod, "The Origins of the London Art Market 1660–1730," M. North and D. Ormrod, eds. Art Markets in Europe 1400–1800 (Aldershot: Ashgate Publishing, 1998): 167–186. These early auctions often contained also common household goods.
3. Brian Cowan, "Art and Connoisseurship in the Auction Market of Later Seventeenth-Century London", Mapping Markets for Paintings in Europe, 1450–1750 (Turnhout: Brepols 2006): 264 and n. 5, 271, table 16, 275. Cowan suggests that many more auctions took place than were advertised. Ormrod: 169 mentions that between 1688–1691, the number of annual picture auctions rose from fourteen to ninety-two.
4. C. Gibson-Wood, "Picture Consumption in London at the End of the Seventeenth Century", Art Bulletin 84 (2002): 491–500, 496.
5. Cowan, 'Art and Connoisseurship in the Auction Market of Later Seventeenth-Century London', N. De Marchi and H. Miegroet, eds., Mapping Markets for Paintings in Europe, 1450–1750 (Turnhout: Brepols, 2006): 274–275 and ns. 44 and 48.
6. Cowan: 266, table 15: Auctions advertised in England by location; also Richard Redford, Art Sales: A History of Sales of Pictures & Other Works of Art (London: Bradbury, Evans & Co., 1866): xv.
7. Frank Herrmann, The English as Collectors (N.Y.: W. W. Norton & Co., 1972): 28.
8. Horace Walpole, Anecdotes of Paintings, 3 vols. (London: Henry G. Bohn), vol. 2: 651; Jean-Andre Rouquet, The State of the Arts in England (London: J. Nourse, 1755): 126.
9. Neil De Marchi, 'Auctioning Paintings in Late Seventeenth-century London', Handbook of the Economics of Art and Culture, V. A. Ginsburgh and D. Throsby, eds. (Amsterdam: Elsevier, 2004): 120–124.
10. Rouquet: 125.
11. De Marchi: 102–107 for a detailed discussion of these regulations and innovations. Also, De Marchi and Hans Van Miegroet, "The History of Art Markets," Handbook of the Economics of Art and Culture, V. A. Ginsburgh and D. Throsby, eds, (Amsterdam: Elsevier, 2006): 69–122: 106/107.
12. Cowan, "Arenas of Connoisseurship: Auctioning Art in Later Stuart England." Art Markets in Europe 1400–1800, M. North and D. Ormrod, eds (Aldershot: Ashgate, 1998): 155 and n. 17 referring to advertisements in the London Gazette for the years 1689–1692, also the collection of sales catalogues in the British Library, shelf number 1402.g.1.

13. Bayer/Page data.
14. Rouquet: 123, 126.
15. For example: 263 guineas paid at Cock's on 12 March 1726 for a depiction of William III on his yacht by William Vandevelde; or 483 guineas for a landscape by Claude Lorraine at Prestage's on 16 Nov. 1763.
16. Bayer/Page data.
17. For example: Cock's auction of a collection belonging to the Earl of Oxford on March 7–11, 1741, included among a number of portraits by Kneller, Lely, Richardson and Riley also five marine scenes by Peter Monamy and three paintings by sporting painter, John Wootton; Bayer/Page data.
18. Bayer/Page data.
19. Law Geo.III cap 50, of September 1777 and 19 Geo. III cap 56 in 1779.
20. Filip Vermeylen and Sandra van Ginhoven, ¨The professionalisation of the art trade in early nineteenth century London: Exploring the business model of Christie's auction house¨ Business History (2023) z https://doi.org/10.1080/00076791.2023.2242278 (last accessed March 2025).
21. A recent example is Arturo Cifuentes and Ventura Charlin, The Worth of Art (N. Y.: Columbia University Press, 2023). Filled with numbers and graphs based on auction sales, the analyses assume that art works by the same artist are fungible, like stocks or bonds. This, of course, is wrong.
22. Louis Lippincott, Selling Art in Georgian London (New Haven & London: Yale University Press): 60–61.
23. Bayer/Page data.

CHAPTER 14

The Economics of Art Criticism, Academia, and Museums

Without the writings and commentaries of art critics, the scholarly investigations of learned academics, as well as our museums' magnificent permanent collections and their curated changing art exhibitions, the all-important aura of art would be impossible to uphold. The unassuming Leonardo panel would have had a different history, unlikely one that would include such a high price or worldwide publicity. These institutions are the agents of communication whose function is to maintain art's distinctive commodity character, that which defines it as a unique product. They are among art's most stalwart champions. Artworks are non-fungible and rank supreme among assets used for storing exchangeable value. Society has apotheosized art, given its quasi-divine status. The realization of this hegemonic position among the world's asset products did not come about by happenstance but by intention. The worldwide faith in the apotheotic character of art requires, like any other faith, a public discourse among its followers to maintain status and appeal. Religion has beautiful churches and temples decorated with symbols of faith. Art has imposing museums, beautifully decorated with similar symbols of faith. Both are accompanied by doctrines. The apostles of the 'Art Faith', the artists, the curators, the museum directors, art historians, art writers, art critics, restorers, and experts, all work in tandem to maintain art's exalted position and defend it against blasphemous attacks. In the history of product design, branding, and marketing, art is an example like no other.

T. M. Bayer, *The Genesis of the Modern Art Market in London, 1700–1900*, https://doi.org/10.1007/978-3-032-00594-6_14

Economists would describe these writers and institutions as 'agents of consumption'. John Ruskin, perhaps the most prominent art writer and critic in the nineteenth century, no economist, but an expert on the subject of art writers, hinted in that direction when he commented that '[W]e are overwhelmed with a tribe of critics who are fully imbued with every kind of knowledge which is useful to the picture-dealer, but with none that is important to the artist'.[1] I will take Ruskin's lead and begin this discussion of the 'agents of consumption' with art writers and critics.

Cultural criticism was well established in Britain prior to the introduction of public exhibitions of art around the middle of the eighteenth century.[2] Earlier, during the seventeenth century, Britain had witnessed widespread growth of its book industry which, among other things, provided more opportunities for aspiring authors. It served as midwife to the birth of a new subgroup of writers, the literary critic. These writers realized that their demographically diverse audience preferred a colloquial and enjoyable style of writing. To accommodate their readers, they developed a vocabulary and general manner of writing that was simultaneously didactic and conversational.

I pointed our earlier that art auctions attracted an audience which overlapped with that of literary critics. The growing popularity of these events appealed to writers as a source for social gossip mixed with intelligibly written discussions focused on the art offered for sale. The same happened when the first public exhibitions of contemporary paintings took place. Writers loved the new topic and embraced the new audience. The result was a new literary genre with its distinct vocabulary and style: popular art criticism as it is still practiced today.[3]

In the wake of the establishment of the annual showings of contemporary art at the Royal Academy was an increasing number of independent, privately organized exhibitions and countless commercial shows organized by dealers. These sales events depended for their success, as well as their longevity, on the quality of the press coverage they received. This trilateral dependency between artists, middlemen, and art writers, particularly its effect on artistic production, was a consciously recognized and even defining dimension of the arts environment. The same mutual reliance existed also on the Continent. Nowadays, it is a permanently entrenched characteristic of the art market.

For most of the eighteenth century, reviews were published in general periodicals and newspapers. Then, in 1785, the *Artist's Repository*, the first publication dedicated to featuring general topics of art and, specifically, to reviewing contemporary art showings, made its appearance. Discussing art and art exhibitions from that point on became an important part of many of the period's other magazines' regular content. In fact, by the late 1848s, as many as twenty different art writers could be seen mingling among the crowds at the opening of the annual Royal Academy exhibition looking for material.[4]

At the beginning, these writings were often solicited from the public by newspapers or journals. The early contributors appeared more concerned with promoting the event and wrote accordingly. But at the same time, they also offered basic, if rather vague, observations useful to an audience not yet conversant in matters of art or polite conversation about pictures.

One such review I found from the first public, artist-organized exhibition that included Hogarth, published in the *Imperial Magazine* in 1760, used such phrasing as, 'In these pieces', the author waxed about four works by Joshua Reynolds, 'you see a copious and easy invention, the most graceful attitudes, great truth, sweetness, and harmony of colouring [sic]; a light, bold, mellow and happy pencil ... one living proof that genius is of all ages and countries and that Englishmen need not travel abroad to see fine things'.[5] 'Great truth' or 'a light, bold, mellow and happy pencil' leave it entirely up to the enthralled readers to contemplate what these words mean. The point about national pride is an excellent example of pandering. It is the stuff that stiffened the upper lip of every patriotic English woman and man.

In due course, as audiences became more accustomed to looking at and talking about art, writing about it also evolved. Finer points of connoisseurship, such as more obscure iconographic aspects and historical accuracy of the depiction of certain classical themes, entered the discussion. These art writers effectively promoted the consumption of art by educating consumers in art appreciation. At the same time, they also enlarged the market for their own products, their writings. Their growing popularity gave them an increasingly important role in the art market, and both artists and dealers had to consider this additional player.

Here is another amusing example. Gavin Hamilton's (1723–1798) *Achilles Lamenting the Death of Patroclus*, depicting a well-known event from Homer's *Iliad*, was scathed by an anonymous reviewer in *The Gazetteer* and *New Daily Advertiser* in 1765. The author questioned the right of a painter, 'when he vies in the scene which he undertakes with a poet, to depart from the description of the latter'. One of the objectionable aspects of the picture was the painter's placement of Patroclus 'upon armour [sic], as if it was just taken off his body; but that was left in the field: neither could Achilles be said to have his own in his tent, as it was his he had lent to Patroclus' (Fig. 14.1).[6] Clearly, an unforgivable faux pas and disgraceful lack of erudition!

Gavin Hamilton (1723–1798) was born in Scotland but spent considerable time in Rome where he established himself as a prominent member of the city's artistic and intellectual groups. Inspired by the history of Antiquity and its myths, he specialized in classical subjects and ranks among the leading proponent of Neoclassical painting. Hamilton was also a dealer in Roman antiquities and often participated in excavations.

Like painters, these authors competed to identify their audience and their niche. Interestingly, there appears to have been a consensus on the corrupt practices of the Royal Academy.[7] Such accusations, not surprisingly, endeared these writers to many of the artists who felt wronged by the pervasive nepotism of the RA's Selection and Hanging Committees. These attacks must have been lauded also by a few dealers whose galleries

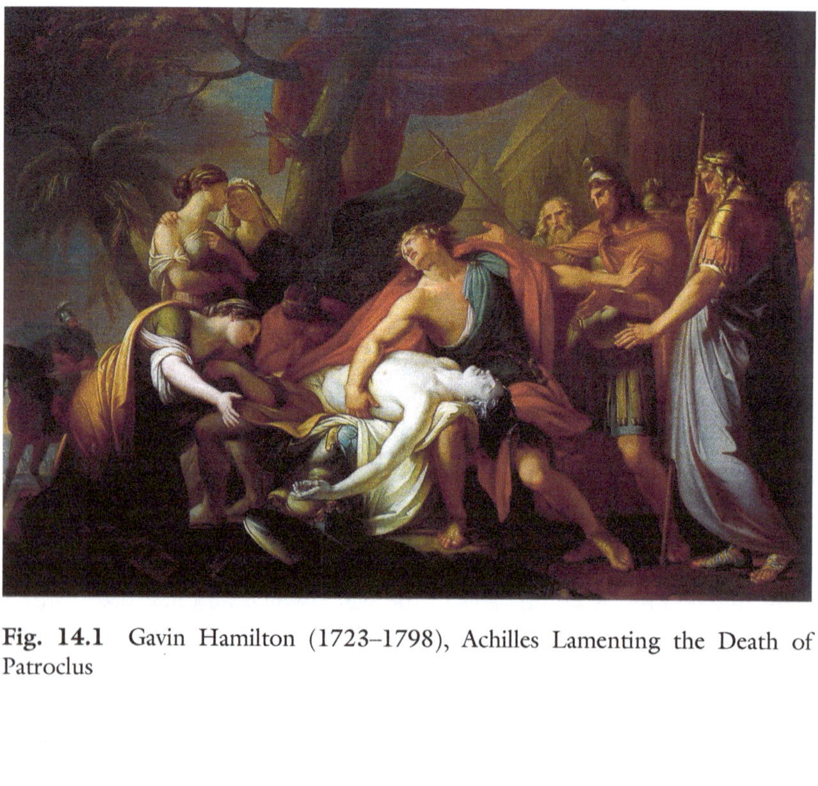

Fig. 14.1 Gavin Hamilton (1723–1798), Achilles Lamenting the Death of Patroclus

and exhibitions provided artists with new commercial outlets. Obviously, such scandalous stuff was savory fodder for the press and hugely entertaining to read.

The development of this new literary genre stands out for its distinct consumer orientation. Unlike Reynolds's pontifications on esoteric aspects of beauty, these writings were intended for popular consumption and worded accordingly. A more discriminating, intellectual approach would have missed the mark. The target was not an educated aristocratic elite, but the intellectually non-elitist reading public.

Painters recognized the crucial influence these new writers could have on their careers. Publishers, too, noticed the positive effects of these essays on the sales of their magazines. And so did print publishers, dealers, and auctioneers. They were all aware that the general interest in the arts, a precondition for patronage, was positively affected by writing about it. The time had come for the publication of a new specialized art periodical.

Arguably the most influential in the nineteenth-century art world was the famous *Art Journal* founded by S. C. Hall in 1838. Since popular appreciation, particularly of contemporary paintings, was still at a nascent stage in the 1840s, the new magazine promoted the general consumption of art among its readers rather than engaging in sophisticated, critical rhetoric on the formal merits, or lack of, of the art reviewed. The general tone of *The Art Journal* and many similar later periodicals was gently didactic and laboriously descriptive, down to the minutest details. The editor, Samuel Carter Hall, also differentiated his new publication from earlier periodicals by resolutely defending the RA as an institution: 'To prejudice and injure the Royal Academy is to prejudice and injure the Fine Arts of Great Britain', he patriotically proclaimed.[8] His journal 'was to be a just representative of the interests of artists and art'. That 'just' representation included promoting the investment potential of works by living artists and even publishing financial analyses of the contemporary painting market.

The proposal which led to the establishment of this leading nineteenth-century art journal in 1838 was initially made by the painter Charles Landseer. Financing was offered by Mr. Hodgson, one of the partners in the print publishing firm of Hodgson and Graves, the same Graves who compiled the auction records which form the basis of this book and, thus, helped shape its content.[9] A small world, indeed.

[Samuel Carter Hall was born in Waterford, Ireland, and began his career as a journalist there before he moved to London in 1821. Hall worked as an editor and reporter for different publications before starting The Art Journal in 1839, a monthly publication focused on art, architecture, and antiquities, featuring reviews, articles, and illustrations of artworks, as well as promoting of art exhibitions and events. The Art Journal performed a significant role in promoting British art and artists. Among them were J.M.W. Turner, John Constable, and the Pre-Raphaelite Brotherhood. Hall remained the editor of the Art Journal for over 40 years and established the publication as a leading authority on art in Victorian England. He was also a passionate champion for the arts, using the Art Journal as a platform to crusade for better support for artists and the establishment of public art institutions. Throughout his career, Hall wrote several books on art and architecture, including The Baronial Halls and Old English Furniture. He was also a fellow of the Society of Antiquaries and a member of the Royal Academy.]

Art criticism rapidly gained prominence in England, playing a vital role in the art scene. Unlike in France, where art criticism was often intertwined with political discourse, British art writers served a crucial purpose in the art business landscape. A notable example is the arrangement between art critic John Wolcott (1738–1819) and portrait painter John Opie (1761–1807) to promote Opie in the press in exchange for a percentage of the artist's earnings.[10] Art writers played a multifaceted role, vigorously championing individual artists, trends, and dealers. They also participated in commercial exhibitions and profited from publishing, promoting, and selling reproductive engravings. By doing so, art writers influenced both, the commerce in art as well as aspects of art's production.

The art market relies on a safeguard to preserve the unique characteristics that distinguish paintings from other commodities. Without this safeguard, paintings risk losing their individuality, rendering art writers, academic art historians, art market economists, and museums redundant. This existential threat creates a powerful incentive for innovation and uniqueness in art.

The mission of art writers aligns with the art economy's mandate: promoting individuality and uniqueness. The more conversations about art, the greater the interest in it. Painters recognized that writers enjoyed telling stories, often re-telling the narrative depicted in a painting. This synergy fostered creativity, unencumbered by writer's block, as the themes were provided in advance. This dynamic is distinct from the later era of Clement Greenberg, who skillfully applied verbal concreteness to pictorial abstraction.

This alignment of interests had certain art scene observers concerned that artists would focus on painting pictures that made it easy for art critics to write about and for dealers to sell.[11] The widespread popularity of narrative paintings during this period underscores the validity of this observation. However, as the art market continued to expand, the success of narrative content led to a saturation of epic scenes and massive canvases. The pool of heroic events, classical poems, ancient myths, religious stories, and medieval romances was finite and, therefore, limited artists' choices. Artists met this challenge with a radical solution. They usurped the hegemony of narrative content, meticulous detail, and imposing size and, instead, differentiated their work stylistically. Turner had pointed the way. This pivotal shift opened the door to a new arena in which henceforth the competition among artists would take place. The new showground gave them the opportunity to explore a seemingly unlimited variety of expression, ultimately transforming fundamentally the entire art landscape.

Of course, this was condemned as 'novelty at all costs'.[12] Writers initially struggled to find the right words to articulate what they saw. Their attempts were criticized for their copious use of vague and incomprehensible terminologies plagiarized from the world of aristocratic connoisseurship.[13] Elitism snuck back into the world of art. Art for the common man had its limits.

To be fair, Whistler's famous *Nocturnals* were much more arduous to put into words and considerably less entertaining for someone disinterested in cutting edge aesthetic debate. Maybe the root of Ruskin's accusation that Whistler was trying a con by 'throwing a pot of paint in the public's face' was a case of linguistic limitations—writer's block—in the face of something altogether new (Fig. 14.2).

In the famous 1878 Whistler vs. Ruskin trial, the American painter had sued England's greatest arbiter of taste for damaging his reputation as an artist.[14] The legendary critic referred to Whistler as a 'coxcomb' with the 'impudence' to 'ask 200 guineas for flinging a pot of paint in the public's

Fig. 14.2 James McNeill Whistler (1834–1903), Nocture in Black and Gold, the Falling Rocket

face'. Ruskin, who was too ill to attend the trial in person, sent two friends, the painters Edward Burne-Jones and William Powell Frith, both celebrated artists beyond reproach, to speak in his behalf. His two witnesses testified that, in their opinion, the price of the piece was simply too high. Whatever was there, it was clearly not finished. No more than a mere oil sketch knocked out in just a couple of days. The impertinent fraud, Whistler, had admitted so himself, right here in the courtroom!

There is an oracular element to their argument. One of the keystones of Ruskin's strict standards for determining the merits of paintings was measurable, evident input of manual labor. His support of the Pre-Raphaelites was in part based on that notion. While painters individually had been successful in establishing the price of their labor, fine finish and meticulous detail were still greatly valued. 'Art for Art's Sake' was not Ruskin's thing. In economic terms, this requirement presented a barrier for some of the artists eager to enter this potentially very lucrative contemporary art market. Whistler's repudiation of the labor aspect of Ruskinian aesthetics, therefore, can also be thought of as an attempt by an art producer to break down restrictive market barriers. 'Novelty at all costs' was what it took to compete, Ruskin be damned! The trial was hugely influential. It was the first time that a court deliberated over artistic freedom and the monetary valuation of creativity. Whistler won. The significance of this trial in the history of art cannot be overstated. It is a frightening thought to imagine how art would have developed if anything new, different, and revolutionary would be subjected to a court deciding whether it qualifies to be called art or not. The artworks created under the Nazi regime and exhibited during the annual exhibitions at the Haus der Deutschen Kunst in Munich offer some clues.

At the time of Whistler's death, his name was better known for his role in this trial than for his work as a painter and etcher. One hundred and two years after Joshua Reynolds had argued in his IXth discourse for the freedom of artists to select their own themes and judge the moral value of their choices, Whistler's trial legally established artistic freedom and the value of individual creativity. When he was asked how long it had taken him to paint the controversial painting, he replied 'two days and the experience of a lifetime'. Twentieth and twenty-first century artists like Duchamp, Mondrian, Rothko, Warhol, Hirst, or Koons are all indebted to Whistler. While the American painter only received an insignificant award for having been a victim of slander, he can claim a history-making judicial win for artistic freedom. By a judge's verdict, artists, as producer, are the only determinant of the definition of their product. Whether or not the market accepts it as art, is a separate matter.

Whistler's successful challenge of the still dominant commodity character of paintings was a sign of larger change. The Victorian art boom was breaking up as the nineteenth century drew to a close.[15] At its zenith, the art market was an unstoppable force, efficiently engulfing a growing consumer base. Conspicuous consumption of culturally sanctioned products was touted as patriotic, moral, and financial virtues. However, its own momentum led to its fragmentation. The modern art market had transcended its final constraints, marking the end of its 200-year genesis. From this point forward, unshackled from Victorian conventions, the market would be characterized by open competition among artists, professional marketers, and art writers vying for an expanding audience of art consumers.

Describing the nineteenth-century London art market with terms like 'collaboration' or 'convergence of interests' does not imply that this union of interests was uniformly positive and harmonious. It was productive, yes, but not always agreeable. Reviews could be quite scathing.

An example is Charles Dickens' full-throated condemnation of J. E. Millais's *Christ in the Carpenter Shop* (1849/50): 'In the foreground of that carpenter's shop is a hideous, wry necked, blubbering, red-haired boy'. Rather unkind words about boy Jesus! Even crueler was his description of Virgin Mother Mary: 'so horrible in her ugliness that she would stand out … as a monster in the vilest cabaret in France, or the lowest gin shop in England' (Fig. 14.3).[16]

Ironically, the outrageous and nearly blasphemous description of boy Jesus, along with the suggestive reference to the Virgin's appearance, only added to the work's notoriety and allure. Art writers, by nature, are biased, as unbiased reviews would be indistinguishable. Frederick G. Stephens, a

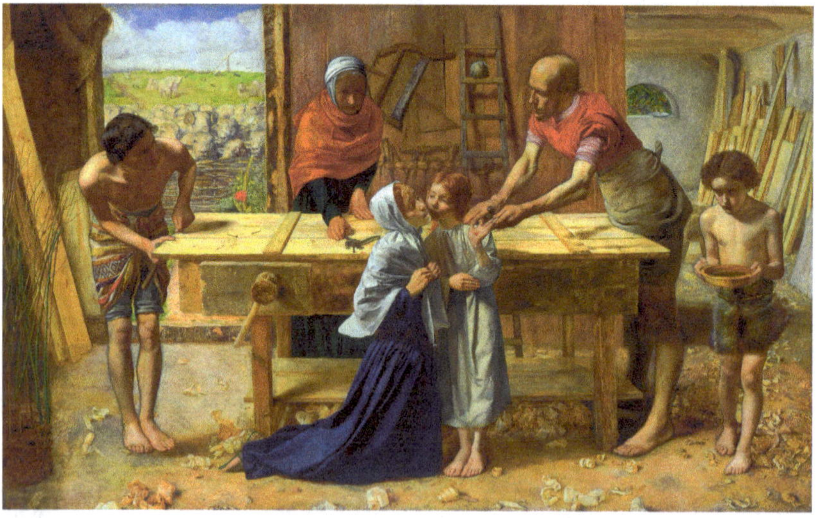

Fig. 14.3 John Everett Millais (1829–1896), Christ in the Carpenter Shop

journalist, penned a series of articles in the *Athenaeum* from 1871 to 1872, championing Millais's *Christ in the Carpenter Shop*, the very painting Charles Dickens had savaged twenty years prior. Stephens' advocacy for Pre-Raphaelitism was so entrenched that he granted Dante Gabriel Rossetti, a prominent member of the group, veto power over any reviews of his work in the prestigious journal, *The Athenaeum*.[17] P. G. Hamerton, whom I discussed in the Interlude, devoted much of his writing for *The Portfolio* to the promotion of etchings.[18] There are countless other examples. Clement Greenberg's role in establishing the credibility and facilitating the commercial success of Abstract Expressionism as a radically new and totally superior, much purer form of art, is just one of the better-known ones.

[Clement Greenberg (1909–1994) was one of the most influential art critics of the twentieth century. His early writing focused on social issues and politics, but he soon turned to art criticism. Greenberg is widely acknowledged as the 'Champion' of Abstract Expressionism and is credited with recognizing the innovative work of artists like Mark Rothko, Jackson Pollock, and Willem de Kooning. His support for Abstract Expressionism and other avant-garde movements encouraged artists to experiment and push boundaries. His writings continue to inspire and challenge art historians, critics, and art lovers to this day.]

It was also not uncommon for critics to engage in art sales. Samuel Carter Hall, the staunch champion of contemporary British painters, even acted as a sales agent for the landscape painter, John Linnell (1792–1882), further blurring the lines between criticism and commerce.[19] A later editor of the *Arts Journal* from 1881 to1892, Markus Huish, was concurrently the director of a commercial gallery, called the 'Fine Arts Society' from 1879 to 1911. These examples should suffice to demonstrate that the conflict of interest between critics and artists was not a major concern at the time.

This symbiotic relationship between critics, dealers, and artists was not unique to England. A Continental example of the 'dealer/critic system' is the French writer and critic Alfred Sensier (1815–1877), who enthusiastically championed the works of Courbet, Rousseau, Millet, Michel, Diaz, and other Barbizon School painters, illustrating the phenomenon's broader European presence.[20]

Dealers paid close attention to cultivating contacts in the press. Placing advertisements was the established, if somewhat heavy-handed, way. Editors, like S. C. Hall of *The Art Journal*, were known for pressuring their writers to pen favorable reviews about exhibitions that had bought advertising. Occasionally, there were complaints about the press getting a little too greedy.[21]

Dealers, too, cultivated symbiotic relationships with influential art journalists on a social level. These connections often led to lucrative opportunities. For example, the mega dealer Ernest Gambart organized and promoted a lecture tour for John Ruskin in 1858 that targeted urban centers with thriving art markets. In return, Ruskin agreed to review regularly Gambart's exhibitions of French art in his widely read publication, *The Academy Notes*.[22]

Painters, as well, catered, deferred, and paid homage to critics. An astute observer of the arts milieu summed it up: '[T]he man who paints for popularity cannot afford indifference to press notices upon which it is fed'.[23] Sometimes, this kowtowing went over the top. Burne-Jones went into raptures after he received a reply to his very first letter to Ruskin: 'I'm not Ted any longer, I'm not E.C.B. Jones now – I've dropped my personality – I'm correspondent with RUSKIN [Burne-Jones's emphasis], and my future title is "the man who wrote to Ruskin and got an answer by return"'.[24]

In turn, writers actively sought out artists. John Ruskin's early success, for instance, was largely attributable to his effusive and often exaggerated praise of J. M. W. Turner.[25] At the height of his fame, the renowned painter had little need for the promotional writings of a relatively unknown author like Ruskin, who was seeking to establish himself. Ruskin eventually rose to become Britain's paramount arbiter of taste, with arguably no other art writer of this period wielding greater influence. His most widely recognized cause was his early and lasting support of the initially much derided Pre-Raphaelite Brotherhood.[26] Ruskin epitomizes the art writer and critic of his era. As Turner's champion, he had significantly boosted his commercial value, a fact that likely influenced the dealer Gambart's decision to collaborate with Ruskin in promoting the second edition of Turner's *Harbours of England* series in 1856.[27]

Yet, despite Ruskin's passionate support of the Pre-Raphaelites, his views were not always taken seriously by every member of the Brotherhood.

Rossetti, for instance, in a letter to a friend commented that Ruskin's ideas were 'absurd', that he was 'only half informed about art'. However, anything good he might write is 'of course, sure to prove invaluable ... for the sale of my rubbish'.[28] This cynical display contradicts the public image of the Pre-Raphaelite Brotherhood's noble sincerity and the sensitive, romantic persona of its prominent member, the painter and poet Dante Gabriel Rosetti. There are further examples that reveal the artist's disdain for the man who had so significantly contributed to his success.

[During the twentieth century, British art critics, like Herbert Read (1893–1968, Lawrence Gowing (1918–1991), and David Sylvester (1924–2019), were leading voices in British art circles, writing for The London Times, The Observer, Burlington Magazine, and other publications. Gowing also served in various capacities as curator and director of the Tate's Gallery from 1963 to 1974.]

As the Ruskin–Rossetti relationship shows, there is a darker side to an art critic's job. Dependence breeds resentment. The audience demanded different opinions, stories, scandals, and conflicts, even if they were made up. The impact of this need for conflict, for having to praise and to condemn, for taking sides, was by no means limited to the careers of artists. A critical review of a gallery exhibition or expressing doubt about the authenticity of a painting in an upcoming auction could be the death knell of these events. Even major museums are sensitive to unflattering reviews. Such power can get to one's head. Critics occupy an unenviable position: with every friend they make, they also make an enemy somewhere. Art criticism is not for the faint of heart.

Three hundred years after the birth of art writing as a distinct literary genre, art critics are ubiquitous. Even academic degrees in art criticism can be earned. Most newspapers, international, national, and local, have an art writer, as do many of the leading magazines and periodicals. At the top end, art critics cultivate a certain celebrity persona that lends weight and influence to their opinions. Usually, they are well educated, urbane, and skilled with words. They can also be hip, provocative, and colorful. The image is part of their brand. They thrive on controversy and hyperbole. There is also a penchant for prima donna-hood indiscriminate of gender identity. Photos of them are usually included in the society pages when they are seen around town.

I find it impossible to imagine a world without art, without the broad engagement of our intellect and our senses that art offers. But this phenomenon is very new. Three hundred years ago, when there were no museums, no art galleries, no art critics, no art or art history taught at our schools, this engagement was an elite privilege. Regardless of what our individual opinion may be, we are indebted to art writers and critics for their valuable contribution to extending this privilege to the rest of society.

Let us now move on to the second 'agent of consumption': academic art historians and the modern academic discipline of art history. What is their relationship to the steadily growing market of art and its increasingly larger role in society? Do academic art history and art historians contribute to arts' exchange value and support it?

Art history, as an academic discipline, is comparatively new. University degrees in art history have only been awarded since sometime during the last two decades of the nineteenth century. The precise date is unknown, but it took place at a German university. A lawyer, Karl Schnaase (1798–1875), had published a book in 1843, called *Geschichte der Bildenden Künste* (History of the Fine Arts) in which he described how each period in art history was connected to past eras and to those after it. This method was adaptable to both course curricula and an accompanying textbook, and his publication paved the way for art history to become an autonomous academic discipline. Herr Schnaase was later awarded an honorary doctorate from the University of Bonn for his achievements in the history of art. Most introductory art history survey courses are still taught this way. The beautifully designed and expensive textbooks used in these classes help students navigate through this history in a chronological, structured, and easily readable way with high-quality illustrations of didactically useful works of art.[29]

This orderly way of representing the history of art should not be considered a historically accurate representation. Textbooks are written by art historian as teaching tools. The reality, whatever it may be, is different. For educational purposes, however, academic humanities tend to superimpose some type of order over events, such as the production of art, that in fact exist in a quasi-chaos. Chaos is unsettling and confusing to us; the human brain prefers order. Therefore, we resort to creating systems of order, even if they are distortions. This book is an example.

While art history as an autonomous academic discipline is young, interest in the history of art has a stellar and ancient pedigree reaching back beyond the year 79 CE when Mount Vesuvius made Pompeii the tourist destination that it is today. The date also marks the death of Pliny the Elder (23 CE–79 CE), a Roman aristocrat, commander of the Roman navy, and author of the popular multi-volume publication, *Natural History*. As he was trying to rescue some friends, flying rocks smashed up his ship, and he drowned. Pliny's *Natural History* contained descriptive passages on the lives of the great artists of the past, where they lived, from whom they learned, whom they taught. And it also mentioned their greatest works.

After Pliny, for around 1500 years, as writing about art history was concerned, nothing much happened. Of course, plenty of art history was being made, but there were no historians writing about it. In general, artists' social status during late Antiquity and the Middle Ages was that of a skilled manual laborer; they were anonymous members of the lower rungs of society whose names did not merit to be recorded for posterity.

Then the Renaissance happened. This 're-birth' refers to the renewed interest in the legendary masters of antiquity, the great artists about whom Pliny had written, the great thinkers and stories of ancient Greece and Rome. During this Renaissance, a painter and architect from Tuscany by the name of Georgio Vasari (1511–1574) wrote a book with the imposing title *The Lives of the the Most Excellent Painters, Sculptors and Architects*. He, too, is often described as the 'first' art historian. Vasari essentially adopted Pliny's method and related the great masters of his world to those of an even more glorious past. A trend was emerging.

In the eighteenth century, it became a movement. Whether writing about the history of art or about current art, exhaustive sojourns to its very origins were mandated, if only to show one's own erudition. The Earl of Shaftesbury, whom I discussed earlier, and his presumptuous opinion that painters should simply illustrate the ideas of their social superiors was among those in England who took the same approach as Vasari. The Earl had learned about this long view method from John Dryden (1631–1700), the celebrated English writer and scholar. Dryden had published in 1694 an English translation of an influential book, *De Arte Graphica*, originally written in Latin by the French painter and art theorist Charles Alphonse du Fresnoy (1611–1668) titled *Art of Painting*.

By that time, the number of writers seriously thinking about the history of art had grown considerably. Implicit in many of their reflections was a hierarchical ranking. To be sure, these were writings that referred to the *most* excellent artists of the past, not merely the excellent ones. Obviously, if an artist's name was included in these writings, said artist was implicitly connected to the superlative, not just the average.

Journalistic art writers and early art critics loved showing off with learned and well-used references. Vasari was fortunate; he had been the only one in his time. Now the stage had begun to get crowded. Different ways of thinking about, and interpreting, the visual legacy from our past were crucial to being noticed and attract attention.[30] Among the most notable early contributors to art historical studies in England were Charles Lock Eastlake (1793–1866) with his *Materials for the History of Oil Painting* (1847); Anna Jameson's (1794–1860) *Sacred and Legendary Art* (1848); William Dyce's *The Principles of Harmony and Contrast of Colours and Their Application to the Fine and Useful* Arts, published in 1842; Richard Redgrave (1804–1888) *A Century of Painters of the English School* (1866); John Ruskin with his *Modern Painters* (1843–1860), also his *The Seven Lamps of Architecture* (1849), and *The Stones of Venice* (1851–1853).

From this point forward, the history of art history mirrors that of art writers and artists. They were all producers of marketable commodities for their respective markets. It was no different from what Turner did to draw attention, flinging his brush like a madman on Varnishing Day at the Royal Academy. But instead of trying to stand out on the walls of the great institution, in art history the competition took place—and still does—via a continuous flow of new ideas, new interpretations, and new evidence. Learned individuals began discussing art history beyond just the lives of artists and how they learned from each other.

These different ways of studying artists and their artworks began to create further categories for art and more ways to examine art objects which, in turn, led to further studies. This process is still ongoing. The historiography of art history is, in fact, still in its infancy. Like art, it relies on constant innovation.

Running parallel to the step-by-step process by which British painters took ownership of their works' design, intention and value were similar efforts to bring the history of art under the control of those individuals who were writing it. This process was first evident on the Continent where

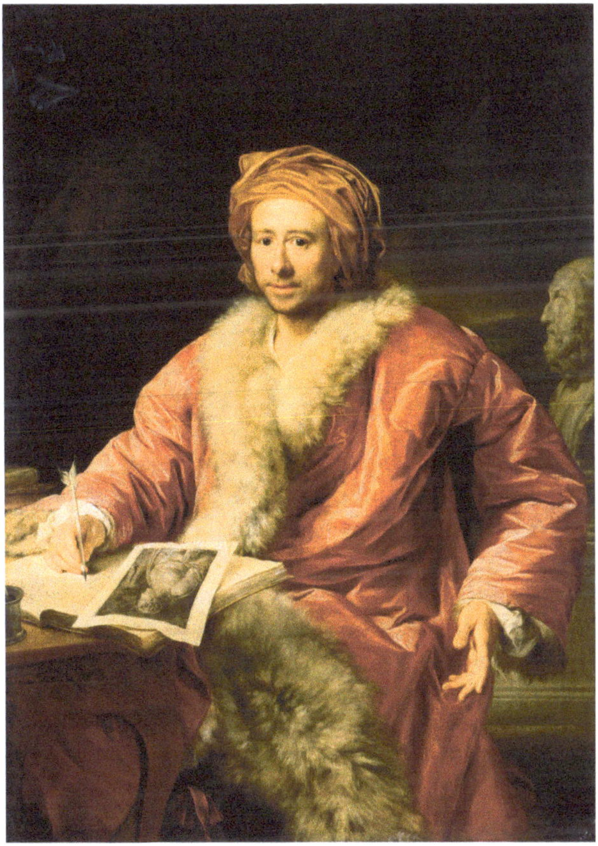

Fig. 14.4 Anton Von Maron (1731–1808), Johann Joachim Winckelmann

the German scholar Johann Joachim Winckelmann (1717–1768) rejected Vasari's celebrity artist obsession. Much more important, he argued, was his *own* opinion as a great learned man and thinker about these artists and their work. Therefore, to differentiate himself from other art writers, Winckelmann made his personal judgement the focus of his writing instead of simply retelling a story like a good storyteller. His methodology paved the way for modern art criticism: offering your own personal views about an artwork (Fig. 14.4).[31]

Johann Joachim Winckelmann was an amateur German art historian, archaeologist, and philosopher. He studied theology and medicine at the University of Halle, but his real passion was classical antiquity. In 1748, Winckelmann secured a position as librarian to Cardinal Archinto in Rome. His new job gave him access to a vast collection of classical texts and artworks and the opportunity to develop his knowledge of classical art and architecture. In 1755, he published his influential book, Thoughts on the Imitation of Greek Works in Painting and Sculpture (Gedanken über die Nachahmung der griechischen Werke in der Malerei und Bildhauerkunst). This work became one of the foundational texts for the nascent field of art history and established Winckelmann as a leading expert on classical art. He was murdered on June 8, 1768, in Trieste, Italy, in the room of an inn by a young man who had become infatuated with him. Winckelmann's legacy continues to shape the field of art history, and his ideas about classical art and aesthetics remain influential to this day.]

Winckelmann's egocentric approach opened Pandora's box. Now everyone had an opinion about art. For an economist, all the different methods for looking at art, how to reveal its many meanings, its inconspicuous or conspicuous messages and allegories, its many nuances, its provocations and challenges of norms, how it resonates with a heterogeneous society, and what its purpose in society is are simply different examples of product differentiation in an expanding market for intellectual products.

Since these new contemplations about art were often tied to either one specific artwork, a group, or a school/movement, they had the potential to encourage further product differentiations. This, in turn, helps to support art's uniqueness, a *sine qua non* of its commodity character. And each successful differentiation comes with the opportunity to market it, to promote it, and, perhaps, even to a create a new asset in the art market.

After art history had first established itself as an academic discipline in late nineteenth-century Germany, it attracted serious scholars who understood that they could gain recognition among their peers by introducing and teaching new ways of studying artworks. Recognition meant having a job. This pressure for novelty is just as intense among academic art historians as it is among artists. The field is already overcrowded, and art history departments are producing more and more Ph.Ds. who have fewer and fewer job prospects. Simply writing a good dissertation on a relevant topic that has not been discussed *ad nauseam* is not enough. To get a tenured position teaching art history at any of the world's leading universities, name-recognition by way of peer-reviewed publications and the acknowledgment of one's work as new, unique, and exceptional is a prerequisite. So, it appears, is increasingly the number of social media followers.

Among the early contributors of distinction was Heinrich Wölfflin (1864–1943). Wölfflin studied at the universities of Basel and Berlin and had a Ph.D. in philosophy and art history from the Ludwig Maximilian University in Munich. He was appointed professor of art history at the university in Berlin in 1901 and in Munich in 1912. Wölfflin developed a systematic approach to analyzing the formal qualities of artworks, such as composition, line, shape, and color. For example, when the description of a painting includes the term 'painterly' (painted with loose and fluid brush strokes), it is due to Wölfflin's categorization of styles. His book "Kunstgeschichtliche Grundbegriffe" (Principles of Art History), published in 1915, outlined his theories on the development of art and the importance of understanding the historical context in which artworks were created. It is considered a foundational text in the field.[32]

Why was this important? When artists towards the end of the nineteenth century started to relegate subject to a subordinate position and compete based on different styles, it was necessary to invent terms which could be used to distinguish between these stylistic variations. Some painters, like Gauguin (1848–1903), were not at all interested in using carefully designed linear perspective in their paintings; they simply loved the idea of painting objects and people just as colorful shapes. Others, Vincent van Gogh (1853–1890), for example, were sometimes using so much paint that the canvas surface became a three-dimensional swirl of different pigments that lent a distinct emotional dimension to their work. Besides these stylistic differences, Wölfflin also wanted to understand what external circumstances might have occasioned these artists to paint the way they did (Figs. 14.5 and 14.6).

Germany in the early twentieth century had become a center for art historical studies. Erwin Panofsky (1892–1968), who taught at the University of Hamburg from 1926 to 1933 and later at Princeton, introduced iconographic studies to the field as another way of classifying or

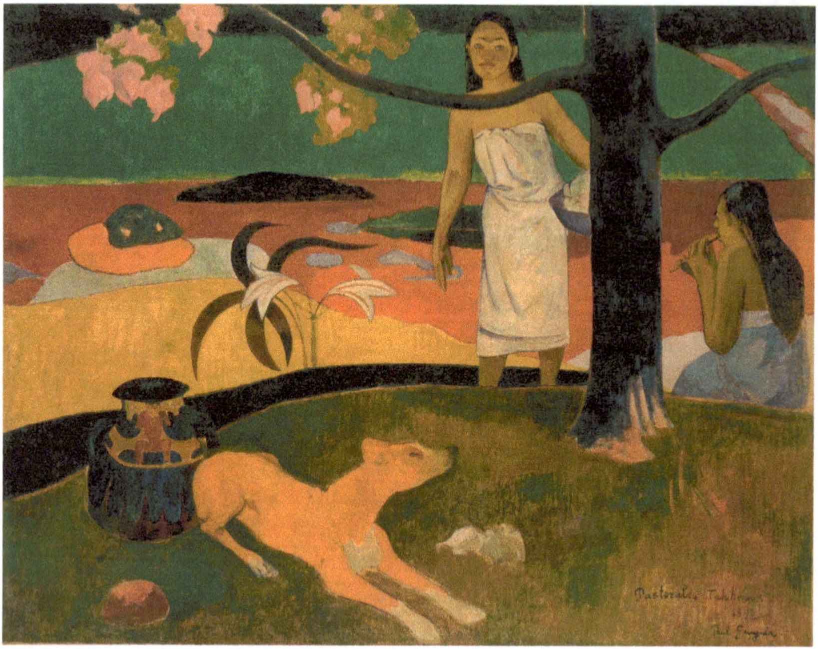

Fig. 14.5 Paul Gauguin (1848–1903), Pastorales Tahitiennes

describing art works. Iconography looks at the one thing his colleague, Heinrich Wölfflin, had pushed into the background: the content of the pictures, the themes, the objects, symbols, and characters the artist had painted to illustrate the theme, the meaning of small details and the type of composition. Without Panofsky, our enjoyment and intellectual understanding of the breathtaking works of the Italian Baroque or the less ostentatious but no less intriguing Dutch paintings of the same time would miss out on many important aspects.[33]

The famous Sigmund Freud (1856–1939) added psychoanalysis as a method for understanding art. His former student, Karl Jung (1875–1961), introduced the fascinating concept of archetypes.[34] There is even a well-established Marxist methodology that studies art works as visual symbols of an oppressive class-based society.[35]

The fact that courses in the methodologies of Art History are taught is an indication that this densely populated academic field is in danger of becoming incestuous.

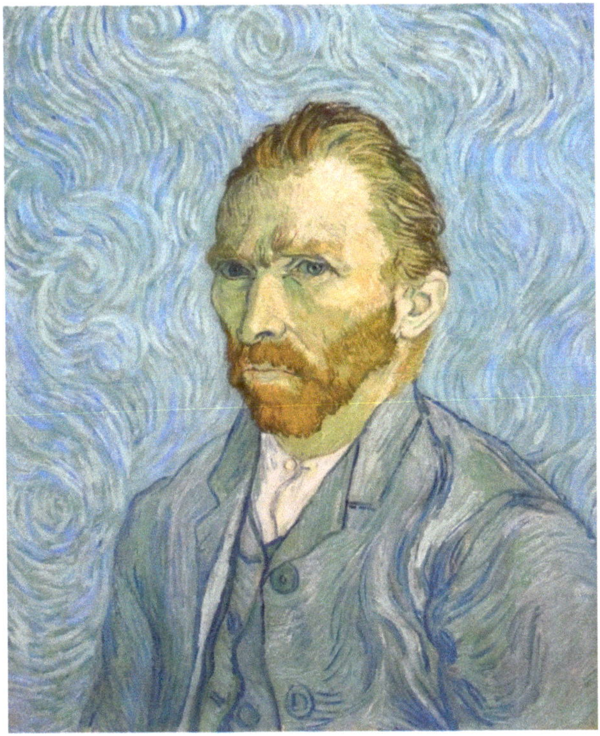

Fig. 14.6 Vincent Van Gogh (1853–1890), Self Portrait

If I were to describe the work of academic art historians in the context of art market economics, I would call them 'art product classifiers'. They oversee the creation of order within the chaos of human creativity and imagination. This is very useful, if not essential, for a market that trades in products that are the result of these uniquely human qualities. It helps us to assign categories to them, to relate them to each other and to distinguish them. Such classifications make it possible to generate fads and promote, as well as change, positions in a hierarchy that is expressed monetarily in the market. Without the input from art historians going back to the days of Vasari, Leonardo's little oak panel, *Salvator Mundi*, would have never exchanged hands for $ 450,000,000. Art historians since Vasari have constructed the apotheotic position Leonardo occupies. What is the price of the physical manifestation of divine genius? It is no surprise that books about Leonardo still become bestsellers even if they have nothing new to offer.

This brings us to the final agents of consumption, the museum industry, the window front for art historians to showcase their newest classifications. But there is more than that to museums. Inevitably, this discussion also briefly takes us geographically beyond the British Isles.

Places for the public to admire works of art are quite old. Back in Antiquity, victorious military leaders and conquering emperors routinely gave their booty to one of the temples in their respective capitals for the crowds to admire and to appease the gods for the slaughter that made this generosity possible. The custom, while generally frowned upon, enjoys occasional moments of revival and popularity in modern days. But instead of temples, national museums now have become the venue to show off the spoils of war. However, we rarely, if ever, include the names of the generous donors on the list of the beneficiary institutions' patrons. The Elgin Marbles are among the few noteworthy exceptions. Yet many of the fabulous treasures from Egypt permanently displayed in the Louvre in Paris do not bear plaques acknowledging the generosity of General Bonaparte.

Certain nations with less successful imperialistic ambitions, however, often had to pay large sums of money to get anything worthwhile for their national museums. The magnificent paintings on view in the Hermitage Museum in St. Petersburg, for example, were purchased by Czarina Katharina the Great of Russia (1729–1796). In 1779, Her Majesty, after long and arduous negotiations, acquired 206 Old Master paintings from the heirs of Sir Robert Walpole (1696–1745), a very high-net-worth and historically very important English politician, famous art collector, and occasional author. Aleksei Musin-Pushkin, the Russian envoy to Great Britain, closed the Walpole Collection deal for a price of 40,000 pounds. This was an extraordinary amount at the time. Yet most of the one hundred and twenty-seven paintings that remain in the Hermitage's collection from this group would individually command multiple times the original cost of the entire collection. As a sovereign wealth manager, Czarina Katharina was, indeed, great (Figs. 14.7 and 14.8).[36]

The great Czarina was most likely aware that for the past decade the legendary Medici family collection with its celebrated art had been open to the public. An old office building (Uffizi in Italian) in Florence, originally designed by Giorgio Vasari and constructed in the early 1560s, had been remodeled to display the greatest art collection in the entire known world for all to see.[37] Perhaps Katherine the Great felt a tinge of sovereign

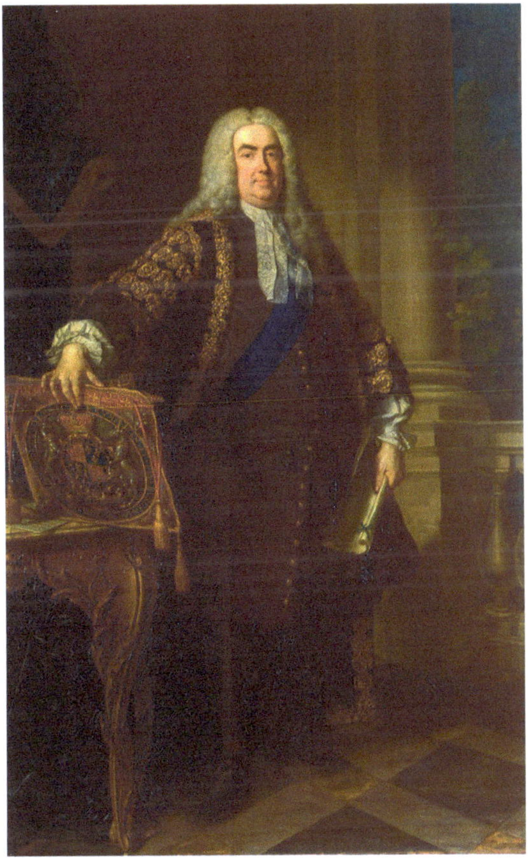

Fig. 14.7 Workshop of Jean-Baptiste Van Loo (1705–1765), Robert Walpole

envy. If a tiny country like Italy could polish its image by boasting with an art collection, then Russia, an empire far greater than Italy, in the Czarina's opinion, had to do the same.

The same competition between nations based on their art collections to bolster image and international standing was also behind the purchase of Leonardo's *Salvator Mundi* and its planned exhibition in Saudi Arabia. The auction generated global publicity, the painting's mystique is choreographed to keep then work in the public's mind, and, no doubt, *Salvator Mundi's* reappearance will attract millions of admirers.

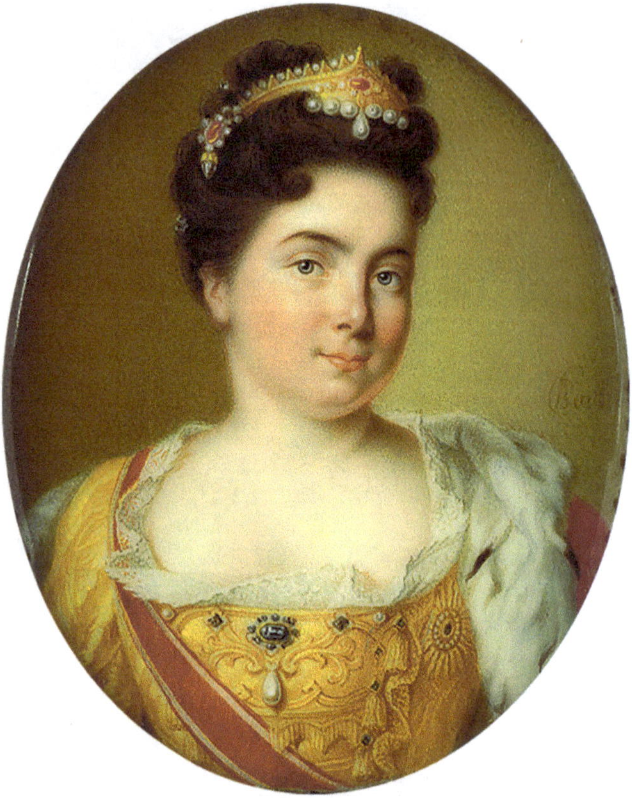

Fig. 14.8 Charles Boit (1662–1727), after Jean-Marc Nattier; Catherine I of Russia

Seen from a historical perspective, the development of the art market can also be described as an expansion of the playing field hitherto restricted to the most powerful and wealthy. Art's capacity to store value and provide prestige was made accessible to increasingly larger sections of society. Along with it, art commoditized by continuously creating new products and new forms of marketing.

Over the next decades, the Italian and Russian examples caught on and were copied in other European capitals. By the time the French Revolution occurred, the official 'transfer' of ownership of the Louvre with its art collection to the new Republican state in 1793 was just part of an elite trend. Petty donor complaints were swiftly resolved with striking efficiency.[38]

Great Britain was running a little behind in the national museum fad. Public money was tight, and King George III had little motivation to hand over the Royal Collection. Fortunately, French methods of persuading royalty had gone out of favor on the British Isles. But, finally, in 1817, the first purpose-built national art gallery, the Dulwich Picture Gallery, opened its doors to the public. Unique in the museum's history is the fact that two art dealers, Noel Desanfans, and his business partner, Sir Francis Bourgeois, whom we already met, are the recognized founders—yet another illustration of the influential role art dealers played in the cultural environment of the island kingdom.[39]

Soon thereafter, the King of Bavaria (1786–1868) ordered the construction of a huge purpose-specific building in Munich to house the collection of the royal family, the Wittelsbach. The Alte Pinakothek, as it is still called, one of the largest royal galleries in existence, was opened to the public in 1836 equipped with skylights and special cabinets to make it easy for the public to enjoy the artworks. This was rather considerate of King Ludwig, given the fact that most of the money for the renowned Wittelsbach collection and the new building came from the pockets of generations of largely involuntarily tax-paying Bavarians. It was only fitting that due attention was paid to the visitors for whose benefit and cultural edification the enlightened monarch had judiciously spent their tax payments.[40]

The public collections I have described are examples of the varied circumstances that have led to the founding of several of the best-known examples: buying a collection, like the Czarina; voluntarily providing public access to an existing collection in a custom-designed space, like King Ludwig or the Medici; decapitating the owners and nationalizing their collection and its building, as was the case with the Louvre; or a private civic initiative, like the Dulwich Gallery.

It is important to remember that these museums' collections, the way in which individual art works were displayed and the buildings that house them were usually intended for the enjoyment by a social, governing elite. Even the Dulwich Gallery collection had initially been put together for royalty. Visible, or invisible, barriers made sure that the common members of the public were always aware of the physical separation between them and the art works on display. Today, watchful uniformed guards on their smart phones, protective ropes, and electronic barriers reinforce this sense. Visitors speak with subdued voices. The palatial walls are crowded with art works hung contrary to any sense of domestic living with art. As mere mortals, we are forcefully and intentionally separated from the Divine. The pantheon of art is purposely kept in a gilded cage to reinforce its aura.

These types of museums represent one category. They are the modern versions of the temples of Antiquity. These temples of culture complete the apotheosis of art. Removed from commerce out of the grubby hands of ordinary humans and given its own shrines, art can now exercise its civilizing power over mankind from its own Mount Olympus, unencumbered. We honor her apostles and missionaries who often suffer greatly for her, and we pay homage to her saints. In the meantime, we stay busy creating more of them. It is no hyperbole to use the term *apotheosis* to describe the position that art holds in our society. Only religion and altruistic nonprofit organizations are given similar privileges.

I already described how these temples of art are also useful tool for tweaking the market. A theme exhibition at one of the major museums with loans from other leading institutions stimulates the market. The inclusion of works from well-connected private collections in a major exhibition translates into real gain in value should the owners decide to sell them. It is also not unusual that a privately acquired old or modern master's work is displayed on a wall of one of our temples of art to reinforce its attribution and boost its value. The Leonardo panel and a recent scandal involving the discovery of fake works by Basquiat are good examples. Sometimes, entire private collections on loan to smaller museums form the core of their 'permanent' collection. Often, when a provenance of a work offered for sale lists 'recently exhibited at ...' there is a chance that an attempt to boost its price is behind it.

There exist also companies that provide ready-made exhibitions to museums for a fee. Success of exhibitions is measured by visitor numbers, just like the first commercial exhibition in London at Shipley's facility on the Strand 350 years ago. Therefore, these companies try to put together exhibitions based on audience appeal. In economic terms, this makes sense. But what art and what themes that should be seen are disregarded because they do not fulfill the requirements of crowd pleasers? Thankfully, there exist organizations funded by generous foundations that explicitly offer exhibition spaces for the display of art that exists outside the norms of audience appeal.

The intentional use of our sacred temples of art in the service of mammon is more occasional than widespread. There are two significant hurdles that prevent abuse: it must involve something special, and it requires excellent connections with key individuals in the museum industry. Both are rare.

There is another category of museum. In the US alone, there are over 700 university art museums; and many of the over 140 universities in Britain have art exhibition spaces. Judged by numbers alone, these university-run facilities collectively are easily the largest category of art museums in either country. What do they do?

They are steppingstones to name-building, to artistic sainthood—feeders of the market, as it were, the first testing ground for innovation. There are few pastimes more enjoyable and stimulating than viewing, with eye and mind open, the first exhibitions of graduating art students. It is at that point where raw talent shows itself. By the time artists exhibit at the Venice Biennale, their edges often have adapted to the market, and the former purity and honesty of their creation are modified.

University galleries have also become part of artists' marketing and branding strategies. Exhibitions in conjunctions with lectures given by exhibiting artists, or participation in critical theme-based group exhibition curated by knowledgeable professionals, are career boosters. And rightfully so. Competition is intense and often refreshingly original. Novelty at all costs is the battle cry.

In addition to university galleries and museums, there is another qualifying arena on the road to artistic stardom. Countless small galleries look for art that sells well and sets them apart as an art business. The commercial gallery industry is hierarchical, and success on one level takes an artist to the next higher level of gallery; further success leads to yet the next one, and so on. To get to the point of being a featured artist at a university gallery, it takes a lot of exhibitions at increasingly more selective commercial venues. Great artists are not discovered, they are forged by their own tenacity. Although, there are some exceptions.

At this early stage, it is impossible to predict any given artist's career path, regardless of what the curator—or gallery salesperson—and the printed promotional material tell the exhibition visitor. There are many more hurdles to take. If there is real talent, these obstacles are more about making the right connections, talking the talk, and walking the walk. This is the price of being master of your own fate, artistically and in economic terms. It is also what most creative individuals hate: wasting time playing the game of fame instead of working in solitude on their art.

The twentieth century witnessed the birth of public and private museums of contemporary art. Both are very useful as promotional and marketing tools. Most of our new art would look out-of-place in a traditional museum, like a hipster in a Victorian salon. The new aspirants for membership in the pantheon, with their wild and crazy ideas and styles, needed their own temples.

This turned into a great opportunity for architects—a dream come true. Here was a chance for them to rise above the crowd, to distinguish themselves by their ability to design not just a useful building, but a compelling work of architectural art to house other great works of art. No design constraints as long as the building works. It is a challenging task. Few other architectural categories demand as much from their designers or are subject to the same degree and types of scrutiny and passionate debate as modern museum buildings.

These architectural art works sometimes house permanent collections which, in the case of privately owned museums, can belong entirely to one individual. This private ownership comes with a host of attractive externalities in the form of financial and promotional advantages. In addition, there is also an energetic exhibition activity. A contemporary art museum needs to be a dynamic and permeable environment, responsive to, and part of, the times, even a driving force of innovation. There should be no single prevailing dogma. It must be a multi-confessional temple. After all, isn't unbound imagination the creative energy that makes art?

If the museum has no permanent collection, frequently changing shows keep the spaces full and visitors returning. Participation in such exhibitions can be pivotal to artists' careers. It exposes their work to different critics, art dealers, consultants, and collectors who frequent these events to look for new talent. Maybe the next candidate for stardom is there? Contemporary art museums are the venues for novelty. Of course, there are a lot of connections and networking necessary to get to this point. Usually, by the time an artist has penetrated to that prestigious level of exhibition activity, someone else, a dealer or patron, has arranged it.

With perseverance, a good agent or dealer—a champion—and a good amount of luck, a contemporary artist can move from exhibition circuit participant to having solo shows and, ultimately, become part of a permanent collection. But it is difficult to get there, and sincere effort alone won't do it. Yet once an artist has attained the prestige of being included in a permanent collection, the longevity of this 'permanence' is subject to the fickle nature of the market's constant demand for innovation. Between today's celebrated genius and tomorrow's museum's storage bins hangs no safety net. The contemporary art market is tough, merciless, and cruel. Stardom has its price. Unlike Leonardo's established renown, contemporary fame is fleeting. Novelty, by definition, is temporary.

Curatorial and managerial know-how are essential to staying at the cutting edge of the contemporary art world. Curators are well-aware of their role and the influence they wield as a result. Just like artists are expected to create works that are unique to their person, curators are expected to leave their own personal mark on their curatorial productions. They are the apostles of our faith in art. If they do their job poorly, contemporary art can easily be perceived as kitsch and a sham, and the faithful would turn away in disappointment and disgust.

The 'agents of consumption' I have just discussed—the art critics and writers who promote buying art for intellectual and sensual pleasure and monetary gain; the learned scholars who organize art's history into more and more classifications and thereby facilitate the creation of newly differentiated art products; and the museums of different types that reinforce our society's consensus that art occupies a position superior to all other commodities—all support the infrastructure that serves the ultimate objective of this effort: to maintain a safe storage alternative for countless billions looking for a place to make home, even if only temporarily.

Notes

1. John Ruskin, Academy Notes (Smith, Elder and Co., 1855): 15.
2. Johann Dobai, Kunstliteratur des Klassizismus und der Romantik in England, 3 vols. (Bern: Bentelli Verlag, 1974).
3. John Plumb, "The Public, Literature and the Arts in the Eighteenth Century', The Triumph of Culture: Eighteenth Century Perspectives, Fritz and Williams, eds. (Toronto: A. H. Hakkert, Ltd., 1972): 33.
4. Helene Roberts, "Art Reviewing in the Early Nineteenth-Century Art Periodicals," Victorian Periodicals Newsletter, 19 (March 1973): 9–10 ff for a discussion of several of the leading periodicals of the period; David Solkin, Painting for Money (New Haven & London: Yale University Press, 1993): ch. 7 and notes. Ronald Paulson, Hogarth: His Art, Life, and Time, 2 vols. (New Haven & London: Yale University Press, 1971), vol. 2: 307; William Whitley, Artists and Their Friends in England 1700–1790, 2 vols. (London & Boston: The Medici Society, 1938), vol. 1: 167–168, vol. 2:

271 for names of several of the early art critics and the publications for which they wrote. See also the London press for art-related topics from the 1760s in the Paul Mellon Center for Studies in British Art, Yale University, assembled by Claire Lloyd-Jacob.

5. Whitley, vol. 1: 167.
6. The Gazetteer and New Daily Advertiser, 21 May 1765, p. 4.
7. Roberts: 11 and n. 7, 12. Roberts also mentions that 'it is difficult to find a review in all the first fifty years of the nineteenth century that does not mention and deplore the oppressive prevalence of portraits in the Royal Academy exhibitions'.
8. Samuel Carter Hall, Retrospectives of A Long Life from 1815–1883 (N. Y.: D. Appleton & Co., 1883): 194–195, Derek Mancoff, "Samuel Carter Hall: Publisher as Promoter of the High Arts", Victorian Periodical Review, 24,1 (Spring 1991): 11–21.
9. Hall: 194–195; Mancoff: 11–21.
10. Exhibition label, (London: Tate Gallery, 2003), 2003–1600.
11. Richard St. John Tyrwhitt, "Skilled and Literary Art-Criticism", Contemporary Review, XI (1869): 107; Philip Hamerton, Etching and Etchers (London: Macmillan, 1868): 78.
12. Elizabeth Pennell, "The Two Salons", Fortnightly Review, LIII (1893): 775.
13. George Landow, "There Began to Be a Great Talking about the Fine Arts," The Mind and Art of Victorian England, J. L. Altholz, ed. (Minneapolis: University of Minnesota Press, 1976), p. 130.
14. The famous trial has been copiously discussed. Here is but one example. Linda Merrill, A Pot of Paint: Aesthetics on Trial in Whistler v. Ruskin (Washington: Smithsonian Institution,1992).
15. The decline of High Victorian painting can be illustrated mathematically, although somewhat un-orthodoxically, by comparing Whistler's average increase in price with that of other more traditional painters. The price of Whistler's work shows a strong advance, whereas the others experience a drop. Bayer and Page, The Development of the Art Market in England (London: Pickering & Chatto, 2011:198–199.
16. Holman Hunt, Pre-Raphaelitism and the Pre-Raphaelite Brotherhood, 2 vols. (N. Y. & London: Macmillan, 1905), vol. 1: 218. For other negative press coverage of the early works of the Pre-Raphaelite Brotherhood see The Times (7 May 1851): 8, and Athenaeum (7 June 1851): 609.
17. Dianne Macleod, 'F.G. Stephens, Pre-Raphaelite Critic and Art Historian', The Burlington Magazine, 128 (June 1986): 398–402.
18. On Philip Hamerton, see Henry S. Spatt, "The Aesthetics of Editorship: Creating Taste in the Victorian Art World", Innovators and Preachers, J. H. Wiener, ed. (London: Greenwood Press, 1985): 47; for Morris: 53;

for Thomson, Pamela Fletcher and Anne Helmreich, 'The Periodical and the Art Market: Investigating the "Dealer-Critic System" in Victorian England', Victorian Periodical Review, vol 41, no. 4 (Winter 2008): 325.

19. Holman Hunt, vol. 1: 202–204, 208, 431.
20. Catherine Parsons and Neil McWilliam, ¨Le Paysan de Paris: Alfred Sensier and the Myth of Rural France¨, Oxford Art Journal, 6 (no. 2, 1983): 37–58; Nicholas Green, ¨Dealing in Temperaments: Economic Transformation of the Artistic Field in France during the Second Half of the Nineteenth Century¨, Art History, 10 (March 1987): 59–76; Harrison C. White and Cynthia White, Canvases and Careers (Chicago and London: The University of Chicago Press, 1965): 94–97.
21. For an involvement of Hall, see Helene Roberts, Exhibition and review: the periodical press and the Victorian art exhibition system, J. Shattock and M. Wolff, eds, The Victorian Periodical Press: Samplings and Soundings (Toronto: University of Toronto Press, 1982): 87; on Carr, see Spatt: 44.
22. Jeremy Maas, *Gambart*, (London: Barrie & Jenkins, 1975): 89, 106–107.
23. Pennell:775.
24. Edward Burne-Jones, Memorials of Edward-Burne-Jones (London: The Macmillan Company, 1906): 127. Also correspondence between Ruskin and Shields reproduced in William Michael Rossetti, The Life and Letters of Frederic Shields (London: Ellis and Elvey, 1895): 69, 71, 73, 87, 89, 167.
25. John Ruskin, Modern Painters, 2 vols. (Boston: Dana Estes & Company, n. d.), vols 2 and 3: 61–64, 83–84, 88, 130, 133–162, 175, 181, 83, 193–197, 214–216, vols 4 and 5: 15–112. Timothy Hilton, John Ruskin: The Early Years (New Haven & London: Yale University Press, 2000); Dinah Birch, ¨Father and Sons: Ruskin, John James Ruskin and Turner¨, *Nineteenth-Century Contexts,* 18, no. 2 (1994):147–162.
26. John Christian, ¨A Serious Talk: Ruskin's place in Burne-Jones Artistic Development,¨ Pre-Raphaelite Papers, L. Parris, ed. (London: Tate Gallery, 1984): 184–205. Susan. Casteras (ed.), John Ruskin and the Victorian Eye (N. Y.: H.N. Abrams, 1993) and William Holman Hunt, Pre-Raphaelitism and the Pre-Raphaelite Brotherhood, 2 vols. (N. Y. and London: Macmillan & Co., 1905), vol.1: 254–256, 415.
27. Maas, *Gambart*: 69.
28. William Michael Rossetti, ed., Pre-Raphaelite Diaries and Letters (London: Hurst and Blackett, 1900), letter no. 104.
29. Michael Podro, The Critical Historians of Art (New Haven & London: Yale University Press, 1982); Mitchell Schwarzer, ¨Órigins of the Art History Survey Text¨, *Art Journal,* vol. 54, 3 (Fall 1995): 24–37.
30. See Dobai; Rudolf Wittkower, Englische Kunstliteratur: Ein Handbuch, (Weimar: Hermann Bohlhaus Nachfolger (1938).

31. Alex Potts, Flesh and the Ideal: Winckelmann and the Origins of Art History (Yale University Press, New Haven and London, 1994); David Irwin, ed., Winkelmann: Writings on Art (N. Y.: Phaidon, 1972);
32. Joan Hart, Heinrich Wölfflin: An Intellectual Biography (Bern: Peter Lang, Bern, 1981).
33. Irwin Levin, Erwin Panofsky: An Intellectual Portrait (Princeton: Princeton University Press,1992).
34. Sigmund Freud, Gradiva (1907), Delusion and Dream and Other Essays, Philip Rieff, ed. (Boston: Beacon Press, Boston, 1956): 69–152; "The Moses of Michelangelo" (1914), James Strachey, ed., The Standard Edition of the Complete Psychological Works of Sigmund Freud (London: Hogarth Press, 1953–1974), vol. 13, pp. 211–236; "Leonardo da Vinci and a Memory of His Childhood" (1910); Strachey, ed., Vol. 11: 63–137. Carl Jung, The Spirit in Man, Art, and Literature (Princeton: Princeton University Press,1966); Jung, Man and His Symbols (N.Y.: Dell Publishing, 1964); Jung, ¨Psychology and Literature, The Collected Works of C. G. Jung, H. Read, ed. (London: Routledge & Kegan Paul, 1964), vol. 15: 133–162.
35. Here are several classic examples. Arnold Hauser, Art and Society: Lectures and Essays (London: Routledge & Kegan Paul, 1951); Hauser, The Social History of Art, 4 vols. (London: Routledge & Kegan Paul, 1951); Meyer Schapiro, ¨Art and Ideology,¨ Marxist Quarterly (April 1937), vol 1, issue 2: 109–125; Shapiro, 'The Social Bases of Art,¨ Marxist Quarterly (1937), vol. 1, issue 3, pp. 311–330; Maynard Solomon, ed., Marxism and Art: Essays Classic and Contemporary, (Detroit: Wayne State University Press, 1973).
36. Rosalind P. Blakesley, The Sale of the Century: Artistic Relations Between England and Russia 1760–1840, (New Haven and London: Yale University Press, 2016).
37. Andrew McClellan, The Uffizi: A Cultural History (Cambridge: Polity Press, 2020).
38. Andrew McClellan, The Louvre: A Very Short Introduction (Oxford: Oxford University Press, 2017).
39. Andrzej Rottermund, ed., Treasures of a Polish King, Dulwich Picture Gallery, exhibition catalogue (1992).
40. Klaus Schrenk, Die Alte Pinakotek. Ein Museum und seine Sammlung (Munich: Verlag C. H. Beck, 1999).

CHAPTER 15

The Financialization of the Art Market

I use the term 'Financialization' in the context of the art market to describe the use of analytical methods, jargon, and productization taken from the world finance. This phenomenon can also be described as the 'securitization' of art, comparable to, for example, the securitization of the mortgage industry or junk bonds. It is the most recent commoditization phase resulting from the investment quality of artworks. Novel financial instruments are being created to promote art's investment quality and aggressively marketed to the investing public.[1]

An anonymous wit once pronounced that 'the purpose of art is to fleece the rich'. Perhaps, this is too cynically worded, but it is not off-target. The arts, indeed, offer to those with vast fortunes to possess something special to safekeep their wealth, something consecrated by human society, something unique, beautiful, meaningful, and good, something that is priceless.

It is unlikely that there was ever a period in recorded history when those who owned art were not aware of its capacity for storing transportable exchangeable value. I only mentioned the Napoleonic Wars as a more recent example of a wholesale geographical redistribution of ownership of many of Europe's privately held art assets. But it does not require a global military conflict for such art to be moved around and change hands. There are plenty of other reasons these days—safety of investment being just one of them—for art to change owners and be squirrelled away in secure places.

T. M. Bayer, *The Genesis of the Modern Art Market in London, 1700–1900*, https://doi.org/10.1007/978-3-032-00594-6_15

Perhaps one of these privately owned and very discreet custom-designed storage facilities in Geneva, Luxembourg, Singapore, or in any of the other 'freeports' that have sprung up around the world might would do. The 'free' part of the term refers to the fact that, conveniently and perfectly legally, taxes and duties of any kind are suspended for as long as the artwork is physically kept there. A freeport is a useful place to park certain art purchases. They cannot be traced to the owner, and no government can tax them or the profits they might make. When the art is in such an advantageous place, there is no need to move it when it is sold to the next high-net-worth person. To assume ownership, the new proprietor is provided with an electronic key to the storage vault. Why go through the aggravation of shipping the art? It is cumbersome, potentially hazardous, expensive to insure, and requires many documents; and there may be taxes and duties on top of it. Who needs all that?

Certainly not the high-net-worth types who accumulate money at a speed that boggles the imagination. They want their art somewhere safe, away from governmental influence and prying eyes, to use it for whatever, whenever they want. It only makes sense that top-tier art dealers and art advisors rent space in one, or even several, of these bonded art warehouses for the convenience of their clients. It is much easier and cheaper for everybody to do business that way. I should emphasize that not everyone who rents space in one of these facilities does so for secrecy reasons. Fiscal common sense alone makes these facilities attractive. Shipping a recent acquisition in a country that charges VAT to a freeport saves that tax. Moreover, insurance for art stored there is advantageously priced. Furthermore, as I described already, art kept in these locations is readily available collateral for loans.

The first official tax-free zone was established in Switzerland, a great pioneer of financial discretion schemes, back in the 1850s—for temporary grain storage, of all things. Art warehousing in these tax-free zones caught on in a big way since the first one opened in the 1960s in Geneva. Not surprisingly, it has since become a growth industry. Think of a freeport as a Swiss bank account for expensive stuff—or rather what Swiss bank accounts used to be.

Top-tier art dealers even built their own facilities to store inventory and transact business. One long-time warehouse operator of a certain notoriety went the opposite direction and branched out into art dealing. The inventory—blue chip art that belonged to others—was already in his warehouse at no cost to him. In fact, he even got paid for storing it instead of having these costs drain his own pocket. With respect to cutting costs, this was a commendable move. If one wants to find examples of 'secrecy jurisdictions', there is no need to look any further. The freeport art warehousing industry is a textbook example.[2]

[The term 'secrecy jurisdiction' describes facilities that enable people or entities to escape or undermine the laws, rules, and regulations of other jurisdictions, using secrecy as a prime tool.]

It is estimated that over $ 100 billion worth of art is stashed away in these facilities worldwide. However, the clandestine nature of the whole arrangement makes meaningful estimates impossible. Still, Luc Martinez, the director of the largest museum in the world, the Louvre in Paris, allegedly described freeport art warehouses as the greatest museums no one can see. He should know. How did it come to that? What has caused this use of art to hide wealth instead of showing it off?

When I was looking for good examples to answer this question, I came across a factoid that helps put the issue into a context. I learned that each year more than 200 new billionaires are added to this illustrious worldwide group. Gone are the days when being a billionaire was something special. Now, it seems, the world is awash with them—and their money. The total global art market in 2023 was only worth around $ 65 billion—less than 0.6% of billionaires' combined wealth of $ 12 plus trillion, and a mere fraction of the personal wealth of today's richest person in the world. And billionaires are steaming ahead faster. To put this into another frame: the annual global market of a very attractive financial asset category—art—is just a little over half of 1% of the wealth of the very demographic group it most benefits! And that's just the roughly 3200 plus billionaires. What about the poorer folks, the triple-digit millionaires? And the double-digit ones? They all want to be in the game too!

It does not take complicated algorithms to understand why the top end of the art market is doing so well. Or why, specifically, the markets for contemporary, modern art and Old Masters have such a bright and growing future. Billionaires' billions are multiplying at a much faster rate than art. Considering this demand and supply relationship, the art market has a bright future.

But a supply/demand comparison shows only one side of the issue. There is another important aspect. Beginning in the 1970s, as part of the campaign among major auction houses to go directly and aggressively after the retail market, the investment potential of art was emphatically hyped. In 1974, the first annual *Art Sales Index*, an alphabetical listing of artists and their auction sales became available. Such transparency surrounding art auctions was not uniformly welcome. Dealers who were used to buying at auction and selling to private clients saw their profit margins revealed. However, the availability of the data also led to the introduction of market statistics and the first periodical exclusively devoted to art as an investment, *The Art Investment Guide* to induce potential buyers. Both—fittingly—were published in London. Continuing the tradition of *The Art Journal* in the nineteenth century, the latter publication, as its name advertises, promoted investing in, rather than collecting, art.

[In 1979, I wrote a 3-part series of articles for The Art Investment Guide*, describing my multi-year, ultimately successful, campaign for the legal approval of fine art as a qualified asset class for closely held, HR10-type pension plans in the US. The* Art Sales Index *had been an invaluable resource in that process. As had been the British Railroad Pension Fund for setting the example.]*

The idea of investing in art, of course, was not invented in the 1970s. It just got better organized—it commoditized. As we have seen from the earlier described accounts, it was already a familiar topic in conversations in the nineteenth century when investing in art was regularly promoted in the press. But most likely, the understanding of art as an investment was less sophisticated back then than it is today. For sure, there were wealthy private individuals who were collectors strictly for financial gain. Others were directly involved in art business projects. In addition to buying and occasionally selling art, they also provided financing for print publishing and exhibition joint ventures. But the prevailing financial and legal system had not reached the point at which a demand for art warehousing in tax and duty-free zones would have developed. That was still in the future.

There were also great collectors around, who spent fortunes on buying the best of the old and the newest of the new. Particularly in the US, a type of collector developed whose passion for buying art mirrored their zest for making their fortunes. In addition to displaying an aristocratic spouse from Europe on their arm, exhibiting European art on their walls offered a certain *je ne sais quoi*. These were the days of Andrew Mellon, Henry Clay Frick, and Andrew Carnegie—America's Gilded Age. Art provided part of its luster.

These individuals bought great art not to store it away or wheel-and-deal with it. They wanted to own it for display, to impress with it, to enjoy it, to live with it as it was meant to be. Undoubtedly, they were aware of the investment quality of art, but they did not use their art as the financial asset that it is today. As America's royalty, they were already very, very rich. Boasting about owing great works of art was socially acceptable. It was quasi-aristocratic, Blenheim-like. But using it to make money? No. This was not what proper Gilded Age multi-millionaires did. It would have been crass. Moreover, there was no incentive to hide their wealth from tax authorities or lawyers. Instead, like Ludwig I of Bavaria, they gave it to the nation to enjoy. Many of the great museums of the United States, and many of the small ones too, were initially seeded with art works donated by these great American collectors of the early decades of this epoch. While the methods by which some of these individuals attained their vast fortunes fall outside of today's norms of acceptability, the societal benefits of their donations are uncontestable.

And then there were collectors like the Cone sisters, Claribel and Etta, who assembled with less grand wealth one of finest collections of modern French Art in the United States. They moved in the right circles; Picasso was their friend, and so was Matisse. The sisters socialized with Gertrude and Leo Stein, and, like these famous cultural trend-setters, they possessed a deep emotional passion for, as well as an intellectual connection to, the art they bought. The sisters, too, gave most of it away.

There are many other Americans who donated great masterpieces to the nation's numerous museums, albeit on a smaller scale. If one pays attention to the donors' names on museum labels, their names can be found there. They are likely not on a list of 'great American collectors of the past', but they, too, deserve to be praised and thanked for their munificence.

In England, Sir Henry Tate, Sir John Sloane, the Rothschilds, and Sir Richard Wallace come to mind when the topic of national cultural enrichment through certain individual admirable generosity. But, like in the

United States, there are many other donors whose names we know only from museum labels.

All this was about to change when a new kind of player entered the stage: financial types, fund managers, wheeler-dealers, and speculators, folks who had little, if any, emotional or intellectual engagement with art. They were after another quality- art's proven capacity for storing wealth.

In a world awash in liquidity, the rapidly growing demand for financial products calls for a continuous flow of new derivatives and new types of assets that can be sold to investors, large and small. This new group of money men—and women—began arriving conspicuously around the late 1980s/early 1990s, checking out the auction scene to find out if the art market was potentially useful to them. They were armed with impressive sums of money, financial savvy, and cutting-edge business wizardry. Although less knowledgeable about the aesthetics or history of art, they knew whom to ask for advice. They also posed different questions, the kind of questions financial speculators or venture capitalists want answered: projected earnings, comparative graphs, risk mitigation, diversification, etc. They liked what they heard, and it did not take long for the financial industry to recognize that a potential marriage in heaven was in the making. The dowry was the financialization of the art market, a very promising gift, indeed.

These money types were energetic suitors. They were accustomed to thinking big, acting bold and getting what they want for their money. Such swagger usually has a predicable effect on a market: it drives prices up. Competing alpha types, regardless of gender, are economic engines. These new operators were, and are, devout apostles of the great Lord Duveen and faithful followers of his 1st commandment: 'When you are paying high for the priceless, you are still getting it cheap'. They also understand the utility of managed publicity to send signals to the consumer.

These ladies and gentlemen proceeded to create the necessary infrastructure to maximize the profitability of their activities. Sometimes, they appear in the guise of traditional art dealers or mega-collectors. But among them are also diplomats, museum directors, academics, artists, con artists, hustlers, cultured financiers, media moguls, business tycoons, cold-blooded investors, showmen and slick-talking sophisticates in designer clothing, or any mixture of the above. The earlier described warehouses for storing art discreetly in freeports around the world are very much a part of this infrastructure. They are outside of nations' jurisdictions, and facilitate the securitization of art.

Acting bold is not just about paying record prices. It is also about influencing the market. With a size of just 0.6 % of total billionaire wealth, the art market requires fewer resources to implement interventionist measures than would be needed for a market 100 times that size. An example of bold—and very smart—action is the acquisition of a leading global auction house by one of the world's biggest art collectors for a little over a billion dollars, a price that is less than three Leonardo oak panels. A bargain, by anyone's measure. Privately owning one of the global duopoly's auction houses is tantamount to having control over the public stage from which market signals are sent by a hammer's knock to the rest of the world.

This is the stage where this wealth is on conspicuous display. Via this platform, in collaboration with middlemen and private speculators, a smart team with deep pockets is in the ideal position to implement various types of market interventions to promote and protect the market or the works of individual artists whenever the circumstances and the need present themselves.

Owning your own museum—or maybe even several—is also gaining traction among this super high-wealth crowd. The sophisticated speculator understands the aura our society has bestowed upon museums, our temples of art, the showcases for our greatest artistic achievements of the past, present, and even of the future. For those who are into the art-for-the-money game, it is advantageous to own one, or even a few of these institutions. Why not be the next Medici? To reach stardom, an artist just needs the right exposure, some good reviews, a smart dealer, their artworks on the auction block and the patron's support in the market until they can stand on their own feet. If it doesn't work out with one artist, there is always another. The whole game has a lively dynamic to it. Fame is fleeting, and the market is always hungry for something new.

Cultural speculators are fully aware of all the tax benefits that come from owning and operating one's own museum. To be up to date, they employ smart accountants, CPAs, and tax lawyers, even lobbyists. Their job is to mitigate the cost, and therefore, the risk of art speculation and shift it as much as possible to the ordinary taxpayer.

The role of art dealers in this financialization has evolved accordingly. They may still look like operators of elegant retail establishments, dealing in a luxury commodity. But, like their predecessors in the nineteenth century, they are proactively involved in the market. The traditional gallery owner is a shopkeeper who offers entry-level wall space and disseminates art. Modern-day art dealers, however, perform a quasi-Keynesian function in the art market, like the great Turner had done almost 200 years ago. Their responsibility is to support the market and prices selectively, manage liquidity as well as engage in the promotion of specific artists or stylistic movements and periods. As I wrote earlier, the art dealer, as an institution within the art market, is the central hub around which the market turns.

Today, behind every great artist or great collector, there is a great dealer. A career-changing one-man show in a prestigious museum is usually the result of initiatives taken by the artist's dealer. A donation to a major public institution or loan to an important exhibition is likely similarly due to a dealer's involvement. A 'breakthrough' exhibition at the Venice Biennale is a dealer-orchestrated event. A feature story in a leading art magazine on a specific artist or school of art is usually the result of a dealer's initiative. A headline-making record price at one of the leading auction houses often involves dealers with a stake in the specific artist's work(s). Conversely, loss of dealer support can spell the end of an artist's fame and fortune and a steep drop of value of one's art investment portfolio.

Despite all this talk about art as a financial asset in the age of Neoliberal Global Capitalism, or whatever the currently popular 'ism' may be, it is not my intent to paint an unfavorable picture of the art market or of its main players. Even if critics have condemned many current artist superstars for churning out market-oriented vulgar and sensationalistic kitsch, is this art not a reflection of our time? Marcel Duchamp's urinal was created for the market, a market that to this day is still about novelty at all costs. We should consider a work of art not on the basis of personal like or dislike but, instead, measure its merit by what it reveals to us. If the art of our time tells us something we don't like, or even offends us, it does not automatically demerit the art. If the individual responsible for creating it is a greedy self-absorbed louse, let's not take it out on the art.

We should also not condemn the new players. They are simply taking advantage of an aspect of art that has been under diligent construction for several centuries. Their behavior is the inevitable outcome of the art market's latest commoditization phase. These individuals are experienced at the big-money game and pursue opportunity whenever it presents itself. Prominent artist/entrepreneurs employ legions of workmen in their factory/studios to turn their ideas into marketable commodities to be sold 'hot off the press' for tens of millions to equally prominent mega collectors-dealers-bankers at highly publicized and choreographed events. In substance, isn't it the same as the sensation picture projects of the nineteenth century? Should we chastise them for making smart investments and using their wealth to their best advantage?

This exclusive look at the monied end of the market ignored, but for a few passing comments, a segment that is very different from the one I have been describing. It is the section made up of millions upon millions of passionate art lovers around the world who experience profound emotional, sensual, and intellectual pleasure from being surrounded by art. They are the regular gallery visitors, they frequent local art fairs and auctions, they support local artists, befriend them, have favorites, and enrich their lives and the lives of others by their patronage.

Those of us who fit into this category should keep doing what people do who love art: get to know it, engage with it, and buy it if we can afford it. Champion it. If one of us happens to become a member of the growing elite group of billionaires, keep doing the same thing and keep buying in the same proportion to your wealth as you did when you first got the art collecting bug. Remember, Leonardo's little, over restored panel at $ 450,000,000 was just chump change for its purchaser.

The billion-dollars artwork is just around the corner.

Notes

1. Ban Lee, High Art and High Finance: Performing Financialization in the Art Market (Lancaster: Lancaster University, 2023), Ph.D. dissertation.
2. On Freeports, see Introduction above.

Postscript

> The simple truth is that capital is the nurse and governess of the arts; not always a very wise or judicious one, but an exceedingly powerful one.
> P. G. Hamerton, Thoughts about Art (1871)

This story started over 300 years ago, when painters in England rebelled against the shackles of aristocratic, state and church dictates and became independent businessman exposed to the vagaries of an expanding, fickle, and anonymous consumer market. After testing a variety of different ways to operate in this new market, the crucial break was an exhibition of their works in the new public amusement park at Spring Gardens in London in 1732. From this fateful start, art as public entertainment commoditized to the point where it has become a major revenue source for many cities around the world, as well as the subject of numerous economic impact studies. Art consumers number in the hundreds of millions today, and there is a general agreement among economists that art consumption is good for the economy and society in general. We owe thanks for this consensus to the entrepreneurial ingenuity and drive as well as the boundless creativity of our artists. In a steadily expanding market, they competed—and still do—against each other through innovation and increasing differentiation. As a result, their products have become more differentiated, and a market for contemporary art emerged that thrives to this day. To achieve this, they cultivated the press, introduced public exhibitions of art,

T. M. Bayer, *The Genesis of the Modern Art Market in London, 1700–1900*, https://doi.org/10.1007/978-3-032-00594-6

and provided the *raison d'être* for a new profession, the dealer in modern art. Dealers and even artists conspicuously protected the market for artworks at public auctions which, by mid-nineteenth century, had become the market's reference point. This practice of market making laid the footing for the investment reputation of contemporary art. The regulatory activity to prop up prices continues to this day, albeit not always as demonstratively as the great Turner pursued it.

Reynolds' IXth discourse in 1780 established the distinctive aura, the very basis, on which modern art production and consumption relies. His lecture expanded the meaning and function of art and created a foundation for a near limitless expression of artistic creativity. Today, this aura has evolved to a point where no restrictive standards of quality are applied. The demand for constant product differentiation in the still expanding art market has overcome any barriers to market entry except the need to garner attention. Nowadays, certain artists can command prices in the millions of dollars for works that have just left their ateliers.

The ongoing, often heated and heavily politicized, discussions concerning taxpayer-funded subsidies for the arts are but a direct consequence of Reynolds' argument that exposure to art has the potential of improving society. His emphasis of 'refinement of taste' with its implied elitism has been adopted by the rhetoric of present-day art marketing and other cultural events to promote these occasions as paths to improve the perception of one's social status in financial and cultural terms.

The ornately worded, often incomprehensible artist statement that has become an integral part of twenty-first century art marketing is a direct offshoot of an earlier union between artists and writers. Like the contemporary artists about whom they wrote, authors and the media, too, sought new ways to engage their audience and provide a theoretical framework to situate these cultural luxury goods in aesthetic and historical contexts. The nascent art writers of the eighteenth-century are today near countless in numbers. Increasingly specialized art magazines and their contributing writers continually seek newsworthy art stories to attract readers and advertisers.

The discussion on what constitutes art provided, and continues to provide, artists and art writers with a constant flow of material. The need for conceptual art to be verbally explained has exacerbated the use of vocabulary that often is as conceptual as the artwork it seeks to explain. The viewer is left musing if the object on display is but an illustration of an abstract thought rather than an autonomous piece of art. But if we agree with Sir Joshua's claim that beholding art elevates the human condition, then, perhaps, the viewers' confusion fulfills art's consecrated mission.

These days, artists use this language to promote their art in talks at prestigious universities. Location and format make these presentations nearly indistinguishable from typical lectures on contemporary art by academic art historians in the same setting. The implicit academic stamp of approval sets individual artists apart from their competitors, while the lecture format deconstructs the apparent commercialism of a conventional art gallery space. And for art writers, these talks provide useful information to share with their audience. Contemporary academic art history would lose much of its purpose were it not for the market's demand for continuous innovation and the resulting steady flow of new forms and ideas of visual expression. The discipline's customary categorization of paintings and other visual cultural products into ever more groups, more schools, movements and stylistic 'isms' is an excellent example of market-driven product differentiation. For the artistically creative, this custom presents untold possibilities which art historians then categorize.

The choice of exhibition spaces has vastly expanded beyond coffee shops and taverns/pubs of early eighteenth-century London. Besides the typical art gallery, today there are banks, hotel lobbies, office buildings, hospitals, churches, boutiques, wine shops, restaurants, music clubs, bookstores, airports, or any other facility with suitable space and human traffic that offers its walls for the display of art for sale.

Career-changing royal patronage has been replaced by patronage of museums and famous collectors. Acquisitions at the top level, like the Whitney, MOMA, the Pompidou Center, or Tate Modern, positively affect prices and benefit all stakeholders in the specific artists' oeuvre: artists, dealers, auction houses, private collectors, and other museum collections.

The newly created profession of art dealing has also continued to commoditize. The already impressive scope of Victorian art dealing has been vastly expanded by today's dealer networks operating globally on unprecedented levels.

Price has been used as a marketing tool for several centuries, and it is today the final determinant of success in the contemporary art market. The investment potential of contemporary art is solidly accepted. From its humble beginnings in nineteenth-century newspaper reports on auction prices, art's investment potential is now promoted using analytical methodologies similar to those used in the financial markets to make trading decisions.

The competitive atmosphere and the pressure to be distinct continue to challenge the most creative minds and extraordinary talents to achieve notice/notoriety and leave their mark in today's media-saturated environment. Nathaniel Hone's purported use of the naked image of Angelica Kauffmann as a marketing device anticipated such later exhibitions as Jeff Koons' explicit depictions of sex acts. While media-saturation and market expansion have reached unprecedented levels, the workings of the art market have not fundamentally changed since they were first established in Victorian England. As before, in response to the ever-present need for innovation, artists continue, much like their eighteenth and nineteenth-century brethren, to create new 'isms'/theories which are welcomed fodder for the popular press, legitimized by academia and the museum community, and validated conspicuously by the market.

The cynical critic of the contemporary art environment may see proof in the above discussion for the corrupting commercialization of the arts. But the still-ongoing evolution of certain aspects of the art market is not inherently a negative influence on the art produced. Likes and dislikes are merely subjective measures. The continuous questioning of what constitutes art has presented us with works that were once derided and are now monuments of our culture. There is no reason for this process to stop. Freed from the confinements of restrictive theories and rules, more art is produced than ever before in our history. This is good. Art calms the savage beast. It also testifies to a society, in global terms, saturated with disposable wealth. Most humankind is still poor, yet these are rich times. The above story simply explains how the once exclusive benefits inherent to art have been made more accessible and inclusive.

We have tracked an entire industry's 'whirlwind of innovation'—as the Austrian economist Josef Schumpeter called it—from a market for simple wall décor 300 years ago to one that trades in high-value financial assets. We witnessed art, artists, and the entire arts environment caught in the same storm. This has raised a lot of questions, and, hopefully, I offered some answers.

A final word of caution. Inherent in the financialization of art is the danger that it could fundamentally re-prioritize arts' aura, its apotheotic commodity character, the very quality which sets it apart. If art becomes a purely speculative financial asset, its merit and quality will be assessed on the same basis as all the other speculative assets. Art would lose its uniqueness and thereby its supremacy over all other commodities. Instead, it would become just another one of them. This would be catastrophic. All that toil by all the people described in this book would go to waste, rendering all the efforts of the last 300 years naught. All the hard work, the smarts, the ingenuity, and the money it took to achieve this hegemonic, this divine status—all down the drain. And this book would have to be re-titled.

But we shouldn't forget that this use of art was not forced upon us by some alien entity set to destroy our culture. We chose it ourselves. Perhaps not always deliberately and with full knowledge of the consequences. But who knows those at the best of times? Hindsight is 20/20. Maybe this concept of art as a financial asset is the defining characteristic, the unique quality, and value of the art of our time. How do we judge?

Bibliography

A Brief Historical and Descriptive account of the Royal Gardens, Vauxhall (London, 1822).

Agnew, Geoffrey, Agnew's, (London: The Bradbury Agnew Press, Ltd., 1967): 65.

Akerlof, Georg, ¨The Market for 'Lemons': Quality Uncertainty and the Market Mechanism,¨ An economic theorist's book of tales (Cambridge: Cambridge University Press, 1970).

Alken, Henry, The Art and Practice of Etching (London, 1849).

Altholz, J. L., ed., The Mind and Art of Victorian England (Minneapolis: University of Minnesota Press, 1976).

Altick, Richard, The Shows of London (Cambridge: Harvard University Press, 1978).

Amory, Hugh, John Singleton Copley, R.A. (New York: Houghton, Mifflin and Co., 1982).

Bruntjen, Herbert, John Boydell (1719–1804): A Study of Art Patronage and Publishing in Georgian London (New York: Garland Publishing, 1985a).

Armstrong-Totten, Julia, ¨Expand the Audience, Increase the Profits: Motivations Behind the Private Contract Sale,¨ La Circulation des Oeuvres d Árt 1789–1848, A. Panzanelli and M. Preti-Hamard, eds. (Rennes: Presses de Universitaire de Rennes Institute National de Histoire de l Árt, Getty Research Institute).

Armstrong-Totten, ¨The Rise and Fall of a British Connoisseur: the career of Michel Bryan (1757–1821), picture dealer extraordinaire'¨ Auctions, Agents, and Dealers. The Mechanisms of the Art Market 1660–1830, Warren and

T. M. Bayer, *The Genesis of the Modern Art Market in London, 1700–1900*, https://doi.org/10.1007/978-3-032-00594-6

Turpin, eds. (Oxford: The Beazley Archives and Archaeopress in association with the Wallace Collection, 2008).

Barrell, John, The Political Theory of Painting from Reynolds to Hazlitt (New Haven and London: Yale University Press 1986).

Barry, James, Inquiry into the real and imaginary Obstructions to the Acquisition of the Arts (London: T. Becket 1775).

Bayer, "The Seventeenth Century Dutch Art Market: The Influence of Economics on Artistic Production", Athanor, X (Tallahassee: Florida State University, 1991): 21–28.

Bayer, "Socio-economic Aspects of Netherlandish Painting during the Sixteenth Century", Athanor, XII (Tallahassee: Florida State University, 1994): 55–59.

Bayer, Thomas Bayer and John Page, The Development of the Art Market in England: Money As Muse, 1730–1900, London: Pickering and Chatto (2011).

Bayer, Page, "Arthur Tooth: A London Art Dealer in the Spotlight, 1870–71", Nineteenth-Century Art Worldwide (Spring, 2010).

Bayer, Page, Yaron Raviv, Joshua Rosett, "Age, Human Capital and the Quality of Work: New Evidence from Old Masters", The Berkeley Electronic Journal of Economic Analysis and Policy, Vol. 13, No. 2 (July 2013): 687–708.

Bayer, Page, "The ingenious marketing of modern paintings", Journal of Historical Research in Marketing, vol. 6, no 2 (2014): 211–233.

Bayer, Page, Raviv, Rosett, "Seasonal Affective Disorder and Seasoned Art Auction Prices: New Evidence from Old Masters," Journal of Behavioral and Experimental Economics, vol. 59 (December 2015): 74–84.

Bayer, "Arthur Tooth", Bloomsbury Art Markets (formerly Art Market Dictionary), Johannes Nathan, Inge Reist, Thomas Gaehtgens, eds. (online, 2022).

Benjamin, Walter, Das Kunstwerk im Alter seiner technischen Reproduzierbarkeit (Frankfurt: Surkamp Verlag, 1977). (English title: The Work of Art in the Age of Mechanical Reproduction).

Behrman, Samuel, N., Duveen (N.Y.: Random House (1951): 30–31.

Bernays, Edward, Crystallizing Public Opinion (N.Y.: Boni and Liveright, 1923).

Berniker, Talia, "Behind Closed Doors: A Look At Freeports"; https://itsartlaw.org/2020/11/03/behind-closed-doors-a-look-at-freeports/ (last accesses March 2025).

Birch, Dinah, ¨Father and Sons: Ruskin, John James Ruskin and Turner¨, Nineteenth-Century Contexts, 18, no. 2 (1994).

Blakesley, Rosalind P., The Sale of the Century: Artistic Relations Between England and Russia 1760–1840, (New Haven and London: Yale University Press, 2016).

Bond, Sarah, E., Trade and Taboo: Disreputable Professions in the Roman Mediterranean, (Ann Harbor: University of Michigan Press, 2016.

Bredius, Abraham, "De kunsthandel te Amsterdam in de XVIIe eeuw," Amsterdam Jaarboekje (1891).

British Museum, Add. MS 23724, ff 14, 40, 60, 61, 62, 74, 98, 103, 112, 129, 130.

Bruntjen, Sven H.A., John Boydell (1719–1804) A Study of Art Patronage and Publishing in Georgian London (N.Y., Garland Publishing, Inc., 1985b).
Buchanan, William, Memoirs of Painting, J. Greig, ed, (London: Ackermann, 1824).
Burne-Jones, Edward, Memorials of Edward-Burne-Jones (London: The Macmillan Company, 1906).
Butlin, Martin, 'An Eighteenth Century Scandal: Nathaniel Hone's "The Conjurer"', Connoisseur, CLXXIV (1970).
Casteras, Susan (ed.), John Ruskin and the Victorian Eye (N. Y.: H.N. Abrams, 1993).
Christian, John, ¨A Serious Talk: Ruskin's place in Burne-Jones Artistic Development,¨ Pre-Raphaelite Papers, L. Parris, ed. (London: Tate Gallery, 1984).
Arturo Cifuentes and Ventura Charlin, The Worth of Art (N. Y.: Columbia University Press, 2023).
Cobb, Eva, ¨Renaissance Printmaking: How Albrecht Durer Changed the Game, "The Collector (Nov 2, 2024), https://www.thecollector.com/how-albrecht-durer-changed-printmaking-renaissance/ (last accessed March 2025).
Coke, David, and Alan Borg, Vauxhall Gardens: A History (New Haven & London: Yale University Press, 2011).
Collins, Wilkie, A Rogue's Life (London: Richard Benleyt & Son, 1879).
Conlin, Johnathan ¨At the Expense of the Public': The Sign Painters' Exhibition of 1762 and the Public Sphere". American Society for Eighteenth-Century Studies, vol. 36 (Fall 2002).
Cooper, Anthony Ashley, 3rd Earl of Shaftesbury, Characteristics of Men, Manners, Opinions, Times, 1711, John M. Richardson, ed., 2 vols. (Indianapolis and New York: University of Indiana Press, 1964).
Cooper, Second Characters, or the Language of Forms, B. Rand, ed. (Cambridge: Harvard University Press, 1914): 135.
De Marchi, Neil and Hans Van Miegroet, ¨Rules Versus Play in Early Modern Art Markets,¨ Louvain Economic Review, 66 (2000): 146–148.
De Marchi, Neil and Hans Van Miegroet, ¨The History of Art Markets,¨ Handbook of the Economics of Art and Culture, (Amsterdam: Elsevier, 2006), V. Ginsburgh, ed.
Denvir, Bernard, The Eighteenth Century (London &N.Y.: Longman, 1983).
Dictionary of Art Historians. https://arthistorians.info/manderk/ (last accessed March 2025).
Dobai, Johannes, Kunstliteratur des Klassizismus und der Romantik in England, 3 vols. (Bern: Bentelli Verlag, 1974).
Eitner, Lorenz, Géricault's Raft of Medusa (London: Phaidon, 1972).
Eitner, Géricault, his Life and Work (London: Orbis Publishing, 1983).
Evelyn, John, Diary & Correspondence of John Evelyn, Frs., W. Bray, ed (London: G. Bell and Sons, 1883–1887).

Fantoni, Marcello, Louise C. Matthew and Sara F. Matthew-Grieco, The Art Market in Italy, 15th-17th Centuries, (Modena: F.C. Panini, 2003).
Farington, Joseph, The Farington Diaries, 1793–1817, 2 vols., J. Greig, ed. (London: Hutchison, 1922–1928).
Fletcher, Pamela, and Anne Helmreich, ¨The Periodical and the Art Market: Investigating the "Dealer-Critic System" in Victorian England', Victorian Periodical Review, vol 41, no. 4 (Winter 2008).
Floerke, Hans, Die Formen des Kunsthandels, das Atelier und die Sammler in den Niederlanden vom 15.-18. Jahrhundert (Munich and Leipzig: Georg Muller 1905.
Foss, Michael, The Age of Patronage (Ithaca: Cornell University Press, 1971).
Frank, Robert H., "The Role of Talent and Luck in Achieving Fame", Journal of Economic Perspectives, 30(3) (2016): 71–86.
Freud, Sigmund, Gradiva (1907), Delusion and Dream and Other Essays, Philip Rieff, ed. (Boston: Beacon Press, Boston, 1956).
Frith, William Powell, A Victorian Canvas: The Memories of W. P. Frith, RA, N. Wallis, ed. (London: Geoffrey Bles, 1957).
Frith, My Autobiography and Reminiscences, 2 vols. (New York: Harper and Brothers, 1888).
Gibson-Wood, Carol, 'Picture Consumption in London at the end of the Seventeenth Century', The Art Bulletin, vol. 84, no. 3 (Sep. 2002).
Goldgar, Anne, Tulipmania: Money, Honor and Knowledge in the Dutch Golden Age (Chicago: University of Chicago Press 2007).
Gool, Jan van, De Nieuwe Schouburg der Nederlandische Kunstschilders en Schilderessen, 2 vols. (The Hague: 1750).
Gowing, Lawrence, The Essence of Turner, Turner: Imagination and Reality, exhibition catalogue (N.Y.: Museum of Modern Art, 1966).
Graves, Algernon, Art Sales, 3 vols. (N.Y.: Burt Franklin, 1970).
Green, Nicholas, ¨Dealing in Temperaments: Economic Transformation of the Artistic Field in France during the Second Half of the Nineteenth Century,¨, Art History, 10 (March 1987).
Hall, Samuel Carter, Retrospective of A Long Life from 1815–1883 (N. Y.: D. Appleton & Co., 1883).
Hamerton, Philip, Etching and Etchers (London: Macmillan and Co., Ltd., 1868).
Hamerton, 'Modern Etching in France', The Fine Arts Quarterly Review 2 (1864).
Hardie, Martin, Frederick Goulding: Master Printer of Copper Plates (Sterling: Eneas Mackay, 1910).
Hart, Joan, Heinrich Wolfflin: An Intellectual Biography (Bern: Peter Lang, Bern, 1981).
Harris, Robert, London Newspapers in the Age of Walpole (London: Associated University Presses, 1987).

Haskell, Francis, Patrons and Painters (New Haven and London: Yale University Press, 1980).
Hauser, Arnold, Art and Society: Lectures and Essays (London: Routledge & Kegan Paul, 1951a).
Hauser, The Social History of Art, 4 vols. (London: Routledge & Kegan Paul, 1951b).
Herkomer, Hubert, The Atheneum, (April 1893).
Hermann, Frank, The English as Collectors (New York: W. W. Norton & Co., 1972).
Herodotus, The Histories, (London: Penguin Publishing, 2003).
Hilton, Timothy, John Ruskin: The Early Years (New Haven & London: Yale University Press, 2000).
Holt, Elizabeth G., Triumph of Art for the Public (Washington, D.C.: Decatur House Press, 1980).
Huish, Marcus B., Étching in England', Magazine of Art (1878).
Hunt, Holman, Pre-Raphaelitism and the Pre-Raphaelite Brotherhood, 2 vols. (London: Macmillan, 1905).
Hutchison, Sidney, The History of the Royal Academy 1768–1968 (London: Robert Royce, Ltd., 1968):13/14.
Ireland, John, and John Nichols, Hogarth's Work, 3 vols. (Edinburgh & London: Oliphant, Anderson & Ferrier, 1874).
Irwin, David, ed., Winkelmann: Writings on Art, Phaidon (1972).
Jenkins, Eversfield, ¨Joseph Gillott and the Rise of the Collector-dealer¨, Edinburgh Research Archives (2023), https://era.ed.ac.uk/handle/1842/40821 (last accessed March 2025).
Johnson, Lee, 'The Raft of Medusa in Great Britain,' Burlington Magazine, XCVI (August 1954): 249–254.
Jung, Carl, Man and His Symbols (N.Y.: Dell Publishing, 1964).
Jung, Carl, The Spirit in Man, Art, and Literature (Princeton: Princeton University Press,1966).
Keppel, Frederick, 'Modern Disciples of Rembrandt', The Art Review, 2 (September-November 1887):145–149.
Kim, Leena ¨Where the Superrich store their Art to avoid Taxes,¨ Town and Country, (April 2023) https://www.townandcountrymag.com/leisure/arts-and-culture/a35032655/what-is-a-freeport-art-collections/ (Last accessed March 2025).
Koch, Walter, Die Kunstaustellung (Berlein: Walter de Gruyter & Co., 1967).
Kopytoff, Igor ¨The Cultural Biography of Things: Commoditization as Process,¨ The Social Life of Things: Commodities in Cultural Perspectives, ed., A. Appadurai (Cambridge, MA: Yale University Press, 1986): 64–91.
Landau, David and Peter Parshall, The Renaissance Print: 1470–1550 (New Haven & London: Yale University Press, 1994).

Landow, George, "There Began to Be a Great Talking about the Fine Arts," The Mind and Art of Victorian England, J. L. Altholz, ed. (Minneapolis: University of Minnesota Press, 1976).

Law Geo.III cap 50, of September 1777 and 19 Geo. III cap 56 in 1779.

Leathart papers, Victoria and Albert Museum, London.

Lee, Ban, High Art and High Finance: Performing Financialization in the Art Market (Lancaster: Lancaster University, 2023), Ph.D. dissertation.

Leen, Anne "Cicero and the Rhetoric of Art," The American Journal of Philology, vol, 112, No. 2 (Summer 1991): 229–245.

Levin, Irwin, Erwin Panofsky: An Intellectural Portrait (Princeton: Princeton University Press, 1992).

Lewis, Wilmarth, Connoisseurs and Secret Agents in 18th Century Rome (London: Chatto & Windus, 1961).

Lipkin, Lawrence, The Ordering of Arts in Eighteenth-century England (Princeton: Princeton University Press, 1970).

Lippincott, Louise, Selling Art in Georgian London (New Haven & London: Yale University Press, 1988).

Lodge, S., 'Géricault in England', Burlington Magazine, CVII (December 1965): 616–627.

London Literary Gazette and Journal of better Letters, 180 (July 1, 1820).

Loos, Famke A., "Freeports as ecosystems for the preservation of fine art value and the acceleration of related businesses," (Rotterdam: Erasmus University Rotterdam (2017) MA thesis, supervisor: F. Vermeylen.

Luckhurst, Kenneth, The Story of Exhibitions (London, New York: Studio Publications, 1951).

Luckhurst, The Royal Society of Arts, 1754–1954 (London: Murray, 1954).

Maas, Jeremy, Gambart (London: Barrie Jenkins, 1975).

Macky, John, Memoirs of the Secret Services of John Macky, Esq. (London 1733).

Mander, Karel van, Dutch and Flemish Painting (New York: MacFarlane, 1938).

Mancoff, Derek, "Samuel Carter Hall: Publisher as Promoter of the High Arts", Victorian Periodical Review, 24,1 (Spring 1991).

Mandeville, Bernard, The Fable of the Bees or Private Vices and Public Benefits (1714) F. D. Kaye, ed., 2 vols. (Oxford: Clarendon Press, 1924).

Macleod, Dianne, 'F.G. Stephens, Pre-Raphaelite Critic and Art Historian', The Burlington Magazine, 128 (June 1986).

McClellan, Andrew, The Louvre: A Very Short Introduction (Oxford: Oxford University Press, 2017).

McClellan, The Uffizi: A Cultural History (Cambridge: Polity Press, 2020).

McKendrick, Neil, John Brewer and J. H. Plumb (eds.), The Birth of a Consumer Society (Bloomington: Indiana University Press, 1982).

Merrill, Linda, A Pot of Paint: Aesthetics on Trial in Whistler v. Ruskin, (Washington: Smithsonian Institution, 1992).

Mills, Esther, ed., The Life and Letters of Frederic Shields, (London: Longmans, Green and Co., 1912).
Montias, John Michael, Artists and Artisans in Delft: A Socio-Economic Study of the Seventeenth Century (Princeton: Princeton University Press,1982).
Montias, Vermeer and His Milieu: A Web of Social History (Princeton: Princeton University Press 1991).
Montias "Socio-economic Aspects of Netherlandish Art from the Fifteenth to the Seventeenth Century: A Survey," The Art Bulletin, LXXII, 3 (September 1990a).
Montias, "Cost and Value in Seventeenth-Century Dutch Art", Art History, 10, no. 4 (December 1987).
Montias, "Art dealers in the seventeenth-century Netherlands", Simiolus, 18, 4 (1990b): 244–256.
Nichols, Robert, and Francis Wray, The History of the Foundling Hospital (London: Oxford University Press, 1935).
Niederlandische Jahrbuch, "Painting for the Market," (1999).
O'Brian, Rebecca D, and Tom Metcall, ¨Yves Bouvier: The Art World's Most Notorious Middlemen,¨ Bloomberg, (online, March 18, 2015) https://www.google.com/search?q=Yves+Bouvier%3A+the+art+world%C2%B4s+most+notious+middleman&rlz=1C5CHFA_enUS1083US1083&oq=Yves+Bouvier%3A++the+art+world%C2%B4s+most+notious+middleman&gs_lcrp=EgZjaHJvbWUyBggAEEUYOTIHCAEQIRiPAjIHCAIQIRiPAtIBCTQ4NDk4ajBqN6gCALACAA&8 (last accessed March 2025).
Ormrod, David, ¨The Art Trade and Its Urban Context, England and the Netherlands compared, 1570–1770¨, Auctions, Agents and Dealers, J. Warren and A. Turpin, eds. (Oxford: The Beazley Archives and Archeopress, 2008).
Ormrod, David, ¨The Origin of The London Art Market, 1650–1730,¨ Michael North and David Ormrod, eds., Art Markets in Europe, 1400–1800 (Aldershot: Ashgate Publishing 1998).
Ormrod, ¨The Rise of the London Art Market, 1660–1769¨, Economica e Arte, sec. XIII-XVIII (March 2000).
Parsons, Catherine, and Neil McWilliam, ¨Le Paysan de Paris: Alfred Sensier and the Myth of Rural France¨, Oxford Art Journal, 6 (no. 2, 1983).
Pasquin, Anthony, Memory of the Royal Academicians; being an attempt to improve the national taste (London: 1796).
Paulson, Ronald, Hogarth: His Life, Art, and Times, 2 vol. (New Haven & London: Yale University Press, 1971).
Pears, 'Patronage and Learning in the Virtuoso Republic: John Talman in Italy 1709–12', Oxford Art Journal, 5, no 1, (1982): 24–30.
Pears, Iain, The Discovery of Painting: Yale University Press 1988).
Pedley, John, Greek Art and Archeology, (N.Y.: Pearson, 2020), 5th edition.
Pennell, Elizabeth, ¨The Two Salons", Fortnightly Review, LIII (1893).
Pevsner, Nicolas, Academies of Art, Past and Present (Cambridge: Cambridge University Press, 1940).

Piazza, Jo, "The Business of Fame: How Celebrities Create and Manage Their Brands", Journal of Brand Management, 26(1) (2019).

Pierpont Morgan Library, New York. Accession number: MA1485D, record identification: 132647.

Podro, Michael, The Critical Historians of Art (New Haven & London: Yale University Press, 1982).

Potts, Alex, Flesh and the Ideal: Winckelmann and the Origins of Art History (Yale University Press, New Haven and London, 1994).

Pye, John, Patronage of British Art, A Historical Sketch (London: Longman, Brown, Green and Longmans, 1845).

Raymond, William, Culture and Society, 1780–1950 (N.Y.: Columbia University Press 1983).

Raimbach, Abraham, Memoirs and Recollections of Abraham Raimbach (London, 1845).

Read, H., ed. "Psychology and Literature," The Collected Works of C. G. Jung, (London: Routledge & Kegan Paul, 1964).

Redgrave, Richard, A Century of Painters of the English School (London: Sampson Low, Marston & Co. Ltd, 1890).

Reist, Inge, "The Fate of the Palais Royal Collection: 1791–1800," R. Panzanelli and M. Preti-Hamard, eds, La Circulation des Oeuvres d'Art 1789–1848.

Reitlinger, Gerald, Economics of Taste: The Rise and Fall of Picture Prices, 1760–1960 (N.Y.: Hacker Art Books, 1982).

Reynolds, Joshua, Discourses on Art, R. R. Wark, ed. (New Haven & London: Yale University Press, 1959).

Richardson, Johnathan, Essay on the Whole Art of Criticism as it relates to Painting (London: 1719).

River, Charles, Tulip Mania: The History and Legacy of the World's First Speculative Bubble during the Dutch Golden Age (Charles River Editors, 2018).

Roberts, Helene, "Art Reviewing in the Early Nineteenth-Century Art Periodicals," Victorian Periodicals Newsletter, 19 (March 1973).

Roberts, Exhibition and review: the periodical press and the Victorian art exhibition system, J. Shattock and M. Wolff, eds, The Victorian Periodical Press: Samplings and Soundings (Toronto: University of Toronto Press, 1982).

Rosen, Sherwin, "The Economics of Superstars", American Economic Review, 71(5) (1981): 845–858.

Rosenthal, Michael, 'Turner Fires a Gun', in David Solkin, ed., Art on the Line (London and New Haven: Yale University Press, 2001): 145–155.

Rossetti, William Michael, The Life and Letters of Frederic Shields (London: Ellis and Elvey, 1895).

Rottermund, Andrzej, ed., Treasures of a Polish King, Dulwich Picture Gallery, exhibition catalogue (1992).

Rouquet, Jean-Andre, The State of the Arts in England (London: Jay Nourse, 1755).

Ruskin, John, Academy Notes (Smith, Elder and Co., 1855).
Ruskin, John, Modern Painters, 2 vols. (Boston: Dana Estes & Company, n.d.).
Schrenk, Klaus, Die Alte Pinakotek. Ein Museum und seine Sammlung (Munich: Verlag C. H. Beck, 1999).
Schwarzer, Mitchell, "Órigins of the Art History Survey Text", Art Journal, vol. 54, 3 (Fall 1995).
Sekora, John, Luxury: The Concept of Western Thought, Eden to Smollett (Baltimore: John's Hopkins University Press, 1977).
Shapiro, Meyer, "Art and Ideology," Marxist Quarterly (April 1937a), vol 1, issue 2.
Shapiro, 'The Social Bases of Art," Marxist Quarterly (1937b), vol. 1, issue 3.
Simpson, Frank, "Dutch Paintings in England before 1760," Burlington Magazine, XCV (February 1953).
Smith, Adam, The Wealth of Nations, R. H. Campbell and A. S. Skinner, eds. (Oxford: Oxford University Press 1976).
Solkin, David, Painting for Money: The Visual Arts and the Public in Eighteenth-century England (New Haven & London: Yale University Press, 1993).
Solomon, Maynard, ed., Marxism and Art: Essays Classic and Contemporary, (Detroit: Wayne State University Press, 1973).
Spatt, Henry S., "The Aesthetics of Editorship: Creating Taste in the Victorian Art World", Innovators and Preachers, J. H. Wiener, ed. (London: Greenwood Press, 1985).
Steegmann, John, The Role of Taste from George I to George IV (London: Macmillan and Co. Ltd., 1936).
Strachey, James, ed., The Standard Edition of the Complete Psychological Works of Sigmund Freud (London: Hogarth Press, 1953–1974).
Tedeschi, Martha, How Prints Work Reproductions, Originals, and their Markets in England: 1840_1900, Ph.D. dissertation (Evanston: Northwestern University 1994).
The Art Journal (August 1852).
The Art Journal (June 1863).
Art Journal (December 1871).
The Athenaeum (7 June 1851).
The Atheneum (20 August, 1864).
The Gazetteer and New Daily Advertiser, 21 May 1765.
The Illustrated London News, October 11 (1862).
The Morning Chronicle (June 15th 1829).
The Pall Mall Gazette (4 March 1890).
The Public Advertiser (June 2, 1781).
The Spectator, no. 10 (March 12, 1710–1711).
The Times (7 May 1851).
The Times (3 November 1862).
Tyrwhitt, Richard St. John, "Skilled and Literary Art-Criticism", Contemporary Review, XI (1869).

Vermeylen, Filip, and Sandra van Ginhoven, ¨The professionalisation of the art trade in early nineteenth century London: Exploring the business model of Christie's auction house¨ (Business History, 2023) https://doi.org/10.1080/00076791.2023.2242278 (last accessed March 2025).

Vertue, George, Note Books, 6 vols. The Walpole Society, 32, vol. 3.on Hay).

Walpole, Horace, Anecdotes of Painting in England (London: Henry G. Bohn, 1849).

Warwick, Genieve, ¨Gift Exchange and Art Collecting. Padre Sebastiano Pesta's Drawing Albums¨, Art Bulletin, 4 (December 1997).

Waterhouse, Ellis, Dictionary of British 18th-century Painters in oils and crayons, (Woodbridge: Antique Collectors'Club, 1981).

Wedmore, Frederick, (ed.), Rembrandt: His Life, His work and His Time (London: Heinemann, 1894).

White, Harrison C., and Cynthia White, Canvases and Careers (Chicago and London: The University of Chicago Press, 1965).

Whitley, William, Art in England, 2 vols. (N.Y.: Hacker Art Books, 1973).

Whiteley, William, Art of England, 2 vols. (New York: Hacker Art Books, 1973).

Whitley, William, Artists and their Friends in England, 1700 – 1790, 2 vols. (London and Boston: The Medici Society, 1938).

Wilde, Oscar, The Picture of Dorian Gray N.Y.: Random House (1909).

Winstanley, Thomas, Observations on the Arts (Liverpool: W. Wales, 1828).

Wittkower, Rudolf, Englische Kunstliteratur: Ein Handbuch, (Weimar: Hermann Bohlhaus Nachfolger (1938).

Wolfthal, Dianne The Beginning of Netherlandish Canvas Painting 1400–1530 (Cambridge: Cambridge University Press, 1989).

Wood, Christopher, Preraphaelites (London: Weidenfeld and Nicholson, 1981).

Wood, Dictionary of Victorian Painters (London: Antique Collector's Club, 1978).

Wroth, Warwick, F.S.A., The London Pleasure Gardens of the Eighteenth Century (London: Macmillan and Co., Ltd., 1896).

Zarobell, John, "Freeports and the Hidden Value of Art", International Studies Faculty Publications. (2020): 27, https://repository.usfca.edu/international_fac/27 (last accessed March 2025).

Zerfass, Ansgar, et al. "The Impact of Social Media on Achieving Fame", Journal of Communication Management, 21 (2017).

https://www.academia.edu/43570364/Did_Cicero_Care_About_Art_An_Apology (last accessed March 2025).

https://news.artnet.com/art-world/damien-hirst-skull-storage-2064567 (Last accessed March 2025).

https://www.dulwichpicturegallery.org.uk/about/our-history/#:~:text=Dulwich%20Picture%20Gallery%20sprung%20out,RA%20(1756%20%2D%201811) (last accessed March 2025).

Index[1]

[1] Note: Page numbers followed by 'n' refer to notes.

T. M. Bayer, *The Genesis of the Modern Art Market in London, 1700-1900*, https://doi.org/10.1007/978-3-032-00594-6

Bicknell, Elhanan, 152

N

O

P

Z

FSC
www.fsc.org
MIX
Papier | Fördert gute Waldnutzung
FSC® C083411

Kolibri 360 GmbH
Ferdinand-Jühlke-Straße 7
99095 Erfurt, Deutschland
produktsicherheit@kolibri360.de